Embracing Judaism

Embracing Judaism

PERSONAL NARRATIVES OF RENEWED FAITH

Debra Gonsher-Vinik

JASON ARONSON INC.
Northvale, New Jersey
Jerusalem

This book was set in 11 pt. Bell by Alpha Graphics of Pittsfield, NH and printed and bound by Book-mart Press, Inc. of North Bergen, NJ.

Library of Congress Cataloging-in-Publication Data

Vinik, Debra Gonsher.
    Embracing Judaism : personal narratives of everyday people / Debra Gonsher Vinik.
        p. cm.
    Includes bibliographical references and index.
    ISBN 0-7657-6097-5
    1. Judaism—United States. 2. Spiritual life—Judaism. 3. Jews—United States—Interviews. I. Title.
BM205.V56 1999
296'.0973—dc21   99-21096

Printed in the United States of America on acid-free paper. For information and catalog write to Jason Aronson Inc., 230 Livingston Street, Northvale, NJ 07647-1726, or visit our website: www.aronson.com

To David

אני לדודי ודודי לי

He who was the first to produce the oracles of God,

he who has been for so long the guardian of prophecy,

and transmitted it to the rest of the world—

such a nation cannot be destroyed.

The Jew is everlasting as eternity itself.

—Tolstoy

Contents

IV   A Choice of One's Own

V   Faith Into Art

Preface

Three years ago, my husband and I wrote and produced a documentary called *Embracing Judaism: Reaching In, Reaching Out, Reaching Up.* It consisted of interviews with people who talked about an increased connection to their Jewish faith and rabbis' perceptions on why the phenomenon was occurring.

The documentary aired on a Sunday morning on most ABC affiliate stations. Though our names and our company's name were listed in the credits, there was no address or phone number by which to contact us. Nevertheless, the following Monday morning we received hundreds of phone calls from people who had seen the program and wanted to buy a copy, as well as those who hadn't seen it but had heard about it and wanted to view it. Calls from all over the country.

It was clear to me that the documentary had touched a nerve. A voice had been given to people's experiences. They wanted both to validate their own feelings and to learn more about what they were witnessing.

A year later I began working on another documentary concerning the demise of the synagogues on the Lower East Side of New York and the life they represented. Interestingly, upon hearing my credentials, everyone wanted to talk about the previous documentary and their similar experience. It appeared that everyone had a story of reconnection.

I was quite aware that it might have been only my little corner of the world, but then again, with the advent of the Internet, my little corner of the world was not so little anymore. Listserves targeting Jews from Orthodox, Conservative, Reconstructionist, Reform, and Renewal backgrounds all had people eager to discuss their reconnection to their faith, whether through small acts of observance or in larger commitments. Whatever the length of the step, the stride was there.

Thus this book was born. No one is positing that the stories of some Jews represent those of all Jews. And though there are many different paths that one may take toward an increased connection to Judaism, there are many Jews who have chosen a different road altogether. But in light of the view by many sociologists and religious leaders, as well as self-appointed guardians of the faith, that the American Jew is being assimilated out of existence, it is important to acknowledge that an increasing number of Jews are revisiting their faith in a way that, in terms of energy and passion, this country has rarely seen.

Many people had wonderful stories to tell. All could not be included or I might still be interviewing, writing, and editing today. Often an interview was chosen because it was emblematic of hundreds of similar stories. Conversely, some were chosen for their uniqueness. All were chosen for the positive message they embodied. I made it clear to the people I interviewed that I had no hidden agenda. I am not a *60 Minutes* reporter. I was trying to create a book of the positive experiences of many Jews in reconnecting with their faith in the hope that others contemplating a return might feel empowered.

During the interview process, five paths become overwhelmingly clear. The book is therefore organized in five sections to coincide with these five paths.

- *Starting Again for the First Time*–Interviews with people who were brought up in secular homes and, as adults, have become more observant.
- *Freedom to Believe*–Interviews with Russian emigres who were unable to practice the traditions in Russia but have reconnected to their faith since arriving in America.
- *After Wading in Other Waters*–Interviews with people who have returned after exploring other faiths or philosophies.

- *A Choice of One's Own*–Interviews with people who were not born into but rather chose the Jewish faith.
- *Faith through Art*–Interviews with people who, through their art, developed an increased connection to their faith.

Many of the paths overlap, lending a sense of arbitrariness to the organization. For example, most of the people interviewed came from nominally religious backgrounds. Their stories might have been placed in the section that deals with starting again, or in a more specific section, such as faith through involvement with art. In addition, many of the interviewees, at one time or another, examined other philosophies or religions. Their stories might have been placed in that section. Ultimately, each story was placed in the section corresponding most closely to its path.

Only the first name and the initial of the last name are disclosed in order to protect the confidentiality of the interviewee. With the rabbis, however, both names are included as, for the most part, they are already public figures and writers of note. Anonymity has not been part of their job description.

Many people were essential in the creation of this book, particularly each person who agreed to spend over an hour being interviewed. To all, the sincerest thank you. Sharing your life with me and others has been truly an exhilarating experience.

Most of the people interviewed recommended someone else who had a wonderful story. In addition, a few people were wellsprings for contacts and connections. Rabbi Shelly Kniaz introduced me to a broad range of people throughout the Conservative Movement. Dru Greenwood was equally important in the Reform. To both the heartiest of thanks for their support and time. Rabbi David Zaslow was a virtual Rolodex of names, numbers, and e-mail addresses for a vast array of people who had marvelous stories from the Renewal Movement. Chaya Teldon offered her insight with connections to those who shared Orthodox stories.

Complete interviews require transcription before they can be melded into form. Without Miguel Carela, this process would have been interminable.

To David Rosensweig, one of the world's truest *menschs,* who acted as advisor in all matters, legal and editorial, my deepest gratitude.

To Isabel Mirsky and John Smith a sincere thanks for their immediate response to questions of research and citation style.

To JoAnn Graham, Bill Simon, Louis Feola, Kathleen Berger, Michelle Stern, and Bernard Witlieb, I owe a debt of appreciation for their innumerable acts of encouragement.

I am enormously grateful to my parents, Bernard and Nora Gonsher, and to Bertha and Julius Vinik for their unflappable support.

And to my husband David, who made sure of all the little things like perfection in a computer, formatting, audio set-ups for interviewing, along with the big things, like giving me the time and the support to write—I thank you for all that and the beauty of the Jewish home we have together.

Introduction

Putting a documentary on television requires, among a thousand other things, vetting. Loosely defined, vetting is making sure that the material one says in the course of the program is true and won't get anyone involved in a massive lawsuit. With our documentary, *Embracing Judaism: Reaching In, Reaching Out, Reaching Up*, the powers that be at ABC were primarily interested in the veracity of the voiceover, most specifically the statement that: "According to a recent *Newsweek* poll, increasing numbers of Americans of all faiths are searching for spiritual meaning, and grappling with the age-old question of what their faith means to them. And as we approach the new millennium, for many Jews their faith has become crucial."[1]

The *Newsweek* article was no problem. In addition, there was abundant statistical data that the United States was enjoying an increase of religious connection and spirituality. The vast majority of Americans surveyed voiced a strong commitment to religious doctrine, affiliation with a religious institution, a sense of a personal connection to God, and even belief in miracles.[2] A 1996 Gallup poll reported that more and more Americans feel that religion plays an important role in their lives.[3] At the end of 1997,

---

1. Barbara Kantrowitz and Patricia King, "In Search of the Sacred," *Newsweek*, 28 November 1994.

2. George Gallup Jr. and Jim Castelli, *The People's Religion: American Faith in the 90's* (New York: Macmillan 1989).

3. Bill Moyers, "The Resurgence of Faith," *USA Weekend*, 13 October 1996.

The New York Times devoted an entire Sunday Magazine section
to a look at the increased religious connection on the part of
American Jews, citing that "Americans are still among the most
religious people on the planet." Whether that religious connection was in fact connected to organized faith was another question entirely. In fact, the magazine section, titled *God Decentral-
ized*,[4] had as a central theme that organized religion per se is
undergoing a change, that a fall-off in attendance at established
churches and synagogues needs to be viewed in relation to the
search by many for a spirituality missing in their inherited houses
of worship. Numerous articles and interviews explored these
quests, including one article by Roger Kamenetz, who wrote on
aspects of Jewish renewal.[5]

ABC was concerned whether this increase of religious fervor
was equally true for Judaism. Had the increased spiritual search
on the part of a vast majority of Americans translated to American Jews? What we found then and what we have continued to
find in our research is that, although there is cause for reflection and even concern in the Jewish community, a budding population of Jewishly committed people are reconnecting in a myriad
of ways and synthesizing Judaism into the very heart of their
lives.

The Problem

The common feeling throughout this decade and certainly as we
begin a new millennium is that American Judaism is in trouble.
Why? Because the numbers are down. The numbers that at the
start of the '90s threw most Jewish leaders into a frenzy were from

---

4. *The New York Times Magazine*, 7 December 1997.
5. Roger Kamenetz, "Unorthodox Jews Rummage Through the Orthodox Tradition," *The New York Times*, 7 December 1997.

the 1990 National Jewish Population Survey (NJPS).[6] According to this study, although the number of Jews—roughly 5.8 million— is about the same as in 1950, the population of the country has risen from 150 million to close to 280 million. Thus, the percentage of the Jewish population has dropped from 3.7 percent to 2 percent. Integral to this numerical downturn and the source of most concern throughout all denominations of Judaism was that the rate of intermarriage had risen to over 50 percent.

The concern was that this decline may have manifold effects, most succinctly an end to Jewish life as we know it.[7] There had been frequent discussion that the perception of the United States as a threefold religious culture—Catholic, Protestant, Jewish— had long been an illusion; this illusion might have been sustainable when Jews counted for close to 4 percent of the population, but certainly not at 2 percent.[8]

It is heartening to remember that the demise of Judaism, like that of the theater, may be greatly exaggerated. Signs of the end of American Judaism have been reported as early as the turn of the century, when sociologists were forecasting that full integration into American society would destroy the Jewish community. More recently, in the '60s, before Alan Dershowitz's 1997 tome bearing the same title, *Look* magazine published "The Vanishing American Jew,"[9] an article outlining the demise of American Jewry. The article was not taken particularly seriously since the evidence appeared distorted and Jews simply didn't seem to be vanishing.

---

6. Barry A. Kosmin, et.al. *Highlights of the National Jewish Population Survey* (New York: Council of Jewish Federations 1991).

7. Elliott Abrams, *Faith or Fear* (New York: The Free Press 1997).

8. Charles S. Liebman, *The Ambivalent American Jew* (Philadelphia: Jewish Publication Society of America 1973).

9. Thomas B. Morgan, "The Vanishing American Jew," *Look*, 5 May 1964.

Yet the issue of assimilation has been a problem. A problem in that there can be a watering down of Jewish values, traditional beliefs, and heritage that are handed down to the next generation. This assimilation fear is heightened by the increase in intermarriage. Currently the rate of intermarriage is such that in the Jewish community, out of every three couples marrying, two couples have only one Jewish partner, and only one couple has both Jewish partners.[10] Even if one factors in more positive analyses,[11] the numbers are still alarming, since a common result of intermarriage is a lack of any Jewish affiliation on the part of children, thereby dooming future Jewish generations.

However ominous the numbers, we must remember that America is a country obsessed with both size and numbers. The quantity/quality issue is one that has especially plagued this generation in various arenas. Whether it be the number of hours parents spend with their children versus the quality of these hours, the number of hours left in a person's life versus the quality of those hours, or the number of Jews versus the quality of their Jewishness, numbers cannot tell the whole story.

Few would argue that having a large Jewish community committed to living a Jewish life, affiliated with a synagogue, and approaching the world from a Jewish perspective, would be optimum. That is not the case. In the absence of this phenomena, is there still evidence of a positive happening in the Jewish community that is not simply "spin"? The answer is a resounding yes. Although the numbers may not be what one would wish, there is a burgeoning community, incorporating, however haltingly, Jewish observance into their lives.

---

10. Sidney Goldstein, "Profile of American Jewry," *American Jewish Yearbook*, 1992.

11. J. J. Goldberg, "Interfaith Marriage: The Real Story," *The New York Times*, 3 August 1997.

What the Numbers Mean

Statistics rarely tell the whole story. What the NJPS showed is the number of individuals declaring an affiliation to the Jewish faith in response to a survey. To afford the widest scope and opportunity for this to occur, the NJPS used no fewer than six "Jewish Identity Constructs," including: born Jews whose religion is Judaism; born Jews with no religion; Jews by choice; and children under eighteen being raised with another religion.

The question is, although forty years ago people may have more readily proclaimed their affiliation, were they in fact living a Jewish life? Because what is behind the numbers is the more important issue. Were Jewish practices, connection to a Jewish heritage, Jewish values, and a Jewish belief system an integral part of their life, or was it no more important than the color of one's hair, and just as easily changed? And what about today?

Unfortunately, what constitutes a Jewish life is open to interpretation. One analysis assesses Jewish life by involvement in three activities: attendance at public worship, support of Jewish institutions, and observance of Jewish rituals at home.[12] Across the board, synagogue affiliation is seen as a pivotal indication of faith. But it is worth noting that in today's individualistic society, synagogue attendance may only be an indication of communal worship; those who appear to be "three-day Jews"—attending only the High Holy Day services—may have other avenues to signify their Jewishness.[13]

Therefore, additional attributes or attitudes as reflective of the American Jew including socio-political commitment, connec-

---

12. Jack Wertheimer, Charles Liebman, and Steven M. Cohen, "How to Save American Jews," *Commentary*, 1 January 1996.

13. Heather Camlot, "Why Synagogue Attendance Soars on Three Days Each Year," Jewish Telegraphic Agency, 9 August 1996. Online http://libary.northernlight.com

tion to Israel, and identification with and importance of the Holocaust, have been included as components of Jewish identification and connection to faith. One worrisome fact, however, is that as time passes, the urgency of the latter two events (the birth of Israel and the Holocaust) is greatly diluted in the minds of new generations.

In addition to the above criteria, we will perhaps see additional components to measure. And certainly, as these interviews will show, many American Jews are, in fact, increasing their level of observance and spiritual connection as well as reveling in a heightened sense of their historical, sociological, and ethnic heritage.

From Where We Started, How Did We Ever Reach This Moment?

It is not the purview of this book to give an exhaustive answer to the causes of this predicament. There are currently many excellent books available specifically devoted to placing the psychological, economic, and social causes in a historical context. However, we do offer, through very personal narratives, insights as to why people were disenfranchised and what caused their return.

The causes are as varied as the story of each American Jew. Experts have discussed the issues of a lessened sense of victimization, socio-political replacement of religion, the weakening connection to the Holocaust and Israel, to name but a few. All offer varying degrees of validity. On a personal note, the disenfranchisement may often be seen as the harvest of an educational model and a particular time.

The old educational paradigm is an avenue of almost universal approbation. Many of the minimally connected and a large number of the people interviewed here talk about their distaste for the Hebrew school of their youth. Their education and knowledge of Judaism effectively was arrested at 13 on the occasion of their bar mitzvah. Rather than that being the commencement of new learning, the rote memorization of their Torah or Haftarah portion, the boredom of the lessons, the sense of irrelevance to their lives became the lasting images of Judaism, frozen in their minds. Jewish leaders are aware that the partial Jewish education or afterschool Hebrew education has done more to alienate youths than perhaps any other single force.[14] As Rabbi Ephraim Buchwald, founder of the National Jewish Outreach Program, has remarked, "afternoon Hebrew school . . . in most instances proves to be a great turnoff to Jewish life."[15]

The role of women in the synagogue also played a part in the disenfranchisement of many. Rabbi Shefa Gold voiced what was an overriding theme for many of the women interviewed when she described the sense of being second class in the temple when she was growing up. Woman after woman discussed the lack of available education sources, the inability to have a bat mitzvah and, when a bat mitzvah was an option, the diminished sense of significance in comparison to the bar mitzvah ceremony.

Some Responses

Responses to this apparent crisis have been broad ranging. Orthodox Jews (comprising groups as diverse as hasidic sects, who divorce themselves from many aspects of modern life, to modern Orthodox, who strictly observe Jewish law but are part of the mainstream) differ in their responses. To the ultra-Orthodox, proclaiming through the Union of Orthodox Rabbis that the other

---

14. Note the recurring theme of distaste toward Hebrew school that runs throughout almost all the interviews, as reflected in the terms used: "lack of relevance," "Jewish aerobics," the "bar mitzvah factory," etc.

15. Craig Horowitz, "Are American Jews Assimilating Themselves Out of Existence?" *New York Magazine*, 14 July 1997.

denominations are "not Judaism at all,"[16] the only answer lies in the mitzvah and obligation of Orthodox Jewry to populate the earth.[17] A vast array of voices have lent support to other Orthodox solutions to the downturn in numbers, including less secularization, avoidance of assimilation at all costs, and an all-out campaign to stop intermarriage.

Conservative, Reconstructionist, and Reform movements have employed increasing egalitarian practices to engage women. Jewish Renewal in particular has made feminism a cornerstone of its practice, incorporating rituals that acknowledge life-cycle passages that may occur in a woman's life and have been previously overlooked. The increase of Rosh Hodesh groups that explore a multitude of topics in the life of the Jewish woman, along with singing and stories about female Jewish religious figures, has also provided women with a path of return.

This is a particularly apt solution to the problem of diminishing affiliations since, in many cases, the increased interest on the part of women often translates to increased interest on the part of children. Addressing women's concerns is thus a thoughtful and good long-term approach. Statistically, people born into a family with a strong Jewish connection, whether this is measured by attendance in synagogue or at a Hebrew day school, more often continue that affiliation in later life. Therefore a woman who feels included in worship is more likely to bring that connection home.

The Jewish Renewal Movement, in addition to making women an equal and pivotal component, has gone a long way to address the issue of dissatisfaction among those who have explored alternative philosophies and religious practices. By experimenting with chanting, meditation, drumming, and other liturgical and ritual

---

16. Cathy Lynn Grossman, "Setting Standards for Faith," *USA Today*, 14 April 1997.

17. Alan Abrahamson, "Debate Rises Over Jewish Census," *Los Angeles Times*, Home Edition, 25 July 1998.

expressions, the Jewish Renewal Movement appeals to many Jews who are no longer connecting with the religion's traditional forms but are still looking for a way to access a spiritual fulfillment.

Across denominations, education at all levels has been seen as one of the answers. The Jewish community has been greeted with a plethora of programs designed with the concept that, if the unaffiliated or marginally affiliated would only take a class or go to a seminar, the untold riches opened to him or her would miraculously affect a transformation. One particularly ambitious program, Birthright Israel, which underwrites teen trips to Israel,[18] may also be shown to have positive long-term effects in both turning young people on to Israel as a source of connection to heritage as well as building a religious identity.

Teshuvah

Against this backdrop of fear and increasing urgency, some are heeding the words and responding with what has been termed *teshuvah*, which is broadly defined as a spiritual awakening, a reconnection to the faith, a return.[19] However, in recent years, the term has taken on a distinctive connotation of strict adherence to Orthodox and ultra-Orthodox traditions.[20] A more useful definition for our purposes is that a *baal teshuvah* is "anyone of college age or older who is more observant than his or her parents, teach-

---

18. Laurie Goodstein, "To Bind the Faith, Free Trips to Israel for Diaspora Youth," *The New York Times*, 16 November 1998.

19. Adin Steinsaltz, *Teshuvah: A Guide for the Newly Observant Jew*, (Northvale, NJ: Jason Aronson 1996).

20. See for example Agi Bauer's *Black Becomes a Rainbow: The Mother of a Baal Teshuvah Tells Her Story* (New York: Philip Feldheim 1991); and Richard Greenberg, *Pathways: Jews Who Return* (Northvale, NJ: Jason Aronson 1997).

ers or friends might have predicted."[21] In that case, these narratives are all from *baalei teshuvah*, at varying stops along the way. The only difference is the path they have taken.

The indications that many people have embarked on a path of teshuvah can be concluded on the basis of a number of hopeful trends. The number of children attending Hebrew day school is surely one optimistic sign.

In the early 1980s there were 499 Jewish day schools throughout the country.[22] A decade later, that number had increased by more than 20 percent,[23] and there is growing indication that at the end of the '90s, the number of schools, while not substantially increasing, will show a decided increase in enrollment. According to the Jewish Educational Service of North America, many economically fragile schools, risking closure ten years ago, are now thriving. The Conservative's Solomon Schechter schools have been and continue to be particularly strong.[24] A strong educational background will certainly have an enormous impact on future generations, decisively replacing the unfortunate experiences of their parents.

A myriad of other indications suggest movement by many toward heightened religious practice, whatever form that observance takes. People are beginning to understand that even if they are not willing or able to take on all 613 mitzvot, there is still joy in taking on some.

---

21. Charles Liebman as quoted in Charles Silberman, *A Certain World: American Jews and Their Lives Today* (New York: Summit Books 1985).

22. Jack Wertheimer, *A People Divided: Judaism in America* (New York: Basic Books 1993).

23. U.S. Department of Education, National Center for Educational Statistics. "Private Schools in the United States: A Statistical Profile, 1993-94." Retrieved December 2, 1998 from the Internet. http://nces.ed.gov/pubs/ps/Hebrew.html

24. Wertheimer.

Many rabbis are seeing an increased number of younger people keeping kosher homes, for example.[25] Others are heartened by the increase in educational forums of all types, from beginning study of Hebrew to more extensive Torah study. Programs like Synagogue 2000, National Jewish Outreach's Read Hebrew America with more than 15,000 participants, and Shabbat Across America, which showed an increase from 40,000 participants in 1997 to 90,000 in 1999, indicate that a return is not just a wish, but rather a reality. Internet listserves dedicated to Conservative, Orthodox, and Renewal discussion along with websites like Shamash, Kavannah, and Maven, which offer links to literally hundreds, if not thousands of Jewish web pages, have shown incredible activity as more and more people log on. All reflect the desire on the part of many to figure out exactly how to incorporate Judaism into their life.

But that desire does not come without struggle. Although the majority of the following narratives reflect a joyous attitude toward a renewed Jewish spirituality, there is also a sense that some days an extra effort is needed. The balance of the secular and the spiritual, and the inherent issues that arise out of a religion with a set of rules over 5,000 years old and born in a masculine era, is not easy.

That is the path of the people interviewed in this book. Each person might be at a different place and connecting perhaps in different ways, whether through community, through cultural traditions, or through ritual. "Rituals are containers that hold people together and bind them to God."[26] The following interviews reflect people who have decided to lift up that container and see exactly what it holds for them.

---

25. Michael L. Sinert, "More Young Jews Keeping Kosher, Attending Synagogue," *The Jewish Advocate*, 2 February 1995.

26. Kimberley Patton, as quoted in Esther Schrader, "Reform Jews Seek Revival of Traditions," *Los Angeles Times*, 20 June 1998.

I Starting Again for the First Time

The redeemed of the Lord shall return, and come with singing.

—Isaiah

No path is more deceptively simple and at the same time so hugely complex than those of Jews who were brought up in relatively secular households and as adults are reintroduced to their faith.

Many of the interviewees in this book start off with similar stories of boredom in Hebrew school, disenchantment with services, and a widely held perception that Judaism was an irrelevance that could be dropped or added at will. It is clear that many of the seeds of the problem began years ago in the postwar era. Parents busy trying to assimilate were unable to be Jewish role models, and merely gave lip service to their faith. By not attending synagogues and incorporating a spiritual life into their daily routine, their children, today grown with children of their own, are now beginning to question their spiritual loss.

For many, the search for spiritual meaning in their life began in college with pathways that revolved around political process. They believed that the paths of civil rights, human rights, even anti-Vietnam sentiment would yield proper meaning. Many were disappointed. For others, this reconnection began with the birth of a child and the self-examination that followed: How do I want to raise my child? With what set of values? How can I ask my child to attend Hebrew school if I don't know what they are learning? For many the simple desire to share experiences with their children brought them back to their roots.

Many needed to confront their own rather hostile attitudes toward Judaism. They may have gone to Hebrew school and been turned off. They may have had a bar mitzvah, but felt that the ceremony held no meaning. As adults, meeting their religion again, they may have gone to a service, read material, connected with a rabbi, and suddenly became interested. A vestige from their past is unlocked.

Others discover that which was once denied them. Many women were not given the option of bat mitzvah at age twelve or thirteen. There was a double standard about Jewish education where boys and girls were concerned. Twenty and thirty years later, women are discovering their Jewishness, often in an egalitarian context, which was never available to them before. Thus, nothing holds them back from a full exploration of who they are and who they want to be as Jews.

Many of the vehicles on this path are through adult education courses that rekindle a desire to reconnect with the rituals and spiritual underpinnings of the faith. Whether it be through introduction to Judaism courses, which teach such basics as how to do Judaism at home, or elementary Hebrew classes, which enable beginners to walk into a service and feel like they belong, or, even more advanced study of the scriptures, Jews don't want to be strangers to their rituals any more.

1 Part of a Long-standing Tradition

Joanie L.

I had a sort of unusual background when I was growing up because my parents were both survivors of the Holocaust. On the one hand, there was nothing more important than Judaism. On the other hand, my father worked on Shabbat because he needed to make a living. They had come here with nothing.

Except for during the holidays, we rarely went to synagogue. We observed Shabbat, my mother lit candles and wouldn't write. We celebrated the High Holy Days, as well as Purim, Passover, and Hanukah—the ones that pretty much everyone celebrated. But Shavuot we didn't celebrate. We might have talked about it in Hebrew school, which I went to, but I really don't remember it. It was a very strange hybrid, but certainly in some way, being Jewish permeated everything we did.

Joanie L. is a lawyer in State Supreme Court. A mother of three, she is active in both her temple and the larger Jewish community, including the Synagogue 2000 project. Though strongly committed to her faith, her hectic life often becomes the catalyst for questioning.

3

That continued throughout high school. Then I met my husband, Jeff, in college, when I was quite young, nineteen years old. After a short time, Jeff went to spend a summer in Israel. Both of us loved Israel. There was always a connection for us. I spent some time there in my senior year of high school. But religious observance never entered our minds. Going out on Shabbat wasn't a problem. We did everything on Friday and Saturday and never thought about it. Even on the High Holy Days, we traveled to either my family or his family those first few years.

We later lived in Israel for a few years, but we were not observant there either. We didn't have to be. We didn't shop on Shabbat since none of the stores were open anyway. But we had a car and would travel to the beach or whatever on Saturday. We never went to synagogue, except again for the holidays; but somehow, when you're there, you feel more observant. We were certainly aware of every holiday, but whether you're actively involved in celebrating is a different story.

◦❦◦

After we had our second child, we started thinking about where the children would go to school. It's sort of ironic, but we never considered having them go to a secular school. We both agreed they should go to a Jewish day school. We were lucky, because we know that this can be a tremendous conflict between parents—what kind of school their kids should attend. Obviously, as a couple you get along and you have similar beliefs, but how you're going to educate your children can often be a cause of intense friction. Thankfully for us it wasn't. We had both gone to afterschool Hebrew school and felt it was inadequate. We wanted our children to have a solid Jewish education, so we looked at the three Jewish day schools in New York and never considered anything else. I went to look at the public school in our neighborhood just so I could say I had looked at other things.

Clearly, there was a real connection to Judaism, whether we were actively practicing or not. Once the children were in school, we slowly started to become more involved in observing the faith ourselves.

❧

As the kids got older we became interested in observing Shabbat. Although I can remember the first time I said, "Hey, let's start lighting candles tonight," I can't remember when it became a steady thing. It was about seven or eight years ago, and that was around the time when one day, we were cooking lobster, and we looked at each other—I can't really tell you what happened. It just didn't feel right.

So life began to undergo a gradual change. It happened very slowly and it continues to happen. But I remember times, going out shopping on a Saturday or whatever we used to do on Saturdays, and I would see people walking to synagogue, wearing *kippot* (skullcaps) or dressed for *shul* (synagogue) and I would just feel something. We always wondered, shouldn't we be doing that? There was a conflicted feeling.

We have a very good friend who called me almost every Shabbat and asked, "Do you want to come to *shul* with us this Shabbat?" But we'd seem to always have something we had to do on Saturday. I couldn't understand how she was always able to have the time to go to *shul.* We always seemed to have some pressing place to go. So we felt a sort of tension because there was a desire to be a part of the long-standing tradition, religion, ritual.

Now, there just doesn't seem to be anything else we have to do. And it has taken on more meaning over the years. I try to remember what was so important, what we did all those Saturdays. Now I can't think of anything else that we should do. But how that exactly came to be I'm not quite sure—I think it's something really beyond our consciousness. It's something subconscious that spoke to us and was meant to be.

❧

One day, we decided we're not going to eat nonkosher food anymore. When I thought about it, I worried how we were going to do this. The kids went into every restaurant, they ordered hamburgers, it was the easiest thing. How were we ever going to be able to do this?

But once we decided, it became the easiest thing in the world. We'll go into a restaurant and we'll eat fish. We're not completely kosher by everyone's definition, but we stopped eating any kind of *treif* (nonkosher food). We made our home kosher. Now, it just seems natural. Why did we do it and what was so hard? I'm not really sure. I think it's something beyond ourselves. It's a connection to a community, because when you're kosher, even if you're not sure why you're doing it, other people that you care for and respect will come to your home and eat. The kids have friends who are kosher. When they come over, they know they can eat here. The rabbi will come to my home and eat off my dishes. That's important to me. It's something larger than myself and my own family. I'm connected to something bigger.

ᐉᐉ

Slowly Jeff and I became more observant. Part of it was that the kids were going to a Jewish school, they were learning about this. Of course, when you raise kids, nothing you're going to do is right, no matter what, but we really felt strongly about not being hypocritical. If they were learning about observing Shabbat and we were going out on Shabbat, they would find that difficult to deal with. Young children can't process the dichotomy.

As the kids were nearing bar and bat mitzvah age, we wanted them to feel comfortable and involved. So we started going to synagogue on a pretty regular basis, almost every Shabbat. The other thing that happened, is that how connected you are to Judaism revolves, to some extent, around life-cycle events. So the children's bar and bat mitzvah, my father's death—of course I was saying Kaddish, going to *shul* every Shabbat—these all helped me to become connected.

That was a time when I certainly wanted to be part of a community. We weren't members of the synagogue when my father died, but we'd been going off and on with friends to a synagogue for a year or two. When the rabbi heard about my father's death, he came up to me and I felt like I really knew these people, I was part of this community. I still wasn't a member of the synagogue, and that made me feel really badly. Of course after that we joined the synagogue and became very involved and I said Kaddish there every week.

The synagogue really became our community. That's what my synagogue is like. If you show up, the next thing you know you're involved in everything. Within six months I became chair of the Social Action Committee. I'm only half kidding when I say that just showing your face or any interest is a very dangerous thing! That's the beauty of the synagogue, and it really is by virtue of that community that I got so involved.

We started attending services regularly and a few years ago Jeff and I participated in a study program for lay leaders, through United Synagogue. People who come for the program often live in areas where they don't have full-time rabbis, so they lead services. It was intensive learning, fifteen hours a day. I knew basic Hebrew since I had gone to Hebrew school and I studied in college, but that's where I really learned to read Torah. I began to understand the structure of the prayer book and the different prayers. I still have a long way to go.

֎

Now I try to read Torah on a regular basis. But to sustain that kind of learning, intensive learning, is difficult. Jeff does it to a great extent by going to school; as a dentist he's got the liberty of taking a day or afternoon off to study, which I really can't do. Every semester, I get the Drisha Institute catalog and I pore over it and plan the class I would take. But of course it never happens because the kids need me, I can't go two evenings a week and get home at eight or nine o'clock. It's very hard.

That was the other reason we felt our children should get a solid Jewish education while they're young. Many people do it when they're older, but it's much more difficult. Now, being involved in the Jewish community at this age with my limited knowledge, my skills are better used in administrative ways, on the Board of Synagogues. I'm always going to board meetings, I'm very involved with the Solomon Schechter high school that's just starting out. My title is Associate Director of Recruitment, and they're going to send me this summer to study. I'm involved in the Jewish community, but not so much in study.

Jeff is on the board of the local Solomon Schechter high school and is involved in the nitty-gritty stuff, like looking for a building. So he's got both areas covered. I guess there's some amount of resentment that he gets to study, which keeps him more connected to the active religious community. I'm connected to that community, but when you go to a board meeting you're not discussing lofty ideas about Judaism, you're trying to figure out how you're going to pay to fix the roof.

ᲘᲢᲘ

In terms of Shabbat, we're still completely observant. But being observant is not always without stress for me. For example, this weekend was Shavuot, and I thought this is just too much, you know Saturday, Sunday, Monday. It is really too much. Of course, I had to work on Monday and I couldn't afford to take off the time. We were really torn; we were going to our house on the beach. Do we drive? Should we invite people over? But it's a holiday. I thought it was crazy that we felt such conflict. And I started to feel resentful about it. I was reading an article in *The Jewish Week*, in which the writer said that Shavuot always gets short shrift. Maybe everybody's just holidayed out by this time, so maybe that's part of it. But I started to feel resentful. I didn't go to synagogue, Jeff did. I just wanted to go to the beach. But I didn't. I didn't go anywhere, but I didn't go to synagogue either.

So I'm still straddling between two worlds, not wholly involved in Shavuot. It's awkward. Maybe it's being more in the Conservative world. If you are a Reform Jew, it's not an issue because the second day is not a holiday. I think if you are Reform, you have a lot more flexibility. If you're Orthodox, it's not an issue either because you just observe the holiday. If you have a job, you say this is my life and what I believe, and that's all there is to it.

Conservative Jews are supposed to say the same thing, yet the community is more varied. There are people who are going to observe absolutely and there's no question about it. And others are going to say I have to work and that's all there is to it. So it's standing between two worlds and not knowing what you want to do and what's right and feeling uncomfortable, whatever you do. It's not unlike when you raise kids and you have to work. You're never at the right place at the right time. When you're at work, you want to be with your kids; when you're with your kids, you should be doing work. It's also the world that we live in. It's a very different world than if you lived in a shtetl and nobody worked, or even if you lived in Israel and nobody worked on Shavuot.

૰✢૰

So right now I'm just a bit torn, contending with a little questioning, a little less striving, which, if you're a Conservative Jew, you're supposed to be making the attempt. I'm not quite striving in the same way that I once was, but in different ways. For example, I've become involved in Synagogue 2000, a program in which a group of synagogue members have met twice a month for the last two years. We talked about the synagogue, specifically about Judaism's approach to healing and what our synagogue could do in that respect. We also discussed how to make people feel comfortable coming in, and what we can do to keep people coming. It was interesting, because even among a seemingly homogenous group of about twenty, there were such divergent views.

One group was more touchy-feely, much more emotionally available and receptive to other people. Then there was the old guard, not necessarily the old people. They wanted things to stay the way they are: What's this about healing? It's just new hype and the fact that the *Harvard Newsletter* wrote an article about spiritual healing doesn't sway people, they snub their noses at it.

So sometimes it seems that there's not a whole lot of change that you can effect in an established institution. But things we have accomplished have been wonderful. We put out a newsletter every Shabbat so we cut down on the announcements. The rabbi doesn't give his sermons now from the *bimah* (platform); he walks around with a microphone so he's more accessible, he's more interesting. Synagogue 2000 has brought forth, if nothing else, a lot of interesting discussion, potential, and ideas.

The best part of Synagogue 2000 was what brought me to the synagogue in the first place: the community I felt, getting together with a group of people from all cross sections of the synagogue. Some people who never came to *shul* on Shabbat, others who have been coming to the *shul* for thirty years, new members, all talking together. Suddenly you were spending a significant amount of time with people who you wouldn't normally come in contact with. The first thing you do when you come in is talk about what's been going on in your life. People really open up, so that you become connected to a wonderful Jewish community.

Sometimes it seems that there's very little we can do in our lives to make a difference. But one thing we can do is try and make the world a little bit better than before we were here. I think a strong Jewish community, a strong synagogue does just that.

2 A Ritual to Mark Reconnection

Adam F.

Growing up, I don't really think I was aware of a sense of religion or spirituality in my house. We celebrated holidays more as family get-togethers. I think my mother probably knew more about when the holidays were than what they were for. There was nothing that I can remember in terms of any kind of rituals or going to synagogue.

The first time I had any kind of religion injected into my life was when I was eleven and a half and I was told I would have to have a bar mitzvah. I was not happy. In fact, I went into that experience kicking and screaming, pretty much every step of the way. It was not an enjoyable process for me at all. It was a jarring thing to have Judaism pushed into my life because I wanted to go out to play. I wanted to do what I wanted to do and my mother was

Adam F. is a graphic designer at the Gay Men's Health Crisis, an AIDS service organization. Bar mitzvahed at thirteen, he decided as an adult to revisit the ritual, this time cognizant of its meaning.

saying how important for her it was to have a bar mitzvah. All I could think of was, well, if it's important for you, why don't you do it? Why do I have to be the conduit for whatever it is that's meaningful to you?

෯

For the most part, the Hebrew teachers were dull, uninspiring people. I just didn't understand and didn't want to understand what my relationship was to all the material I was studying. Even if they made it interesting, I resisted. I think I understood the letters and reading, but I was just not making the connections.

At one point I was nine lessons behind on my homework because I just wasn't getting the language. So I decided to give it the college try and do my lessons and catch up on my homework. In one week I got three or four lessons ahead. I figured in one month I would be caught up. I think there was one teacher who was somewhat supportive. So I went to him and said I was all excited that I had done these lessons and was on my way to getting caught up, and he said something like, "So?" That's all I needed! That was it. I wasn't going to get any support from him. There was nothing in it for me.

Looking back, and since I have the audiotape of the whole ceremony, I guess I grasped it easier than I thought. I was actually pretty good at the chanting and the *trope* (melody). I don't remember all of the lessons per se, but I must have learned Hebrew well enough to recite all of it. But with absolutely no understanding.

෯

The big incentive for doing a bar mitzvah was, of course, the party. It wasn't all that big, because my parents couldn't afford that much, but it was something. The only thing that kept me interested was knowing that I was going to be getting some kind of monetary compensation. When I did the service as an adult, it was antigift, which was a completely different experience.

One of the stipulations to me as a child preparing for the bar mitzvah was that it would be my graduation, that it would be the last time I had to attend anything in Hebrew school. My mother tried to get me to continue, finish out the school year. I didn't.

ॐ

As I grew older, I had no interest in anything religious. Even thinking about spirituality didn't interest me at all. It wasn't until I met a guy who was a seminary student. He had been a Roman Catholic and he converted to Episcopalian. He was Filipino and religion was very deeply rooted in his upbringing, both actually doing it and also studying it. He was always gently prodding me to explore my own roots, my own spirituality, but I was very resistant.

Eventually I started looking into Buddhism. My friend had told me about the Buddhist monk Thich Nhat Hanh; I started reading some of his books and the way he wrote was nice and clear. I started to connect, at least to thinking about things spiritually. Then I read a book by Joan Chittister, from the Order of St. Benedict, who wrote a book on Benedictine rule, which by my understanding is a way of living out Jesus's words or Christianity. She writes really beautifully, very clearly and simply, but with great power, which touched me. Not that I wanted to convert, but there was just something there that appealed to me: the idea of conducting one's life based on something other than whim and fancy.

Then I bought Michael Lerner's book, *Jewish Renewal*. I don't know where I had heard about it, but I really connected to that. So I thought, I'm connecting to all these things within the realm of spirituality, then it seems to make a lot of sense to connect through my roots. So I started to pursue that avenue. I started looking for a Jewish congregation to join.

Somebody that I worked with recommended that I come to his congregation, which is very small. It doesn't even have a building. It's called Kolech Hiyenu, which means Voices of Our Lives. I attended that congregation because the rabbi was very nice and engaging. In the beginning, I kept coming just to give it a try. I wanted it to be something regular in my life, meaning not just come once but instead to give it a few weeks, a few months. I kept coming back and haven't stopped. I've become a part of the congregation, sort of the hub of the congregation. There are sixty or seventy families, but there's really only a dozen people who do the work.

⚛

We used to meet in people's homes but now we meet in a church. We have a service every Saturday morning with maybe a dozen to two and a half dozen people on a given Saturday. It's very diverse, very intelligent, warm people.

This is my second year of full membership. When I first started going, the guy who told me about the congregation was going to have an adult bar mitzvah. Until then, he'd never had one. There was a group of four people. I thought it must be rather interesting to do as an adult. I went to the service, to the bnei mitzvah, and I remember sitting there thinking these people are really intelligent. I could never come up with saying anything or thinking along the lines of what they talked about. But the idea intrigued me. I thought it would be a really nice way to come back, to have a formal ritual to mark my reengagement, my reconnection. When they started talking about when the next class would begin, I said I wanted to join.

⚛

There were four in my group. It started out as nine. We studied for about a year, formally, as a bnei mitzvah class. I think for three or six months before that we were learning just Hebrew, sort of gearing up for the class. As a beginning class, we were really varied in level. I tell everybody that the only thing I remember from Hebrew school as a child was "*sheket bevakashah*," which means "quiet, please." It's funny but unfortunately that's the case with a lot of people.

So I started learning. The rabbi basically started the course asking questions like, Why are you here? Simple questions. We learned Hebrew throughout, although some things fell by the wayside because we just didn't have time in the class. With everyone's schedule, it became impossible to do all that we set out to do.

We studied from a book of stories, like fairy tales written in biblical Hebrew. We learned a lot of the basic biblical Hebrew language through fairy tales that we were also familiar with, which was interesting. We also had to look at the Shabbat morning prayer service. At the time we did this there were five of us and there are five parts to the service. Each of us took a part and from that part we had to choose a particular prayer that we liked. We had to translate it literally, word for word, and also come up with a prayer we actually wanted to say because the literal translation is always in a language that you might not feel comfortable with in a prayer. We also had to research commentary from different sources.

We put all that together into a prayer page that then went into a prayer service program for the day of the bnei mitzvah. That was really nice, because it made you look at the prayers and the service and see the different parts of it and the purpose for each. It made us think about creating our own prayers, taking what's there and using the poetry of the Hebrew, which is difficult for some and requires a lot of dictionary use. But it was really fun.

෴

The whole thing, the actual day of the bnei mitzvot, was very emotional for all of us. I was expecting to be affected by the bar mitzvah a little bit, but not to the extent that I was. I was crying. I tried to inject humor and some kind of wisdom that I acquired from wherever and put it all together. My part was writing about the process that we went through. It struck me a few days before the event itself that I couldn't really write about that without connecting somehow with my experience twenty-five years earlier. Since it was sort of a theatrical space, I decided to play two parts: myself as an adult and as a boy of thirteen. I ended up bringing a pair of shoes up to the *bimah* and then putting them down on the ground next to me and starting my speech. At some point, I went back to being thirteen and knelt into the shoes so that I was at the height of a younger me. It was much more powerful than I ever expected it would be. There was something that I couldn't put into words, a connection to all that frustration, resentment, and anger I felt when I was thirteen years old and reconnecting to something that could've been meaningful for me from that time until now.

As a thirteen-year-old, I expressed my bewilderment about the meaning of everything I was learning in Hebrew school. A story that epitomized the depth of my resentment was when my sister was left in charge of me for a week. I had asked my mother if I could skip Hebrew school for that week and she had said yes. In the meantime, she told one of my older sisters to try to get me to go to Hebrew school. My sister tried to bribe me to go but I dug my heels in. I was not going! I got so upset that I grabbed a carving knife and chased her around the room. I wasn't going to hurt her, I just wanted her to leave me alone. My sister ran upstairs to the bathroom and locked the door and that was the end of that. Of course, it seemed like a victory, but it wasn't really.

I think my adult bar mitzvah was a very powerful experience for everybody. I was up on the *bimah* and when I got down on my knees for the thirteen-year-old me, I just lost it. I wasn't sure that I was going to be able to finish my speech. The place was dead quiet. The only thing I could do was look at my mother, who was sobbing in front; that was a very strong connection. My sisters were also there and I had them come up. We tried to engage our families or friends, whoever was important to us, to come up and be a part of the service. My two sisters read from the prayer page. There were commentaries, some humorous, some more serious. Each of them was involved and read one quote. They were taken with how thoughtful, how full of meaning everything was that we were saying.

Each of the members of the class had to talk about a different aspect of the bar mitzvah process. I spoke about the process of us as a class and also for me personally; somebody else spoke about prayer. We each talked about something different. It built nicely.

ଡ଼ୀଡ

Today my connection to Judaism is even stronger, though still with some resistance. There's questioning, but I think that's one of the main parts of Judaism, this questioning of everything, maybe sometimes to a fault. For me there's a struggle to find a balance between doing the things I want to do and trying to be a good person and a good Jew. I think there are at least two poles: one is to do completely what I want to do—like if I step on people, that's just too bad. On the other side is spending all my time helping the homeless or feeding the hungry or things like that, becoming a rabbi or becoming a holier person. I'm trying to find a balance between the two, between having fun and having a holy life. And that's difficult.

So I work at it. I attend services every Saturday. I am much more involved in Judaism than before. But I haven't koshered my home yet. And I still don't have a full understanding of the holidays. But I figure that I only started two years ago, so I'll get into the rhythm of it, because I'm definitely much more involved. I think you have to allow it to seep in slowly and not feel like you have to do everything at once. It'll come.

3 Belonging to a Larger Whole

Lisa S.

I was raised JINO, Jewish in name only. I had no Jewish education since my father believed that institutionalized religion was the cause of man's inhumanity to man. He wasn't anti-Judaism per se, he was anti all institutionalized religion. He also thought that teaching religion, not just Judaism, to children was doing them a great disservice. He believed that religion was too abstract a concept for children. So I was raised completely secular.

We were never affiliated with a synagogue and I wasn't permitted to go to Hebrew school. Actually, my father finally once gave in and said if I could find a synagogue that would let me go to Hebrew school without the family joining, then I could go. I wasn't able to do that. I'm forty now, so this was about

Lisa S. is a musician, special education teacher, and mother of twins. A quest for knowledge and the desire to guide her children to the best of her ability brought her to a deeper understanding and connection to Jewish observance and community.

thirty years ago and even the Reform synagogue wouldn't permit that then.

I was raised with some traditions. My mother is from a Conservative Long Island family. I think her family kept kosher until she was about ten. Her brother had a bar mitzvah. Her father was a cantor. He was raised Orthodox on the Lower East Side of New York and became more of a Conservative Jew as she was being raised. So we had a Passover *seder* every year but I also had visits from the Easter bunny—a completely secular Easter bunny, kind of like the tooth fairy. We had a Hanukah bush in the wintertime and Santa Claus visited us, but I didn't realize that Santa Claus had any connection to Christianity. It was just a nice warm family time. We lit the menorah and my mother would tell us what she knew of the story of the Maccabees. She would read some books. We had a lot of family traditions but no connection as a family to a greater Jewish community.

Once I turned about fifteen or sixteen, my father was much more comfortable with letting me pursue and explore on my own because he felt at that point I could critically assess what I was hearing. I joined B'nai B'rith, primarily for social reasons. It didn't give me a lot of Jewish education but it gave me an involvement in a Jewish community, at least in terms of Jewish peers. I became involved in the leadership of B'nai B'rith, went to some district conventions, and learned a few *berachot* (blessings). We would say Hamotzi, the blessing over bread. Of course I didn't know what it meant; speaking Hebrew was like speaking Greek. And there was no teaching or explanation as to what we were saying, why we were saying it, the source of it, or any meaning. We were just thanking God for the food. So I picked up a few Hebrew terms here and there. Coming back from those weekends my conversation was laced with some Hebrew phrases. My father's reaction was, "If that is something you want to pursue at your age that's fine, but it's not something I want to hear, so please don't use it around the house."

❧

I went to a middle Atlantic college where I had a greater interaction than before with Jews from different parts of the country. But off campus, the surrounding suburbs were not terribly Jewish. I remember once, during the semester break, I stayed where I lived in Alexandria, Virginia. I didn't even know where the Hillel was on campus, so I went to a supermarket, which I would have done at home in New Jersey, to look for Hanukah candles. When I couldn't find them, I asked the store manager whether they carried any and he answered, not with any animosity, just as a matter of fact: "I'm sorry but we don't carry any of that Jewish stuff for you people." That was my first experience with any kind of anti-Semitism. I found out that people had very little understanding of Jews.

I met my husband at a Halloween party at a recording studio in New York City some years after college. I was never taught that I had to marry a Jew. There was no message that Judaism needed to be continued and that our participation was key to its survival. Nothing like that at all. So when I met my husband, it was very interesting. First of all, I couldn't understand his name, Shimon, which is Hebrew. It seemed very odd to me. I found out he is the son of an Orthodox rabbi, which explained why he didn't have an English name. He said that his parents went with the tradition of not giving English names in order to create a more Jewish identity in the children. He is the second of four sons of a modern Orthodox rabbi, and his mother is the daughter of an Orthodox rabbi. But he had rejected it at an early age, which wasn't easy, growing up in such a family. We started dating and over a period of about two years we got to the point where we wanted to get married. His family was just happy that he brought home a Jewish bride. It didn't seem to matter that I was Jewish in name only. I had Jewish blood.

❦

By marrying into my husband's family, I had an introduction to a way of life, to Judaism, that I hadn't and probably couldn't have gotten any place else. I completely felt that I had intermarried. Even though he was not Orthodox and rejected both the philosophy and the life-style, and we shared the same values and views, I couldn't help but learn about Orthodox Judaism. If nothing else, by osmosis! And it interested me enough to want to learn more about it. I had opinions about Orthodox Judaism, but my opinions were based upon a complete lack of knowledge.

When I finally grasped that I really couldn't make decisions about Judaism because my convictions were based on ignorance, I realized I had an incredible resource at my disposal—an entire family of Orthodox rabbis. So I decided that I was going to take advantage of it. Someone looking for resources to learn about her past and heritage had married into a family that opened up all the doors to that knowledge. I started learning on my own. I took a lot of books from my father-in-law's library. I had a lot of discussions. And two years later, when my husband and I set up house and got settled in a community, I joined a Conservative temple and went to the adult education classes and took some Hebrew classes. It really didn't change my views but it did provide me with a completely different perspective.

One of the things that I discovered was that the values, the morals, and the world view that I had were, in fact, a product of my Judaic upbringing. In spite of a complete dearth of Judaic education and ritual as a child, my parents had imbued in us completely Judaic values with respect to morals and ethics. I found that amazing. I am eternally grateful for the way in which my parents raised my sisters and me and the values that they instilled in us. That motivated me to go on and to learn more.

⊙⥿⊚

Like many people, what really got me involved in my own growth and my own movement toward the Jewish community was when we had children. When you have children, you wind up examining yourself, your values, and your views. You look at who you are and what you're about. You can't responsibly raise children if you don't know where you're coming from and where you want to guide them. My husband and I went through a lot of introspection and soul-searching as to what we were going to teach our children about Judaism. I found, in looking back, I had really missed out on having any sense of community, of having any sense of belonging or connectedness to my past. We couldn't trace our family beyond our grandparents. I have no family genealogy, nothing that I could draw on. As an adult I learned that there was definitely a hole in my soul and I had no tether to the past, what came before me. That was something I did not want to pass along to my children. I wanted them to start with the warmth and security of the family unit as their womb, but outside the womb, I wanted them to feel a sense of belonging to a larger whole. That was important to me, my need to pass on to my children a sense of belonging that I never had.

We ended up sending our children to a non-Orthodox Jewish day school, not just for religious reasons but also for academic reasons. In spite of the fact that I was comfortable with my decision intellectually, I found it emotionally very threatening. I didn't really know what my children were going to hear. Everything your children have learned up until the point where you send them off into the world has been through your eyes, your mouth, your love. I was concerned about how they would assimilate what they were being taught about Judaism and religion, and if the values being taught were going to be contradictory to my values, my perception, and my world view. I felt that it was my responsibility and my duty to learn as much as I could so that I would know what was being taught to my children, so that I could answer their questions intelligently.

At about that time, I became very good friends with the wife of our rabbi. Through my desire to learn more about myself and my concerns about my children's religious education and to be the best mom that I could be for my children, I became involved for the first time in a temple, which is egalitarian Conservative.

❦

One of the things my mother instilled in us, which I later learned was the primary thrust in Judaism, was that our purpose on this planet is to leave it a better place because we were here. It's called *tikun olam*, repairing the world. I had always been very involved in that aspect of life—through my work, in organizations, and volunteering. I was a special education teacher. I taught for three years and had been involved in some type of organization that contributed to, what I hoped, was the betterment of humanity. That was one of the things I couldn't do as the mother of young twins. I missed it and I saw in the synagogue a wonderful way of getting back that part of my life.

I got involved and jumped into the Jewish community with both feet. I joined the choir. I was very fortunate because our congregation and our community is very warm, much like a large extended family, and I had never had that experience. It's wonderful. It was exactly what I wanted for my children, and I guess for the child within me. I started studying with the rabbi; I became more involved in the temple and going to evening services. I went to my first Purim service about three years ago, and my first Simchas Torah celebration.

❦

I'm educated in the ways of *kashrut* (the Jewish dietary laws) both through my in-laws and formally by studying, so they trust me in their kitchen. I know the laws, a lot of the commentary about it, and the reasoning. I dispelled for myself a lot of fallacies that I had heard; for example, many people believe that *kashrut* was for health reasons and now with our modern society we no longer need that anymore. I am very comfortable knowing the traditional view about it. My children know all the laws of *kashrut*. Of course they go to school where many of their friends are kosher in their homes and the school itself is completely kosher.

In our house, I try to make a traditional Shabbat dinner most Fridays. We light the candles, we say Hamotzi, we say the *berachot.* From school my children know a great deal more about *davening* (praying) and the blessings than I do. I'm learning with them. It's a wonderful experience and they enjoy that. So do I. I like that the purpose of Shabbat is to be with the family. Time devoted just to the family, to non-physical endeavors, to emotional and spiritual pursuits and being, just being with ourselves, within our family, within our community, within the universe.

ּֿ❦

I am more comfortable with where I am right now than where I was. When I had children, a different purpose regarding my Jewish faith presented itself: to pass on Jewish knowledge, wisdom, and traditions interspersed with its values and ethics; to have Judaism help guide their lives, to teach them where they came from and to be part of a larger community, to enable them to be as fluent and comfortable sitting down at a black hat, modern Orthodox, Conservative, or Reform table, and that they will know what's going on and what's expected of them. I didn't know that. My purpose now is to pass on the knowledge, and let them form their own experience of it.

4 A Calling

Paula D.

I grew up in Portland, Maine, in a town where basically one way or another we're related to three quarters of the Jewish population. Three out of four of my grandparents were all brought up and raised in Portland.

It was the kind of town that no one moved away from in those generations. My parents' good friends when I was growing up are the same people they went to high school with, and belonged to the Jewish fraternities with, and went to Portland junior college or off to Boston University. But everyone came back to Portland and raised their kids together. That was Jewish society. They weren't religious Jews by any stretch of the imagination, not even

Paula D. is the mother of four. An active member of her congregation, until recently she was a guidance counselor at a Solomon Schechter school. After years of contemplation about the "right" path for her, she was accepted at the Jewish Theological Seminary and awarded a Wexner Fellowship to aid in her rabbinical study.

bagel-and-lox-eating Jews. Portland was removed from what we think of as New York Judaism, cultural Judaism. It was men playing poker together and women playing mah-jongg, and all the kids, myself included, hanging out at the Jewish community center. In my synagogue there was a very strong core of kids who belonged to United Synagogue Youth, which I did, because I followed my boyfriend there. He was president one year, the next year I was. I did it for very social reasons.

The United Synagogue Youth is the youth movement of the Conservative Movement. Today, it's an informal educational tool for the Conservative Movement that teaches kids what it means to be a Jew. But when I grew up, it was totally social. None of us knew how to pray or how to lead prayers. None of us learned how to read the Torah, except what we memorized for our bar or bat mitzvah.

I was bat mitzvahed in a group of seven girls. Although that was kind of neat, the boys got to do it themselves. We had to get in these dorky, white robes. And we each got about one of the blessings and three of the lines of the Haftarah to say. My brother's bar mitzvah was not a big deal, it was a luncheon after services. It was very low key in Portland in those days. But for the girls, it was even less of an event because it was seven of us at one time. Although I remember it being fun, I don't remember it as having any impact on me. I didn't have any idea what it meant to become a Jewish adult. It meant nothing to me as an understanding about taking on obligations. All the very stuff that I teach kids today at Solomon Schechter, I knew nothing about.

⚬⚬

I was a pretty bad girl in Hebrew school. I was a very big goody two-shoes in every way out in public, but in Hebrew school I was a very bad girl.

We would hide inside the girls' lounge and cut class. And we would torture these nice Yiddishe mamas who were our Hebrew school teachers. When I think of it now, I cringe. The only person who we really adored and cherished was the cantor, and to this day I adore and cherish him. Besides my grandfather, he was my first big Jewish influence. He is a Holocaust survivor, and he didn't talk about his experience very much except for once when we were in sixth or seventh grade. He told the music class his whole story. I'll never forget his story or him telling it to us. He is really one of the reasons that I'm along the path as far as I am. He is just a fine human being, an incredibly wonderful man. When I've been back in Portland, it's been a wonderful reunion for us each time.

I sang in the youth choir, that was the other connection, and he of course was in charge of it. In fact, I conducted the youth choir through about eighth grade. This is another measure of how little connection I had to religious Jewish life. We would sing, we had an organ in our temple even though it was Conservative, and during a bar or bat mitzvah the youth choir would sing right through the Torah service. Then as soon as we were done, we would leave. We were in one of those old-fashioned places where you were up some stairs and you could look down on the congregation. As soon as we were done with our part we just left. We hung out in the lounge and the service had nothing to do with us. While we were singing, we just thought of ourselves as singing, no way did it have anything to do with prayer. It had nothing to do with me that it was Shabbes. It was kind of weird.

◈

I went to Swarthmore College in Pennsylvania. This was how Jewish I was: I went home for Rosh Hashanah and Yom Kippur, I went to services, I celebrated Passover and ate matzah, and that was it. That was really it. I was a very typical college student, totally into being a universalist. I was into meeting people from all over the world. My roommate for three years was Indian so I learned about the history of Hindu culture. Swarthmore is a Quaker school so I went to Quaker meetings. I was into learning about everything.

I never thought about not being a Jew, but I was not very interested or knowledgeable about what it meant. For the first time,
I really had a very broad group of friends. Although probably a
third of the college was Jewish, they were not a very observant
Jewish community. At Penn, where my boyfriend was, I hung out
at Sigma Ki on Friday afternoons, drinking beer across the street
from Hillel. I saw everyone walking to services, but it had nothing to do with me. One year I went to Penn for Yom Kippur. We
fasted, went to Hillel services, and then broke the fast by eating
pork chops for dinner in the fraternity house. When I think about
that, I just about die. But there I was, that was fine with me.

ఌఀ

My first movement toward figuring out who I was as a Jew was
when I finished college and moved to Washington, DC, with my
best friend. I had majored in English literature with a minor in
sociology. I was ready to save the world, but people only wanted
to know how many words per minute I could type. It was a learning process. My roommate is Jewish by birth and from a very
assimilated family with really no Jewish background or knowledge. We didn't establish any kind of Jewish apartment together,
but it was my first time really on my own. I had to get a job, pay
rent, without a family to fall back on. I started looking, whether
consciously or subconsciously, toward the Jewish community.

My first job was at a bank. I was doing loan mortgage servic-
ing, some stupid job. When I started looking for a real job, one
that would make me happier than just paying the rent, I started
looking in the Jewish community.

I ended up getting a job at Neighbors' International as a glori-
fied secretary. I worked there for a year. It was the first time I
had an understanding that there was a world of Jewish communal service, that people dedicated their lives to the Jewish community. I didn't grow up in a UJA family or anything like that.
My mother was involved in Hadassah when I was a kid, but that
was it. Then she had to go back to work and didn't do any vol-

unteer work while I was growing up. So I didn't have that role model, I didn't understand it, I didn't know what it meant. This was the first time I learned about it and I gained this whole family. It was more than just a work group. I adored my boss, and he taught me a lot. Another man started talking to me about what I wanted to do, and I knew I wanted to go into social work. He suggested looking into a Jewish communal role. That started me thinking.

After about a year there, I started looking at the classifieds again because I still hadn't saved the world. I was incredibly fortunate and blessed to get a job for the Jewish Foundation for Group Homes, which was a brand new fledgling agency. At twenty-three, I became the Senior Residential Counselor in a group home for mentally retarded adults. In the house we kept kosher, we made Shabbat dinner, we observed the holidays, and we had mezzuzot on every door. It was a real Jewish home. I started shopping in a kosher butcher and our group home was affiliated with a *shul.* All of a sudden, I was living the suburban Jewish life. It was kind of a funny role since all the people in the house were about my age. But it was magnificent: I had never kept a kosher home before and it was so easy. It felt so natural. I'm still in touch with two of the people from the group home.

❧

I had decided to go to the Baltimore Institute at the University of Maryland and to continue working in the group home. Instead, I met my husband Jonathan and the next thing I knew, I was applying to Columbia University and the Jewish Theological Seminary for a joint program in social work and Jewish studies. I really thought I was going to get this degree based on lighting candles on Friday night. I was told that I needed to become fluent in Hebrew and take classes in Torah and Jewish history; I was freaking out. But I really wanted to do it. I took it on as a challenge and it added a full year to my studies. Before I knew it, I was caught up in a whirlwind of Jewish communal service, which

I had been doing as a pregraduate student, but now I started understanding what it meant.

In the program I was in, students receive two master's degrees: one in social work from Columbia and one in Judaic studies from the seminary. It took me three years because I had so many prerequisites to complete. I started in the summer with Hebrew and philosophy. It blew my socks off. I started as a student who had never even thought about the word revelation. By the time I was done with the course, I had started on a process that has continued: wondering about my conception of God, my understanding of Shabbat, what revelation means, what happened at Mount Sinai, all things I had never thought about. I was turned upside down and on my head. That was the beginning; I had three magnificent years at the seminary. During that time, I married Jon.

At the seminary, I had many new friends who were committed Conservative Jews; rabbis, rabbinical students, all became my close buddies. These people came out of a very active Jewish life, lived in apartments in the city, kept kosher, and observed Shabbat with friends—all things I had never done and never understood. So out in New Jersey, where Jon and I were living, we started looking for a synagogue. We found our synagogue in Caldwell and a great rabbi who brought us in. He didn't say, "Nice to see you, I'm glad you're here"; he said, "Come with me and meet these people." The more committed I became to observing commandments from God, the more committed Jonathan became to this social community where he felt at home and was accepted. That was huge for us. We moved to Caldwell to be closer to the synagogue.

ॐ

Change continued to happen for me. It happened gradually through reading books, learning, and being a part of my community. Other changes occurred through larger events, like the loss of my dad, a new friendship, and other huge things that propelled me forward at breakneck speed.

One of the huge things was when Jonathan and I became close friends with Rabbi David and his wife Rita. David came to Caldwell as a rabbinical intern, Rita was working for the seminary. She was a Hebrew day school graduate, who attended Penn at the same time I was there, but since she was walking to Hillel services, our paths would never have crossed. Being in their home and spending Shabbat with them was wonderful. From watching them I realized that was exactly what I wanted.

So Jonathan and I decided to keep kosher. It was pretty amazing. I wanted to do it because, with all my studies at the seminary, I had started thinking I'm a Jew, I'm commanded to do this. Jon was thinking about his new friends and that he wanted them to be able to eat something more than tuna fish in our house. We came at it from different places, but it didn't matter because Jon was willing to do it with me, whatever his motivation. Now I think he keeps kosher more because Jews are commanded to do so.

Turning my house into a kosher home was a huge statement for me. It was an external thing that started to change who I was inside. I suddenly felt more authentic. It said, I'm going to live the life of a Jew. Not just know about it, not just dip into it once in a while, but every day, every meal. This was a very heady, exciting time.

᭒

I was in school at the seminary from 1984 to 1987. During that time in Caldwell we started regularly attending the early morning Shabbat services at our *shul*. It was so comfortable there that we quickly became active in all the social aspects of the *shul* including volunteer work.

When we first got involved with the synagogue, we didn't live within walking distance. We would go to synagogue and then into the city to do errands. It was not a day of rest; that aspect came more gradually. There came a point during my schooling when I stopped doing errands, but Jon still did. But we were driving to *shul*. I also had no problem getting into the car Friday night to drive to Maine to see my parents. Especially after we had kids, we were always trying to get to Maine to see my parents and grandparents. I didn't have any sense that I shouldn't be doing that. I felt like it was the right thing to do.

While I was in school, I did social work at the Daughters of Israel Geriatric Center, an Orthodox Jewish nursing home. I went to work there after finishing my degree. Then, because of my love of working with people with disabilities, I got really active in a program called Just Be—a house for adults with developmental disabilities. I also got very active in UJA and I was seen as someone who could put together educational programs. I got active in my sisterhood as the education chair, and I taught Hebrew school in my own *shul*. During that time other people perceived of me as a very knowledgeable Jew. But all the time, I still had my own uncertainties, as if I didn't quite know what I was doing.

ﻬ

Once we had kids, Shabbat became much more regular. There was a lot less running around doing errands after services. We really started spending that time with friends. As the kids got older, I came to be in a different place. Having kids changed me profoundly. I lost all my doubts about God and became very sure, not just that there is a God, but that I have a relationship with God. Raising the children I felt an enormous responsibility, wanting them to have the Jewish upbringing that Jonathan and I never had as kids. We sent them to nursery school at the synagogue, which had a wonderful program, and we became even more active. I learned again how to read the Haftarah and it's a real joy for me.

There was a lot of gradual change. But in 1991, I lost my dad. That was my first experience with real loss. It was a shock and it was horrible. I'd been toying with a lot of different ideas, but losing my father pushed me to take on something new. It's interesting to look at what has influenced me in the past; at the JCC I learned a little bit about *teshuvah*, from a Lubavitch man who ran the Passover matzah factory with me. I learned from him that, in the face of loss, you take on mitzvot, positive action to help ease your own pain by putting something back into the world. So when I lost my dad, I took on the mitzvah of going to the *mikvah* (ritual bath) every month. I also took on the mitzvah of wearing a *kippah* and tallit during Shabbat services. And I decided to extend our Shabbat. I don't want it to end with services, to jump in the car right after. I didn't want our kids to think they can go do anything. I wanted a full Shabbat. And that was the first time that we extended it.

Today, we don't do anything until after Shabbat ends. And if we're going somewhere, we keep Shabbat there. Until that point, we just dropped Shabbat if we happened to be on vacation. Shabbat would just not exist for us if we weren't in our own community—which tells me how important it is to be part of a community. When I lost my Dad, I took on those mitzvot, and I have them all in my life today.

༺༻

Once a week at Daughters, kids from the Solomon Schechter day school came to visit. These were the most amazing kids I had ever seen. And who were they? They were Conservative Jews being brought up in a knowledgeable way. These beautiful handsome boys looked like every other boy in the world, except they wore a *kippah* on their heads. It was incredible that these teenagers seemed to be totally immersed in a Jewish way of life, yet they were still quite normal. I fell in love with the kids.

I ended up going to work at the school. I started as the guidance counselor in the middle school. I was learning huge, huge things about the Jewish way of life. I learned from the kids. Some are totally nonobservant in their familial lives and some are very observant. There's the whole gamut, but the parent body is committed to educating children Jewishly, to know how to be Jews, to have it in their back pocket.

When I went to work at Schechter, I was able to seal the fate of my kids because Jonathan, at that time, said they can have a Schechter education. He was pretty uneasy about it because both of us grew up in public schools and feel very commited to public school education. I think he was more worried than I was about our kids being too sheltered or too Jewish, but now he's so happy and proud of their education. So Schechter became my whole world.

My kids have learned so much there. I'll give you one example: now, I pray three times a day and still struggle with the words because I never learned to do this as a child. I'm so humbled by what my children already know, what they own, what is theirs, and what I never had. That feels wonderful to me. Sometimes I look backward and feel really gypped by what I didn't get as a kid, but I guess I was busy getting other things. It was a very different time of life.

⚶

Now I am going back to the seminary. I will be studying for five to six years: I'm going to become a rabbi. That's been a goal for the ten years since I finished at the seminary. I was studying there during the incredible time when the final decision was made to ordain women. I ushered at the graduation ceremonies when the first woman was ordained as a rabbi in the Conservative Movement. I said, oh my God, I never thought that could have anything to do with me. Look at that, I could do that. It just felt right, and I held on for ten years and here I go. Sometimes I'm afraid I don't know enough. I see eighth graders at Schechter who know so much more than I do. What I don't have is the authentic underpinning, the true knowledge. And that is why I want to go to rabbinical school; I want that knowledge, but I know I will have to work very hard to even begin to gain it.

What I do have is an incredible connection to God and an ability to express it and to share it with others. Others feel comforted by my presence, or enriched, or whatever the response has been during my years of service in the Jewish community. It has felt important and right to me. I've been searching for a Jewish or Hebrew term that means a calling, which sounds more like a Catholic kid becoming a priest. But this is a calling. Where does my spirituality, my connection to God come from? I think it was a gift from God to allow me to start understanding my place in the world and my connection to something so much bigger than myself. I think it started with something as natural and simple as giving birth to children and losing parents.

All these parts of the life cycle force you to start thinking about what life is all about. It can't just all be about getting dinner on the table and washing the dishes and sending your kids to a Jewish day school—it's got to be something more. I've been a creative soul, I've always written journals. I've always questioned and as I've matured, I think my questions have become more mature. Because I had a community available to me, filled with magnificent people who could provide answers to my questions, my questions have become deeper. My rabbi never says to anyone, "You have to do this, or you're not a Jew." He says, "Where are you now and where would you like to go?" He's never judged, he's never measured. He's just provided all these pathways and that's his magic.

My community is made up of vibrant, committed Jewish people who live 100 percent in the America of today and want to take advantage of everything it has to offer. At the same time, they refuse to give up laws that were given by God and a belief in the divinity of Halacha (Jewish law) and Shabbat and everything else. I think all those things have come together for me, to make me feel that God wants me to have a further impact on the Jewish community. The way I can do that is by becoming a rabbi; becoming a rabbi will just take my learning further.

5 A Rabbi's Perspective

Jacob J. Schacter

A remarkable phenomenon is going on today in the American Jewish community. There is a sense of return—return to a tradition, return to a set of values, return to a way of life. People are seeking something that life until now has not given them. I see all kinds of people, from all age groups, crossing the threshold of our synagogue. We're seeing now a tremendous number of singles, in their twenties and early thirties, who are extremely well rounded and very productive in their secular careers. But they have a sense that something is missing in their lives. Life is not just a job, it's not just a career. That may have been good for a couple of

Jacob J. Schacter is rabbi of The Jewish Center in New York, co-author of *Modern Heretic and a Traditional Community: Mordechai M. Kaplan, Orthodoxy and American Judaism,* and editor of *Judaism's Encounter With Other Cultures,* and *Jewish Tradition and the Nontraditional Jew,* among other works.

years. The same thing is true with older people as well. There's a search for something authentic, there's a search for substance, there's a search for something spiritual, and there's a search for a sense of community.

If you put all that together, then you have the ingredients for what we're seeing today in our community. A community is a group of people who are like-minded, who share the same set of values, who feel a sense of obligation and responsibility for one another, who feel a sense of closeness for one another, and who feel a sense of kinship and a desire to spend time with one another.

People out there in the world are very much alone. I hear this all the time. New York is a big city. People are not connected with one another. People are seeking and searching for connections. The Jewish community provides a sense of community. The synagogue houses communal prayer; we don't pray alone, we pray as a group, as a community. We pray in the plural, not in the singular. It's that sense of community that many are looking for. They want to be part of something.

There are really two dimensions: the personal, human dimension and the spiritual dimension. People are looking for something more than the rat race. They're looking for some meaning, some substance. And they're finding it in religion, however they understand religion to be or wherever they are in their level of observance or understanding of religion.

☙❧

The downturn in American Jewish observance depends on which segment of the community you look at. For the Orthodox community, that is anything but the case. In my own congregation, we have forty-eight new members, which puts us now somewhere around 515. The growth that we experienced in the last five, six years has averaged about sixty to seventy new members a year. We have about 1,200 people now on Shabbat morning in various services.

There is a tremendous vibrancy, tremendous striving, tremendous feeling of life—the opposite of vanishing. People are more and more interested; they are coming to classes. We house an outreach program that attracts about a hundred people just to classes every week. A beginners service on Shabbat mornings has about twenty-five. High Holy Day beginners services were attended by about 125 people. Things are very exciting.

This trend is not necessarily happening in the general American Jewish community. If you check the National Jewish Population Survey, you find that the numbers are down. The numbers of people who are committed to Judaism are down. The numbers of people who identify themselves as Jews are down. What we're seeing is a bifurcation of the American Jewish community in which vast numbers are falling away at the same time that more and more are becoming stronger.

To some extent there is also a renewal within the non-Orthodox community. Some people are experiencing a commitment, a return to tradition. I favor any further involvement in Judaism, wherever it comes from and however it's expressed. So we find an increased intensity of involvement in a smaller and smaller segment of the community while the larger and larger segment is slowly falling away.

❧

There's no specific path, people cross the threshold of the synagogue for all kinds of reasons. People come in for the first time either because they have a friend who brings them or because of an experience that somehow was important to them, positive or negative. All different backgrounds and experiences bring people to the synagogue.

I say "coming into the synagogue" as a euphemism for coming back to the Jewish community. For some people it's a synagogue, for some people it's a Jewish community center. People have different avenues of returning and becoming part of the community and they come for different reasons. People come unfortunately when they lose a relative, a parent. They come to recite Kaddish. They wind up participating in the services for a year. As they slowly become more involved with the community, it often takes on a more important part of their lives. People come in because they want to enhance their level of knowledge, their studies. Some are already observant but want to learn more. What brings people in is really the kaleidoscope of life. We try to work with people, to be sensitive to their needs and try to help them and reach out.

People feel a sense of alienation in their lives and they want to be part of something, to have a sense of community and spirituality. God is coming back now. For a while God was out; now God is alive and significant and important. People relate to God. Modern, sophisticated, high-powered people who live all week long in the maelstrom of American culture at the highest level are looking for God. God means something to them—whatever it means, however it expresses itself. Whether it's coming to prayers once or twice, whether it's an observance, an act of charity, an act of kindness, a value. It's not just person to person anymore. There's a tremendous sense of God as well. I've seen a growing sense of spirituality, of godliness, of human connection. It's really a remarkable phenomenon.

ॐ

In an average class at our synagogue, you'll find tremendously successful people who want to enhance their level of understanding of Judaism. It's not only a matter of enhancing their observance but of broadening their background, of raising their level of appreciation of Jewish law. Some of them have a good background in Jewish law but don't know much about Jewish history or theology. I'm teaching a class about dealing with catastrophe in the Jewish national historical experience and how that fits into our lives today. After all, in America we're so blessed and fortunate, yet so much of our historical experience has been negative. How do we understand it, how do we relate to it, and how did it develop?

Many people who have good backgrounds have never thought along those lines, never thought historically, never thought theologically. So they come to study. Some people are looking for companionship. Others are interested in learning more about their heritage. All levels, all backgrounds, they come and they keep on coming. It's a wonderful opportunity.

6 A Rabbi's Perspective

David Woznica

There's a search for values in America and many Jews are participating in this search. What kind of values will I raise my children with? What is important to me in life? How do I make decisions? Often, to their surprise, Jews are finding that the Torah, the Talmud, and thousands of years of Jewish history have a lot to say to them about how to live their lives. As one example, America places high value on freedom of speech; Judaism places high value on the responsibility in speech. There are a number of Jewish laws on the issue of gossip, dealing with what is appropriate or inappropriate to say about another person. General society cannot legislate such laws, yet Judaism does.

Adapted from interviews with Rabbi David Woznica, Director of the 92nd Street Y Bronfman Center for Jewish Life in New York City. Rabbi Woznica speaks extensively throughout the country on issues affecting Jewish life.

Another example comes from an article I read a few years ago. A woman dealing with a parent nearing the end of life was struggling with the quality of life versus quantity of life question. I too began to wonder what Judaism says about end-of-life issues. To answer this question, I assembled a panel at the 92nd Street Y consisting of experts in the field of medicine, as well as rabbis with an expertise in bio-ethics. Hundreds of people attended these lectures, reflecting the desire to study and learn about this topic.

I have learned that Jews are thrilled to find they have a tradition that speaks to them about the issues they confront daily. And when Judaism is presented in a manner that causes people to think, they come back for more.

❧

Lack of commitment to Jewish life has been an issue under discussion in the American Jewish community for a number of years. The problem is reflected not only in the high rates of intermarriage, but also in the lack of visible commitment to living a Jewish life. Sadly, it is now considered a victory if a Jew simply marries another Jew. While the hope is that the couple will embrace a Jewish life, it is rarely an expectation.

Having said this, I do not think that the Jewish community will vanish. The question is: What will the Jewish community do Jewishly? Though hundreds of thousands of people are Jewish by birth, Judaism has too little impact on the way many live their lives. The result is a community of Jews, but not a Jewish community. However, if the community commits itself to reflecting on its relationship with Judaism, to study, to finding meaning in the tradition, then we have a Jewish community with the capacity to influence the world—as long as our decisions are informed by Judaism.

There is also a search for spirituality, for something deeper: Is there a way to bring special meaning to my life? What about my spiritual life? What touches my heart? How can I connect to God? Many Jews are seeing for the first time that they've been handed a tradition that can raise their lives from the mundane to the holy.

✿

There is something beautiful about growing up as a child with a strong commitment to Judaism and wonderful memories from the home. However, as an adult you bring a depth of questions and issues that make your study particularly meaningful. That is why there is equal beauty to coming to Judaism as an adult. To those entering the gates of Jewish study, enjoy the process. My suggestion to adults who are connecting or reconnecting with Judaism is not only to study Judaism, but to live it. Judaism is not just a philosophy; it is a way of life.

About twenty years ago I received some advice from Dennis Prager. It has been so helpful to me and I have shared it in virtually every course and lecture I have given. Dennis teaches that a little bit is better than nothing. That is to say, it is better to observe a little rather than nothing at all. One is not a hypocrite if one goes to synagogue on Friday evening and then to a movie afterwards. No one would argue that is ideal, but it is a beginning. If something in Judaism is appealing to you, try it. It is intellectually dishonest to say I am not prepared to do everything, therefore I won't do anything. If it is all or nothing in life, you get nothing.

✿

This is an incredible time to be involved in Jewish life. Those of us who are fortunate to be Jewish educators want to convey that it is a sacred task, a privilege rather than a burden, to be a Jew. And we give more to the world as Jews when we look at the world through Jewish lenses. At times it may be tough to be a Jew, as the Yiddish proverb teaches, but it is also very beautiful.

II   Freedom to Believe

*A mighty longing for freedom
is what characterizes the Jew.*
—Judah Magnes

None of the paths to connect with one's Jewish roots have been simple, but few are as difficult as those of Russian emigres. Denied access to the religious element of their heritage, for most, knowledge of their faith was relegated to the obligatory demarcation on their internal passport. The stories of Russian American Jews may vary in terms of years they had to wait to emigrate, the separation endured among family members or the amount of money and possessions they were allowed to take. But what is not a variable, rather what is almost mindnumbing in its similarity, is the consistency when discussing their Jewish upbringing in the former Soviet Union: Holidays were barely known, synagogues were non-existent, and the passing of events in the Jewish life cycle—a circumcision, a bar mitzvah, a marriage under a *huppah* (wedding canopy), was an anomaly.

Certainly not all Russian Jews in the United States have embraced Judaism and embarked on a path of increased observance. But in the case of many, there is a thirst for a Jewish cultural heritage that has been denied them. Many Jews left the former Soviet

Union due to a desire to practice their religion. Others, only upon experiencing freedom in the United States, realized that they sorely missed the spiritual component lacking in their lives. And for many Russian emigres, there is an almost palpable anger at the country that denied them this Jewish heritage. It is sometimes hard to imagine, for as Natalia Z. comments, "Everyone who was born here, you were born here, you have it, you took it for granted."

7   Vision for the Future

Valentin P.

I was not raised with a Jewish life in Bulgaria. I don't think anybody in Bulgaria lived a religious life. Religion was not tolerated over there; it was washed out from the people's lives.

My mother is Jewish but my father is not. Things were so mixed up there that for a long time I did not even know I had Jewish ancestors. I found out much later. I don't know for what reason, but this was the life I had. That's probably why I'm so thirsty to learn everything that I missed. Some people have it handed to them on a plate and they don't appreciate it enough. Not me.

There was, I believe, one synagogue in all of Bulgaria. It was in bad shape, behind the supermarket. The outside didn't look very good.

Valentin P. is a Bulgarian-born opera singer. Ten years ago, he came to the United States to study at the Julliard School of Music at the recommendation of composer Gian Carlo Menotti, never imagining the direction his life would take.

෯෧

I once had a Jewish girlfriend in Bulgaria. It was funny—this was in the school years, we were kids, but somehow I related to her. Of course, we broke up, as childhood romances usually do. But I remember talking about her to my Grandma, and how we were talking about marriage. And my girlfriend had said, "Oh, I'll keep my name." And I said, "Why? Everybody in Bulgaria takes their husband's name." My grandmother said, "Well good for her, she should keep her name. She has a good Jewish name and she should keep it. It will help you to keep the faith."

෯෧

I never thought I would come to America. Gian Carlo Menotti heard me sing and thought I could have an international career. I had some difficulties getting out of the country. The government wasn't letting people out at the time. So it took me one year before I could leave. I was allowed to take my passport—that's all. And I came here. My wife and son had to stay in Bulgaria. We lived apart for nearly three years until the politics had changed enough for them to come.

After I came to America, I went to school. At one of my first jobs singing, I talked with colleagues about how I felt there was something missing from my life. I was reading a lot about Judaism, but I was scared to go to synagogue for the first time. I tried to read more, to know, but I actually didn't go to services until fate intervened. A colleague pushed me to go; it was probably the right time. It was like I was jumping, and I jumped in. That was it; I was glued immediately. This was my new life. It was as if I'd had this all my life, even three lives before, and it bloomed, it exploded in me. That is how I felt from the first minute there. Now I try to live in a Jewish way and to do everything that I missed all the years in Bulgaria.

My parents, who are still there, are happy for me and the fact that I could really connect with Judaism. I have total moral support and I just see the future for us through my son. It is always through the generations. The better I can teach him, the better he will teach his children, and that's how you pass on the good values.

❧

Everything is different now. I'm trying to build my knowledge about everything: Jewish history, the prayer book, the rituals, and everything that is connected to the Jewish life. I was so excited, I took a class this summer to study the prayer book and services. I took the class to learn more and at the end, I read the Torah and it felt wonderful. The more I learn, the more I have the feeling I have to learn more because it is never enough. It is like entering the sea—the more you go in, the more water you see around you. It is an incredible feeling, not always easy to express. For example, people who were lucky enough to be born with the freedom to worship probably don't think about what it would be like if this could not be, if they could not be part of Jewish life or if they could not grow knowledgeable enough as Jews. Now I realize what I could do better, what I could fulfill more in my Jewish life.

We are really trying to keep kosher now and say prayers, and we learn things so that we can bring our Judaism into our home. We really want our son not to miss all that we missed. So we work together as a family, and together also with the community. I try to educate myself more and more and everyone at home does the same. My son was accepted to Hebrew day school and we're so incredibly happy for him. This is a big, big thing for us. He used to go to Hebrew school, but it was only three times a week; now he's going full time. He is extremely happy.

For me, to be Jewish is not just to learn and observe the traditions, it is also to have vision for the future, where you should go, not just where you came from. That's what I'm trying to do with my life—to see where my family and I should go, where my community and Jewish life should go, and how Jewish life should relate to all other people, whether Jewish or not.

❧

I had an official ceremony here to formally join the Jewish community. I went to the *mikvah.* There was a ceremony in the synagogue, which I attended just because I didn't have anything in the past. I wanted to go through the ceremony. Because things were so mixed up in Bulgaria, some of the family were Jewish, some not, I wanted to make sure that everything in my life was starting completely clean. I wanted to start my life here with a clear mind, clear about who I am and my Jewish life.

The day of the ceremony was a completely joyful day. On that day I could say, yes, that's me and this is what I mean, that's what I want my life to be about from here on. It's difficult to describe. People who have always had their Judaism are very lucky.

❧

I travel a lot. One of the bags is filled with books and it is heavy like a stone. I always have a prayer book and the Torah with me. It is not the small format version of the Torah, it is the big one. I try always to read and to educate myself and to pray and to learn so I can become better in every way I am able.

❧

I'm trying two synagogues; I like both for different reasons. Probably it's just that I am so excited that if I had the opportunity, I would be a member of all synagogues. We are members of one synagogue but because my son started in Hebrew school at a synagogue near our home, we also started going there. We like it so I think we'll keep them both. Friday we'll go to the one synagogue and Saturday we'll go to the other. Also, I can walk to one of the synagogues, I don't have to take a train or anything. I feel better when I don't have to use transportation. On Shabbat you try to do things that are in accordance with the Jewish tradition. Because of that, I'm happier here.

❧

The more I do and learn, the more I see that I know less and the more I have to do to improve and go forward. I think this is not just true for me but for everyone who feels passionate about Judaism. Sometimes I think that it is better for people like me to have a choice. If I want my complete life as a Jew that means that I want it with my heart and my mind, I chose to have it. That's why I think it's even stronger, the will and the faith.

I hope everyone, sooner or later, will have the need for a Jewish life and Jewish faith; I cannot separate the Jewish life from the Jewish faith. To me they're one thing and it is not just religion, it is a way of living. It makes me happy, and I'm so anxious and passionate for all of it. It is being passed to my son, I see in him the sparkle to learn everything about Jewish history and Jewish life and song. For him, we try to live it in any way we can.

I think, in a way, the most important thing is that I found myself. If I have to put a label on my life, it is that I found where my heart and where my mind is. That's what my life is about.

8   Second Life

Natalia Z.

My parents came from the shtetls to Moscow in 1937. My mother came from a slightly larger town than my father. When they were little, neither family was exposed to Jewish life at all. I remember that my grandmother spoke Yiddish and I knew how a few words were used, but I cannot speak. My upbringing was very literate, both my parents were very educated. My mother taught in the military academy, my father was an engineer. Then my father was in the war, and when he came back, I was already seven years old. He spent all his life teaching me, but he taught me in his taste, the arts and literature. I read tons of books, thirty volumes of Balzac, Flaubert. You should see the library we had. Huge, full walls of books and I read all of them. It was my father's

After a successful career as a physicist, Russian-born Natalia Z. emigrated with her daughter to the United States. Only then did she have a chance to explore the religion to which she was born. And in the exploration, she found a community she hadn't known existed.

doing. But nothing had to do with Judaism or Jewish interest whatsoever. I only knew that I was Jewish because somebody pointed at me and said, "You're a kike." That's how it was from the beginning, and that's how I remember myself. I fought outside with children who cursed and threw slurs at me.

It was the most terrible time in Russia, in the late '40s and '50s, when my father came back from the war. We would be afraid even to get on the bus. Even though my father had served, we heard shouting, "Oh you Jews, you never went to war, you were hiding behind our backs." Life was just unbearable in the sense of anti-Semitism. It was just the worst. My awareness of being Jewish was only because somebody else told me, and I had it on my passport. That's it. That is how we knew. I didn't know about holidays or keeping kosher; I didn't even know those words. Then I started getting a little bit interested in religion, but my interest went to the Russian Orthodox Church. I went around the country visiting old churches. Then I was interested in Buddhism, then something else. Everything but Judaism. I never went to the synagogue.

৽

For all that lack of Jewish upbringing I couldn't bear to marry someone who was not Jewish. That's how my mother and father taught me, because of anti-Semitism. It was implanted in me that if you marry non-Jews, one day in an argument they will call you kike. So it was not even possible that I would marry a non-Jew. I married a Jewish scientist.

In 1972 our friends left for Israel. That's when my conscience started brewing a little bit inside me. Not so for my now ex-husband, who is still in Russia. He couldn't bring himself to leave the country, he just couldn't. He didn't come with me. He is a very prominent physicist, very educated, but he was afraid. He wrote a lot of books, he didn't know English, he was just scared. He was not sure of himself at all. So I left and he stayed there. That was in 1980. I had to divorce him before I left. I still have a good relationship with him, but he just couldn't overcome the turmoil and fear.

⊛

I left Russia with my daughter. When we came to America, for the first five or six months we lived in Brooklyn. I cleaned apartments. I would go through the streets of Borough Park with wide eyes because for me, it was just out of this world. Then I got a job in Connecticut; someone who helped Jews gave me a chance to learn computer skills. Even though I was a physicist in Russia, I couldn't do physics. I didn't know English well enough, but computers I was able to do. So I was working as a computer programmer but I didn't have any exposure to any Jewish things there. I went to one synagogue then to another but it didn't do anything for me at all.

Then I moved to New Jersey and my friend said, "First thing in the morning, go to a *shul,* any *shul* around." So I started going. I didn't know how to read in English and certainly not in Hebrew, but I started learning. The first year I learned about the holidays, then I started going to classes—classes in Torah, but nothing in Hebrew yet. I like to go to synagogue on Saturday. I enjoy when they read the Torah because I have time to read Torah in English. Now a lot of Reform people ask me questions since I've been told that my knowledge of Torah exceeds theirs.

⊛

My hate, and I'm afraid of this word but I have to say that my hate for Russia is still very strong. It hasn't dissipated. Actually, it probably has increased with the years because I can't forgive the system that deprived me of my Jewishness. I visited Russia in 1985 to get my father, but since then I haven't been back and I don't have any intention of going back. To be fair, I really don't know the country anymore. I left one country and right now it is absolutely a different country. That's why I don't know what's going on now there Jewishly.

Now in my second life—I call it a second life—I got my identity. I didn't have any in Russia. When I came here, the Jewish identity that I had was by default. After years and years I just feel and know that I am Jewish. I would say my development is in two directions: the Torah and Israel. I was already there four times. Israel is my country.

⚛

On Saturday I go to the *shul* but I have to drive. Whenever I must, I try to balance. For me, the best feelings I get are from the High Holy Days. Those holidays, I spend the whole day in *shul*, full days, standing. First of all, I never used to fast at all, and now I feel it, I enjoy it. I am completely there. I even fast on Tisha B'Av and I go to *shul* in the evening.

I go to classes at my *shul* but what I'm most interested in they give only once a month. It's not enough but it's a start. I would really like to take many classes. I love the academic learning of the text, of comparing translations, what each word could mean. A Hebrew word can be translated this, this, or this. So I interpret a sentence according to each different translation. I like this kind of approach.

I have a lot of friends who are observant. Where I live in the suburbs we have only one Orthodox *shul*, a Chabad *shul*. My friends are not Chabad, they are just observant and they go there. I like when they invite me to Shabbat dinner but unfortunately I live alone and I feel I couldn't follow all the kosher rules. If I had a family with me I would probably do all of it. I like it because I am part of something, something Jewish, I belong to a group. On Friday, I light candles and make a special dinner. That's why I say I'm observant in a sense; I don't observe everything, I don't have a kosher kitchen but I don't eat meat in my home. And if I'm invited someplace it's mostly to kosher houses so I eat meat there. I like to be part of the Jewish community, part of world Jewry. People have said I've come a long way—from zero to something.

9   Acts of Loving-Kindness

Tina G.

Every person's life is a book. Mine started in the former Soviet Union, in Kiev in the Ukraine, but my mother tongue is Russian. I grew up during the Soviet era, with the iron curtain between the United States and Soviet Union. In the Soviet Union, religion was considered to be the opiate of the masses. That meant that there was really no religion, for both Jews and non-Jews. Churches were open, but mostly for museum purposes. Attendance to those churches was monitored tremendously by authorities. Synagogues also functioned, but I never knew a synagogue. I didn't even know where the synagogues were in the city. Once I remember riding a bus when a girlfriend of mine whispered in my ear, "Right around

Tina G.'s path has carried her far, geographically, occupationally, and spiritually. Having emigrated at fifteen from Kiev, she has been a political activist, a hairdresser, and a therapist. She is currently the recipient of a fellowship and enrolled at Hebrew Union College, where she is studying for the rabbinate.

that corner there's a synagogue," but there was no sign, there was no address, no one I knew ever went to the synagogue.

We knew we are Jews because it was written in our passports that we are Jews. Soviet citizens carried passports with them past the age of sixteen. It was your identification. In your passports, you had to identify who your parents were and your religion becomes your nationality. This is a difficult concept to understand. Russians had to put Russian in their passports; Ukrainians put Ukrainian; Georgians, Georgians; and Jews, Jewish. If you came from Jewish parents, your nationality was Jewish. I wasn't even familiar with the concept that Judaism was a religion. To me, Judaism had to do with a group of people that shared a certain historical path, which I at the time had no desire to share. It was just too difficult to be a Jew. I knew my limitations in Soviet life due to being Jewish: there were several universities I could not enter and certain career paths I would not be able to explore. If I wanted to go into the field of languages and deal with international affairs, politics, arts—there were Jews who were involved on a high level, but they were very few. Very few Jews made it.

ΦΦ

Growing up, we knew nothing of the Jewish holidays, or what they meant. Jewish values, the Ten Commandments, the Torah, none of that was familiar to me. However, both of my grandmothers spoke Yiddish. They often spoke to my mother in Yiddish. The cooking in my house was Jewish. The way they conversed between themselves, and the wit and humor was Jewish humor. So their life, and my life with them, was permeated with their culture.

Their love for me was also in a Jewish context. Love may be universal, but the way the love was expressed, the way my needs were put before their needs and how children were the goal to all of your achievements—that was Jewish. I would say all nations do that, but Eastern European Jews took it to the limit, all the way to the edge and beyond.

I was very blessed in that my grandmother spent a lot of time with me. Every day my grandmother would ride on this terrible bus to find me after school and to feed me and to help my mother with certain chores in the house. But I was very uncomfortable with her Jewishness. Once when she took me shopping, she met one of her old neighbors. My grandmother was a very loving and gentle woman; she had a long, long braid, grey but with some of her rich brown color. When she met this neighbor, they broke into Yiddish immediately, in a very loud, lively way. I remember my head went into my neck like a turtle, because I knew that public expression of our background was not going to be welcomed. Almost immediately, a voice from this woman on the bus, with her bags of groceries and little baskets of apples and potatoes, said, "If you want to speak that language, you have to get out of here! Here we're speaking Ukrainian or Russian. You have to get out of here if you want to speak your Jewish language."

The shame I felt was unbearable, shame attached to who I was and who my grandmother was. So when we got out of that bus, I remember looking at her and telling her, "When I'm with you, don't ever speak Yiddish in public." She didn't say anything. But her eyes—it's like telling me not to speak Russian. It was her mother tongue. She couldn't have disciplined me, she couldn't have grounded me. I was simply behaving as a product of my environment that was less than friendly to Jewish culture.

༺༻

Even with all the food limitations we had, I remember family gatherings and wonderful meals. My mother was still able to conjure up the most extraordinary dinners. She would collect food over a period of months, and cook for a week—extraordinary dishes, where everything was made by hand. Stores didn't sell premade. So if there were dumplings, my mother and my grandmother actually put together the dough, peeled potatoes and mashed them with fried onions. The scents were incredible; the cooking took forever on this tiny, tiny kitchen stove. And more times than not we only had cold water to wash our dishes.

My mother would take out dish after dish, filling tables with food. Chairs would be borrowed from neighbors, so then the neighbors were invited because they had nothing to sit on at home. Then my uncle would sit at the piano and play. All of a sudden, people would sing in Yiddish and dance in this tiny apartment, putting chairs on top of chairs, moving sofas to make room for such graceful movements. An unbelievable joy and truly, deeply, heartfelt expression of life, no matter how limited life was for us. I don't know where they learned Jewish dancing, I can only guess from their parents. So there were elements of Jewish culture, there were definitely elements of Jewish life.

I never knew when it was the Jewish New Year except that when I would return home from school, a plate with honey cake would be on the table. My mother came from the world that knew Jewish holidays, so she would make honey cake and distribute it among the Jewish neighbors. During Passover, matzah would appear as well. I didn't know it's origin. No one told me when and where it was found. It was like manna, you don't know where it came from, it just appeared.

I remember daring to bring matzah to school. During that same time, for Russian Easter, my non-Jewish friends would bring wonderful flappy cakes. That's right, the state said no religion, the state said no spirituality, this is opium for the masses. But it takes a lot more to kill religion. So they would bring these sweet things that their grandparents had made. I remember looking at my matzah, this dry cracker, and looking at those flappy cakes. There was no context as to why I was eating matzah. I would have been very happy to have their cake.

❧

In 1979, there came a chance to leave Russia. I swear it was from the grace of God. I was sixteen and a half. We were not the sort of family to get out. We were not entrepreneurs going to the

United States to make money. We were a very loving, but financially non-ambitious, neutral family. We were not refuseniks. We kept a low profile. We wanted to have an easier life and we were not politically sensitive.

To make such an extraordinary move, based on little real passion and less information, was amazing. No one could get information about the United States. We didn't know where we were going. We had no idea what was on the other side of the ocean. We got out with zero money. We left our home, our life really, based on little but pure faith. If you don't have high ambitions and deep dreams that take you along, how do you go? There's a certain element, a miracle that moved us, that took us out. We had some very influential friends, influential to us, not influential government-wise or politically. They said they were going and that we were going with them. You have to get out while you can get out, they told us, and so on their spirit we left.

How does one move? None of it is a fast jump. It is layers and layers of experiences. First of all, when we got out, we were greeted in Vienna by the distribution organization that helps to resettle Jews. Then we arrived in Italy, and somebody gave us money to live for two months while we dealt with the process of applying to the United States. The Soviets let us out, but with nothing. Somebody gives you money, so you begin to understand, to see, that somebody out there is putting up an effort. There were books printed: how to behave in the United States, what Americans do, what they mean when they do that, what you are not to do, their sort of customs. Someone actually had thought to put it together and write it up. Then there was the issue of where to distribute us. Those who had families were sent to them. We didn't, so who pays for the flight and with what money? There are communities that put up money to pay for flights to the United States. I mean, there were five of us to get across the water and you can't wait always for United Airlines to have a sale. But tickets were needed so tickets appeared.

Arriving in New York presented us with another gift from the Jewish community. The only person who spoke English was my sister, who is five years older than I am. There were five of us, all standing behind her. She's a little thing. Out of nowhere, this woman who we've never seen before appears with a sign with our names and takes us to a hotel. We had another flight the next day to Indiana. We were to be settled in Indiana because we had no family anyplace else. A Jewish community in Indianapolis had said, We'll take care of a family of five, we'll resettle them, which was very lovely. So we said okay, then we're going to Indiana. I had no idea where Indiana was. Not a clue. This woman, a total stranger who volunteers for the Jewish community, took time out of the day, took us to the hotel, then in the morning took us to our flight to Indianapolis. She made these two trips to the airport to get us. The depth of commitment is amazing.

When we landed at the airport in Indianapolis, three families were there to meet us. We had never seen them before. They were Jews from the Reform Jewish community. They were unbelievable, total strangers took us to an apartment that was already furnished, tuna salad made in the refrigerator, beds made, little pictures on the walls. We asked who put this together. They said volunteers. What volunteers? People who do these things for their fellow Jews, they told us. We couldn't believe it, we thought they were paid. I mean, who would take their free time and do that? And these were families with three or four children, attorneys, doctors; they had enough to do, dealing with their own lives. We had a daily visitor so we wouldn't feel abandoned. My family went to work and they received support from the Jewish community. Where does the foundation start? Foundation is laid upon the acts of loving-kindness.

When Rosh Hashanah came, they took us to services. There were so many people driving to service in the suburbs, policemen were directing the traffic in order to help get the cars parked. I never imagined I would see this, that the government, an institution, was on our side, protecting me, that there would be laws to protect Jews.

ॐ

After we left Russia, the border was closed and there were no more exit visas. That meant families were separated. Fathers and sons were in one place, sisters and brothers in another. Nobody knew when it was going to end. Families were separated, and other families were living in very poor conditions in the Soviet Union.

The Jewish community in Indianapolis was very involved in refusenik causes, getting these people out. We had rallies with politicians and I became very active. That started my political activism. In the meantime, I was undergoing some interesting experiences in my private life.

Indiana is in the Bible Belt. Not only are there churches on every corner but it's also populated by very righteous Christians who see Jews as an integral part of their spiritual relationship to God. Of course, there were also folks who wanted Jews to convert. Yet there were many who saw Judaism as having a very important place in a universal, spiritual patchwork. I was lucky to meet some of those Christians who became very much loved in my life and tremendously encouraged me to seek out my spirituality. I would say that the reason that I'm in rabbinical school is very closely related to their enthusiasm about my Judaism.

These friends became very influential and I felt very comfortable not only being a Jew, but seeking out my path. They went to services with me. They encouraged me to discover the richness of my tradition. These were devout Catholics and Methodists.

So I started going to the temple. At first, things did not make sense. My spiritual place in the temple was one of my latest developments. At the time, my Judaism was caught up with activism; it was all about deeds. The actual act of praying and, in the Reform tradition, responsive reading, was very foreign. For former

Soviet citizens, it really takes some time to feel comfortable in large temples with large windows, rather than small and closed spaces. I couldn't find my place in it; it took a long time.

❧

I worked my way through Indiana University as a hairdresser. It paid the bills, but it seemed like I was a part-time student forever. I got a master of science degree in family therapy, practicing as a therapist my last year. Working as a hairdresser was a good precursor to my work as a therapist and it also introduced me to the American world. If I had been limited to a clerical job, I would have been exposed to four or five people, but dealing with clients in a nice salon, I was exposed to people from across the spectrum and around the country. In Indiana people are very open, very friendly. I built wonderful support systems that I think really made me an American.

My spirituality grew with a struggle. I imagine for many Jews spirituality is a struggle, questioning as you read more, trying to understand. People want to know why, what is Judaism, what is being chosen, what are the consequences of being chosen, both in a traditional and a practical sense in history. So I struggled, questioned, and grew slowly.

During this time, holidays had become very important to me—Rosh Hashana, Yom Kippur, and Hanukah. I went to temple and developed a very close relationship with a woman there who writes children's books and is also a rabbi. She influenced me tremendously without knowing it; she was a model. She was one of the first rabbis I met, and a woman, and articulate. It took a while for all that to sink in.

❧

My decision to become a rabbi came about through a very gradual and unconscious process. It really takes time before things germinate and you begin to see what's been going on under the surface. A lot was happening without my knowing. I met an extraordinary woman, a therapist and Episcopalian minster, with whom I developed a very close relationship. She was an extraordinary model of spirituality and therapeutic mastery. At the time I was aspiring to be a very decent therapist. This woman brought the two worlds together and practiced such a method. I thought she was extraordinary. I didn't even know that I wanted to copy that model. It took some time.

But the seeds were there. They began to flourish with help from the outside. For example, I lived one year in Australia. When I was there, someone asked me if I had ever thought of becoming a rabbi. I had never thought of it, but I remember an electric surge went up and down my spine, a mixture of fear and excitement. That was in 1992; I said the rabbinate is not for me, I wear miniskirts, dangling earrings. I love wearing leather, I love to flirt—I can't be a rabbi. I'm not ready for this. This is impossible. The idea was destroyed right there.

But it wasn't destroyed. What began to happen was that my deep, inner desire and sense of where my life was going began to become obvious to others before it became obvious to me. It happened again and again: "Have you thought about the rabbinate?" Again I disregarded the idea. But the idea was stronger than me. Even my grandmother knew. She was the first one who guessed that I was going to be a rabbi. One day she saw me reading *Beginning Talmud.* "Talmud," she says, "do you want to become a rabbi?" This was from an eighty-three-year-old woman who spent most of her life in the former Soviet Union.

꩜

I spent a year working as a therapist. I loved it and it was very important to me so I decided to go for a doctorate in counseling psychology. I started applying to schools. I probably called thirty places. I went to Boston to interview, I went to Chicago to interview, I went everywhere. But I knew before I started school I wanted to spend six months in Israel. It was very important. I knew that once I started graduate school, it would be five years of commitment and I wouldn't be able to go. So I made reservations to travel and continued to check out schools with the idea that I would apply upon my return.

Two days before my trip, I took a little ride to Cincinnati with a very deeply spiritual friend of mine who's not Jewish. We went to the Hebrew Union College campus. We walked through the halls of the building. My friend looked at me. We sat in on a couple of classes. I left with an application and that was the application that took precedence over all other applications.

I went to Israel considering rabbinical school. The electric current that went up and down my spine is really a passion for Jewish study and work. I did not feel it while I interviewed for a degree in psychology. Even though therapy was what I wanted to do, I was going to go to rabbinical school.

My friend, the Episcopalian minister and therapist, was instrumental in my decision to become a rabbi. She said to me, "Tina, I think this is how you feel about life." And she quoted Abraham Joshua Heschel, which is incredible—an Episcopalian minister giving a rabbinical quote. Supposedly a few months before Heschel's death he was asked, What message do you have for people? And Rabbi Heschel said, Let them remember that there is a meaning beyond uncertainty. Let them know that every word, every deed counts, that all of us have power to change this world. And remember that the meaning of life is to create a life as if it was a work of art. That stuck. I think it became sort of a motto for me to live by. I used that quote in my statement to rabbinical school and still use it in some of my sermons. This woman really nailed it to me. An Episcopalian therapist was being a midwife of an emerging rabbinical student. That's how it started, like a beach, grains of sand upon sand, layers upon layers.

10 A Rabbi's Perspective

Bernard Mehlman

I think all of these reports and pronouncements about the demise of the American Jewish community are ill-conceived. There is no question that we are facing challenges that we have never encountered before. We're a community of people living in a democratic society in which certainly the gross incidences of anti-Semitism have disappeared. Jews feel that society is open to them, they can advance spiritually, intellectually, and economically. As a community we are living through a period of transition from a set of teachings and value orientations—primarily the birth of Israel and the Holocaust—that have less and less significance in the life of the next generation.

Bernard Mehlman is the Senior Rabbi of Temple Israel in Boston, Massachusetts, which has more than 150 Russian families as members. During the 1980s, Rabbi Mehlman was involved with Action for Soviet Jewry; he has traveled to Russia several times to help educate, bring materials, and relocate hundreds of Russian families.

We are confronted with a lot of very complex issues and problems. Along with this tremendous overlay of democracy is the
sense of unparalleled freedom, which we Jews don't really have a
long history of dealing with. We have an excellent track record
on how to deal with adversity and difficulty. We have less of a
historic track record in the other area. So there's a lot of conster-
nation in Jewish quarters.

There are a lot of negative signs but there are also many, many
positive signs for the future of the American Jewish community.
The most positive sign is that we have a very well-educated Jewish community in the United States, which probably represents
the most educated Jewish community in the history of the Jewish
people. And those people are, in significant numbers, trying to
figure out what Judaism means to their lives. We have an incredible opportunity in front of us over the next decade or two to
engage those Jews who have superlative educations, and to bring
them into a kind of educational process about their Jewish history and their Jewish identity.

That's one of the challenges that the Jewish community has
before it. How are we going to engage these people? Are we going to muster the resources and the spiritual and intellectual ar-
mory to make that happen? That's a very exciting challenge.

Many young Jews are seeking Jewish learning. Here in Boston, for example, we have a program called Meah, one hundred
hours. An incredible number of people are participating. Commit-
ting themselves to two years of serious study, one hundred hours,
with academics drawn from all kinds of rich resources from this
community, from Harvard, Brandeis, and Tufts universities, and
from Hebrew College. And the numbers are growing every year.
They're doubling. It's a very positive sign.

In my own congregation the response, again in limited circles,
is a real return to, What is prayer? What is God about? What does
Judaism have to say about my daily life? I'm seeing the most serious people approaching those issues and joining congregations.
Part of it is that there is a religious revival going on in the United

States. It's palpable. I think that Jews respond to that. They're inquiring. They want to know why their neighbors are doing this. What's happening? What's the general atmosphere that has conjured this religious revival as the century comes to a close? Jews are asking those questions, and in that search they're also looking to their own roots.

Another factor is that life has become very, very complicated—frenetic—for a lot of people. Thoughtful people are beginning to ask themselves questions about what it all means, and what it means to be a Jew.

⚜

We have a very active program in the congregation on behalf of Jews from the former Soviet Union. We're running second-language classes. We have a weekly Shabbat lecture delivered in Russian on Judaism, on Jewish themes, for the more elderly population. But what I'm seeing with Russian Jews, more than the pursuit of knowledge or study, is the steps taken to begin to acquire authentic Jewish memories. These people came with little to no Jewish ritual memory, no historic memory, no memory of celebration, of food, of some of the things that serve as the mortar that holds a lot of American Jews together. Gefilte fish, Yiddishisms, those were suppressed.

They were Jews almost exclusively—the ones that I have seen—because they had the letter for Hebrew, Jew, in their internal passport. They had names that were identifiable as Jewish names. In other words, most of them came out of an experience in which identity as a Jew was trouble.

When they come here, that basically evaporates. But they don't have the memory of a baby naming, of a *bris* (circumcision), of Purim, of Hanukah. I'm not talking about deep, ritualistically religious involvements; I'm talking about the general Jewish culture—a boy is born and you have a *bris*, you have a baby girl and you give her her name, on Pesach you have a seder, on Hanukah you light lights and you give presents, on Purim you get dressed up and you have a *grogger* (noisemaker). It isn't just that they don't know the content, they haven't had the experience. Their experience was limited to Simchas Torah in the courtyards of the synagogue. That was their Jewish experience.

The vast majority of the people are grappling with their Jewishness, and there are some who have just walked away. But the ones who are grappling are slowly building Jewish memories. Their kids are being named. They're being enrolled in Hebrew school. They're going through the first bar and bat mitzvah in their family history. They're beginning to collect the memories that will ensure, on some emotional level, their Jewish continuity. And they're very eager about that, they want that very much. Sometimes they don't understand it, you have to take them by the hand and lead them through it. But it's a very beautiful thing to see the first wedding in a family, the first *bris*. They're totally amazed by it all. They don't trust it, they don't know how to deal with it, they don't fully comprehend it. They just need mentors to guide them.

☙❧

Two other phenomena are characteristic of the effort of Russian Jews to reestablish their Jewish connectedness. First is the number of men who have come to me to be circumcised, and the number of families that have brought their sons, who are seven, eight, nine, to be circumcised. Innumerable. They had heard, they knew that's what made you a Jew. A number of people sought me out, and I had to connect them with doctors in town who would help them get this done.

That was one phenomenon. The other was not as big a number as the male circumcision, but significant. A half dozen or more women had Jewish fathers and Russian mothers, but considered themselves Jews. They were technically not Jewish, but came and studied with me and went to the *mikvah*. For example, a young man came here when he was fourteen. He was picked up by the Jewish community, got a decent education, as an adult got an excellent job. He met up with a young woman in my congregation whom I had brought out of Minsk, whose father was Jewish, but her mother wasn't. They both studied Judaism with me. He got circumcised before he married, she went to the *mikvah*. They wanted to bring all that up to speed somehow. They had a need to do that.

There are a lot of these stories among the Russians. These are people who, from a point of view of basic knowledge, knew almost zip. I call them stories of reattachment, of rebirth, of new beginnings. The beginning of a Jewish identity—that's what we have to invest our money in with the Russians.

III   After Wading in Other Waters

*Asking questions
is man's finest quality.*
—Solomon ibn Gabirol

The disconnection that had translated, for some, into a dropping out and away from their faith spurned others to embark on a journey of a different sort. Though Russian emigres win, hands down, in terms of the geographical distance they had to travel, for many, the journey to a rekindling of faith covered far more territory.

As questioning is an integral part of the Jewish persona, it is no surprise that many Jews have been drawn to and explored different philosophies. Disillusioned by what seemed a lack of spirituality and answers at home, Jews searched through Buddhism, mindfulness, Sufi, Quaker, the teachings of the Native American traditions, and others. From many of these belief systems they found insight and value. Often, however, they felt a sense of disjointedness: it was too foreign or it lacked some crucial aspect that kept them wanting.

The return to their Jewish roots was often enabled by a rabbi who respected both the journey made and the forms of spirituality that had been acquired, whether meditation, chanting, drumming, or silence. To the delight of many, practices that had been sought in other venues were found to be a part of their own Jewish heritage.

Remarkably, for many people who struggled and sought answers elsewhere, wise people of other faiths helped them see that the first place to search for meaning was in their own backyard.

11 A Seamless Whole

Spencer J.

I was born in Brighton Beach, which is an old Jewish neighborhood in Brooklyn. I really don't have any memories of living there since, when I was two, we moved to Philadelphia. But I often went back to Brooklyn to visit my father's parents, and I would see around the corner from the Oceana movie theater, these old men sitting on wooden fruit boxes and wearing black Eastern European clothes. Being a kid, I never had any notion they were special—they were just part of the environment. But in Philadelphia, when they weren't around me, I began to make a connection that there was something unique about my heritage that set me and my people apart from the rest of the world.

☙❦

Spencer J. is a video producer with an eclectic background as a forest ranger and jazz musician. His longtime interest and participation in Zen Buddhism has undergone a change, as he rekindled his connection with Judaism.

My family was less observant than the generations that pre-ceeded it. My father's side was religious, my mother's side was more secular. My grandparents on my father's side were obser-vant: they kept kosher; my grandfather, especially after he retired, prayed every day. So in my grandparents' home there was a lot of evidence of a religious life. But when it got down to my family and my parents' level of observance, I would say they were more cultural Jews.

We didn't have any specific religious rituals in the home, but I vaguely remember the occasional *yahrtzite* (memorial) candle or Shabbat candles. We didn't keep kosher. My father would go to synagogue, but not on a regular basis. He was involved in the political fabric of the *shul*, working as an usher and going for holi-day services. The responsibility was put on my brother and my-self to keep the traditions alive and go to Hebrew school. How-ever, it wasn't really something that was an integral part of our lives, it was separate. We lived our secular life going to school and playing baseball but then were sent off to Hebrew school to learn something that seemed very foreign, and we hated almost every minute of it.

I say almost every moment, because I do have some good memo-ries of Shabbat services as a kid. One is the stories—stories are very powerful, and to this day I remember a lot of the Bible sto-ries. That was the part I enjoyed. Also, we belonged to a syna-gogue that had been designed by Frank Lloyd Wright. It was a magnificent building; when you went inside, the light playing in the room just did something to you. The simple experience of being in this building was beautiful. In my mind I connected that synagogue with beauty. The building also had a cool system of tunnels that went underneath, so kids could go down different stairwells and explore. It was fun to play hide and seek. But other than that, there was a sense of learning things that were very unconnected to my life.

At that time, the Zionist movement, particularly in Conserva-tive Judaism, was being played out very strongly. As a child I was sent to Hebrew school to learn about the culture and the history of Israel. I didn't even know about American history, yet I was learning about Israeli history! As a kid, I understood that it was important, but I didn't understand why. I would watch as other kids went to play baseball, and there I was, stuck in class, staring out the window, listening to a teacher talk about the history of Israel, which had absolutely zero relevance to me. I think there was a certain level of resentment, having to learn things that seemed so obscure. It wasn't as if in our home we had a sense of Israel or the larger Jewish community.

ം⸸ം

That went on until my bar mitzvah, after which I stayed for a couple of years. What I found was that right around bar mitzvah age, it started to get meaningful. Most kids dropped out at that point, they had hit the goal of their parents' expectations and they were free from their indentured servitude. The class I took had six kids in it who had chosen to keep going. It was a very intimate experience. The experience was like forgetting everything we had learned so far, and finally getting into the real thing. And that was actually wonderful.

ം⸸ം

In the beginning I became involved in Buddhism partly out of a sense of protest. I began reading some very simple books about it and even though I was a precocious kid at twelve or thirteen, that was a little unusual. I remember buying a book on Buddhism, which my father later found and he got very upset. Of course, that only made me more curious! Then my friend came back from summer camp and he had read *Siddhartha* by Herman Hesse. He said, "Oh this is a terrific book, knowing you and your interest in Buddhism you should read this." And it moved me. It touched off a desire to keep reading and thinking about things.

I have a brother who's four and a half years older than I am, and he was a very cool kid. He had read *Dharma Bums* by Jack

Kerouac, and so at age thirteen I also read it. It gave me a picture, even though it's probably half fiction, of people who could have a fun, rebellious life, which also included spiritual seeking. And as a kid, I thought that was great. Curiously enough, the next thing I did was buy a book, a translation by John Bloefeld called *The Zen Teaching of Huang Po*, which is one of my favorite books. I still have it. It was my first exposure to Zen Buddhism; I bought it because it was the only book in the bookstore in Philadelphia that had the word Zen in the title. What I liked about it was that the teacher, Wong Po, spoke in terms of life experience rather than in terms of text. A whole section in this book is stories about individuals' direct spiritual experiences that wasn't dependent on their level of knowledge or numbers of years of study, or intellectual capacity. They could look at the reality around them and come to an understanding based on the experiences that they had, without all of the other requirements that most traditions emphasized.

Throughout high school I continued to read about Buddhism. I found a lot of things that were personally meaningful to me, things I could relate to. Aspects of it were very different from the religion that I was raised with. Even at that age, I was beginning to have a sense of the larger world around me, and some of its cruelties. This was right around the time of Biafra. I knew what was going on, that there were places in the world where people were dying all the time, that there was incredible sadness. And I knew there was pain and heartache going on in my larger neighborhood, and I was beginning to get sensitized to that.

I found in Buddhism something that began to give me some of the answers I was looking for. Buddhism teaches things like compassion, mindfulness, kindness—things that, believe it or not, no one ever talked about in my Hebrew school upbringing. In Hebrew school there was more of a sense of responsibility. There was a sense of legality. But there wasn't a focus on kindness. So I became attracted to this other religion in an attempt to find something that was personally meaningful to me, different from the background that I felt was being forced upon me.

❧

I continued with Buddhism for many years. Even now I continue to study Buddhism, to study its written teachings. Meditation practice is something I'm very interested in and I was able to take away from it a tremendous amount of wisdom. However, as I've gotten involved in Judaism, I've found that those things that I found very attractive in Buddhism also exist in Judaism. It's just that often they're not talked about as much. The aspects that I was most interested in, like mindfulness, empathy, benevolence, are as integral to Judaism as they are to Buddhism. Some things I thought were exclusive to one particular form of belief are really not. They're really part of my own culture's belief system as well.

When I went away to college I began toying around with actual Buddhist practice and meditation, but it took a few more years before I tried meditation on a serious basis. I got involved with a wonderful group in New York City, a lay organization. There's no priest there, there's no *roshi*. It has less of the religious affects than other Buddhist organizations. There were some statues, the incense, whatnot. But being a lay organization that attracted people from different denominations, that part was downplayed. I think there was an attempt to make this a real American Zen place as opposed to Chinese or Japanese. So it was a little easier for me to go there and practice meditation.

Two months from the first day I walked into a Zen center, I decided to go on a *sesshin*. This is an intensive eighteen-hour, seven-day, morning to evening training period in the Zen tradition. It was very intense. Over the next two years, I went to ten *sesshins*: meditation practice, work practice, chanting, walking meditation, and interviews with the teacher.

As years went on, and I got a lot more involved in meditation, I also got involved in *koan* study with a Japanese teacher. That's a formalized individual study where you work on yourself. You're given a question or a problem that is a test of your understand-

ing—not your intellectual understanding, but the understanding
you have from your heart. I had a chance to study a little bit with
a teacher who had been trained in this kind of Buddhism interview process, Yoshi Suzuki Roshi. He's still alive, he's a very old
man now, but he was a remarkable teacher. In *koan* study, he would
present questions to me, challenging questions: What is the sound
of one hand clapping? is the one that most people know. Roshi
would not use any of those. He would invent them based on each
individual. He might ask a *koan* like, How do you experience God
when you're driving a car? That had nothing to do with anything
I'd ever read about Buddhism, or anything I'd thought I'd ever
experienced. At that time I was a musician, so he might have asked,
You hear an orchestra playing, where is God? Now these aren't
necessarily Buddhist questions, these could be Jewish questions
too. And because of his lack of reliance on the history, the liturgy,
the written tradition of Buddhism, because of the spontaneous
nature of his questions, I was able to begin to think about these
things in terms of myself, my life, and my experience. I was able
to throw away all the books that I had ever read about Buddhism.
And I began to ask myself, when I'm driving a car where is God?
That affected a change in me. That was the beginning. It was very
rewarding to actually be put on the spot by a teacher who was
asking me, Where do you stand? What is your understanding?
How do you realize God at this moment? These were not the kind
of questions anyone had ever asked me. He wasn't asking about
anything that had to do with statutes or prayers. He was saying,
at any given waking moment, how do you understand what God
is? His questions transcended any specific religion. For me it was
a really profound time of growth. It's an experience I look back
on and realize I received a tremendous amount from that kind of
teaching.

᠗

When I reached the age to decide what I wanted to do with
my life, I chose forestry. I spent four years at forestry school,

working every summer in the woods, working with a chain saw, cutting down trees, doing forestry work. When I graduated, my wife Susan and I moved to Ohio for a forestry job.

In Ohio, I had a sense of myself as a Jew for the first time. I never really had one in Hebrew school or any place else. When I lived in the Bible Belt of America, where everyone around me looked at me as a Jew, then I started to say that's what I am.

Everyone had a sense of identity in Ohio. It was based on what church they belonged to, what cultural group they were from. I had none. I would watch as people went to their churches. There's nothing sadder than being in the Midwest in a little farming town during Christmastime, watching a glow coming out of every house and you're sitting there with your family eating takeout Chinese food. It's a sad feeling, but we had no sense of a culture that was ours. We got invited to people's churches all the time but we would turn them down. Then they would ask, "Well, what are you?" and it was a very good question. We told them we are Jewish because that's what we needed to say for them to understand why we weren't going to their church. But we weren't practicing Jews, though we did decide to keep kosher for a while. I think it was an attempt to give ourselves comfort, because we knew we weren't Baptists, but we didn't know what we were, so we were going to try kosher on, like trying on a new suit of clothes.

All this time I worked with a bunch of guys who were born-again Christians. They were constantly trying to impress upon me the idea that as a Jew I was an incomplete Christian. They would test me and ask me questions about the Bible, and I had no idea what they were talking about. They kept hounding me with religious questions and I would get infuriated. I knew back then that I needed to find out more about where I came from, if only to shut these guys up. I needed to learn more about my roots.

❧

After Susan and I had a son, Zack, we started asking questions. What is our family, what religion should our son be? They were tough questions. Zack actually came with me to the Zen center a bunch of times, but Zen centers are not family places, at least as I've experienced them. I know there are places that encourage family practice, but Zen practice is a very solitary, lonely practice. You sit by yourself on a meditation cushion; there isn't a lot of room on that cushion to fit a wife and child. So there was something in the practice of Buddhism that made it tough for me. I began to find that there were certain answers I needed that I didn't get out of meditation practice. Meditation was good for helping me deal with certain things, but it never answered the fundamental question of how to live my life, or what to do after I leave the meditation hall.

At the same time there were certain personal tragedies in my life. A friend had developed inflammatory breast cancer, my mother developed breast cancer, my grandfather died, a friend of mine from the Zen center developed brain cancer. Other tragedies like this were going on, all within one year. I was upset beyond words. I needed to find a place where I could process the endless grief that I was going through. When I thought about going to the Zen center it just didn't work for me, because I couldn't go to a place that felt that lonely, where people sat isolated by themselves, alone on their cushions. I really needed other people around me.

๑৳๑

I first went to a synagogue almost as a fluke. My wife dragged me once to a *havura* (study group) in the neighborhood. She said, "Zack is getting older now, he's got no religion, he's gone with you to the meditation hall a couple of times but he has no sense of himself as a Jew. This is something I'd like to do. Would you go?" I said no way. You're not going to drag me to this thing. But I went. When I heard the Jewish prayers at this *havura* meeting, it was the first time I had heard them in years, there was something very moving about that experience. I suddenly remembered prayers from when I was a small child, I remembered the words to them and it was wonderful. I had the same cathartic experience sitting there in someone's living room with a group of people chanting the Shemona Esre that I did when I was sitting in a meditation hall chanting something totally foreign to me and totally foreign to my culture. And it felt right to me.

From that experience I learned how to get a little more deeply into prayer. I learned that prayers are not something that you just recite, but that they have personal meaning. I didn't want to tell my wife right away that I liked it, because that would have been giving in too easily. But I went back. It got to the point that I went back many, many times and began to explore along with a group of people who were in the process of redefining Judaism for themselves.

Ultimately I left them because I needed a greater sense of structure. I really needed a *shul* and a more traditional service. I wanted to find an environment where I could learn more quickly. But I learned a lesson with the *havura*, which was that Judaism and the practice of it could be very personally rewarding for an individual. I just had to figure out how it was going to work for me.

⊚✛⊚

One day, at a street fair, I saw a table representing a synagogue on the fringes of my neighborhood. The guy at the table, who had a long white beard and really long hair, looked like an old hippie. I took their literature and read it, and it appealed to me because their publicity said it is an accepting place, not to worry whether you're Orthodox, Conservative, Reform, whether you wear blue jeans or a suit, everyone is accepted no matter what their level of observance. Although I had been thinking of going back to a synagogue, I was very intimidated by the idea of a place where I would feel like I had to change myself to be accepted by other people.

I finally decided to try the synagogue. I put on a suit and a necktie, and walked into this place where everyone was wearing blue jeans. They all looked at me; they didn't know who I was, I think they thought I was a visiting rabbi. People came up to me afterwards and were really sweet. There was a guy there, a couple of rows in front of me, wearing a big white tallis and under it was a crew jacket from a TV show. I never thought I'd see that in a synagogue. I thought, wow, I like this. The image of this yellowed wool tallis struck me as so funny yet, more of who I was. I'm a video guy, I listen to rap, I'm not a klezmer kind of person, I don't listen to cantorial music. So the esthetic of the place really appealed to me and the folks I met were absolutely accepting. No one hit me up for membership, no one hit me up for the building fund, no one asked me for my Dun & Bradstreet profile, they just said, "Come if you want to come, we'd love to see you again."

After the service, people came up to me immediately and asked my name and introduced themselves. I liked that a lot. My experience as a kid was getting dragged to a synagogue by my parents, and now I actually could look back with some fondness on those memories and thank them because it probably prepared me for what I was experiencing.

As a child it seemed that the synagogue was the adult world. It was not a place for a kid with a lot of questions, it was for adults who had all the answers. This was the first time I went to a synagogue and I saw a lot of adults who still had all those questions and they were still trying to answer them. I thought that was a wonderful thing.

But there was more to it than that. I showed up at 9:30 A.M. The building itself has a beautiful skylight, and the light coming in was an early morning light. The rabbi was from England and had a beautiful voice. I began to hear some melodies that I had grown up with but forgotten. Things started coming back, I remembered the words, I remembered the melodies. I hadn't *davened* (prayed) in twenty years or more at that point, but everything started coming back. After the Torah service, the congregation was saying Etz Chaim He, and I began to cry. The beauty of it just grabbed my heart in a way that nothing had in a long time. And during the parts of the service that I was unfamiliar with, I thought about what I was going through with my friends. When Kaddish was being said, I cried again, and there was something tangible in the experience that spoke to me about where I was in my life. I thought this was a place I could come and get comfort.

❦

It was also a participatory *shul.* People in the congregation lead the service. It wasn't religion being spoon fed to a congregation from the *bimah.* It's really people who leave the *shul,* go home to study, *daven* independently, think about things, ask questions, and bring all of that back to the synagogue. The Torah discussion the first day was short, then it was opened up to a general discussion in the congregation. People were talking in the most animated way about how the Torah portion related to their lives. They weren't talking about some history book that was thousands of years old. They were using the text of the Torah to help them answer the questions they had at that moment. How do I live my life in this craziness of Brooklyn, with my car being broken into, with sirens wailing all day long, with not being able to find a school to put my kid in, with rampant crime everywhere—how do I create for myself and my family a sense of stability, a sense of morality, a sense of interacting with other people in a human, compassionate way? Where is my anchor in all this madness? They were using the text of the Torah to begin to answer some of these questions, to look at a time when people had even less than they did, when people slept in a tent in the desert, not knowing what army was going to come over what hill tomorrow and wipe them out. If this was how people lived back then, Brooklyn was not quite so bad. But there were certain similarities, and people were using the Torah to answer some of those questions.

I had been brought up in a synagogue where there was a rabbi and that rabbi's Judaism, and the congregation listened very passively and practiced their own form of Judaism, which was nothing like the rabbi's. I found in this synagogue a really collaborative experience, where members of the congregation were getting up and leading different parts of the service. Instead of the sermon after the Torah reading, there was a little bit of a talk and people shared their thoughts about that portion of the Torah that they had read at home that week. I thought this was kind of cool, I had never seen this in a synagogue. These people were involved.

I continued to go back. I particularly liked the early part of the service when there weren't so many people around. The experience was halfway between a Zen center and synagogue because it was intimate and personal, and there was space and quiet. And the morning light would come in through the windows, just like when you start meditating in a Buddhist meditation hall; you start before dawn and often at the end of your first sitting period the light is starting to peek through the windows. The synagogue felt a little bit like that.

❧

Jewish practice and prayer are now a big part of my life. It's something that I'm involved in every day, but I'm also involved in the secular world. I go to work, I play the harmonica, listen to the blues, hang out with my family, go to the park and roll in the leaves on a fall day. I straddle two worlds: the world of prayer and traditional Judaism and also the everyday secular world. But I never feel a dichotomy, I never feel a real separation between the two.

I guess an example of this is my music. My connection with music is really interesting since it's become caught up with my faith. When I was about twelve, my older brother got me a record by Sonny Boy Williamson, a famous blues musician. That was the only record I owned and I played it till it was paper thin. By the time I got done with this record, I had memorized every note on it. We didn't have a lot of money back then and my only instrument was a harmonica. I was able to buy a little vest pocket harp, and I taught myself how to play the harmonica by recreating what I had memorized from listening to this blues record. I carried this thing around in my pocket, and when no one was around, I'd pull it out and play.

I spent the next bunch of years getting hip deep in blues and R&B. I think there was actually something very familiar about learning blues, because a lot of it is minor key music, which was similar to the minor key melodies I had listened to as a kid in the synagogue. And though there's a certain sadness to a lot of it, there's also a lot of joy in it as well. But the thing that I liked most about it was the passion, that it was passionate music—passionate like prayer is passionate, from the heart, from the soul.

Now when I play my harmonica, and I really love to play, some of the things that I feel are exactly what I feel in the synagogue when I'm involved in prayer. It's very personal. It's giving voice to something inside of me. Depending on what it is I am playing, it may be a cry, it may be a shout of joy. It's very similar to what I might be doing if I'm involved in prayer. While there are differences between them, on an emotional level they feel very close to me. Blues music is the music of a people in exile. When I pray in a synagogue, it's also the prayers of a people in exile. So spiritually, the music and the prayer are part of one seamless whole.

❦

It has not been particularly difficult to combine the two parts of my life. Usually I get up about 5:30 in the morning, before the rest of the family gets up, so I can pray. It takes me roughly an hour to do the morning prayers. I do them at home most days except for Wednesday and Saturday, when I go to my synagogue and do the morning prayer service with a group of people.

I put on a tallis. I put on tefillin on the days that are not the Sabbath. I do the traditional prayer service. But I do something a little bit more than that: I always try, as I'm saying the prayers, to insert something personal in them. For example, if I'm reciting the main prayer in the Jewish service—the Shemona Esre, which is divided into a number of parts—during the prayer that has to do with the health of people, I'll take a moment and say a personal prayer for the people around me who may be ill. I'll pause to think about them. If I didn't have that formalized ritual every day I might let slip the opportunity of thinking of the people that are close to me and what they are going through. The structured act of praying every day gives me the opportunity to think more about some of these larger questions.

In addition, my son Zack and I have our own bedtime ritual. He used to want me to read a story to him every night, and some nights I'm just exhausted. Somehow he learned that if he asked me to read the Shema, I wouldn't refuse. He learned that this was a good way to manipulate Daddy into staying with him for twenty minutes. He didn't understand the words but when I *daven*, it's with a quiet, gentle sing-song. Instead of just reading the Shema, I would do the evening service and he would fall asleep during it. This was great for me also, because I was least familiar with the evening service and now it has become a really enjoyable service for me. It's very intimate, like the early morning service.

ॐ

When I was most involved with Zen, a lot of the practice involved going off to a retreat, going someplace where I might get up at three in the morning to sit in a dark room with a group of people, then go and have private interviews with a teacher. It was really not a family practice. In fact, as I looked around at the people I was practicing with, I realized for many people there was a choice involved. If you practice that form of meditation as it's often done in this country, you have to leave your family behind and practice meditation on your own and then come back to your family. They're really two separate things. Part of what I love about Judaism is that I do have a different sense of community. When you practice meditation, there's a lot of silence, but anybody who knows Jewish people knows they talk all the time. You can talk to other people about things, about issues, about things in your life, about your world. It's a lot more dialogue-based as opposed to being internally focused. There's give and take, an exchange in dialogue that I really find wonderful.

❧

Buddhism is not a religion in terms of its core teachings, so I think it is possible to be both a Jew and a Buddhist. Jews practice mindfulness all the time. As a Jew you are always trying to be aware of God's presence. In the Psalms there's a line that says God is always there at arms length away, which means that I'll always be aware of God's presence. Tzitzis are constant reminders of God's presence. A mezuzah on a door is a constant reminder of God's presence. When you eat a piece of bread, you say a *berachah*, because you are aware of the source of blessing. You know you are alive, you're breathing, you're experiencing life, you have a family, you hopefully have your health and, if you're mindful in the Jewish tradition, you understand that this is all a gift, and you feel a sense of appreciation. In the Shabbat service the Nishmat prayer (the soul or breath, it's translated both ways) of everything that lives proclaims the glory of God. I take this very literally; as human beings breathe air in and out of their lungs, every breath is a prayer to God. It's not just at mealtime that you're aware of God, it's a constant; even in your sleep, every breath you take over twenty-four hours, there is some connection with God. That's mindfulness to me.

❧

Being in the synagogue is a family experience. I can go there and be involved in prayer and there can be kids climbing all over the place and running up and down, and my son can sit next to me. We wrap ourselves together in a tallis and hang out together. This is something I can never do in a meditation hall on a meditation cushion. I can have a sense of family. My wife, my son, and I can participate with other people in experiences that bring a lot of joy and a sense of connectedness. There's a sense of group prayer together. In a synagogue with kids around you, the joyous noise that they're making is part of the experience of prayer in that sanctuary. To me, that's the most wonderful noise of all.

12 To Live in Both Worlds

Maxine W.

I was born into a family of mother, father, and a sister who's three years older. Both my parents were born in America to immigrant parents. Neither my parents nor my grandparents had any religious practices that I can remember. I never saw anybody light Shabbes candles. Nobody belonged to a synagogue. My parents were very much concerned with assimilating into society. There was never any talk about God, or faith, or commandments that came from any religious connotation. I had no concept of what the Sabbath was. I knew that my father couldn't go into work at a certain time, I knew that somebody had to watch that the food at my father's business, kosher catering, was actually kosher, but none of it had any meaning to me.

Maxine W. is the Executive Director of Nursing at a major metropolitan hospital. After exploring a number of belief systems and philosophies, she now tries to balance the responsibilities of her professional life with those of an Orthodox woman.

The majority of my friends and about 95 percent of my elementary school and junior high school, and maybe 70 percent of my high school were Jewish. It's interesting because since the schools are state run, we still had Christmas and Easter activities. Nothing really Jewish was ever brought into our school.

Although we were a close family, we never went together as a family to a religious function other than a bar mitzvah. We did a lot of other things together as a family: we went to every free art exhibit within a hundred miles of Brooklyn and we always went away together for the summer. But there wasn't anything based on any kind of spirituality or religion.

I received a lot of negative input about Judaism. There was talk about the Holocaust. My father ran from it. My maiden name in English is Smith, my grandfather changed it from Schmidt. We always felt like there was no big bargain in being Jewish.

⊛

We had a *shteibel* on our block, a little Orthodox *shul*. That was my first real contact as a little girl with Orthodoxy. Members of the congregation would often come looking for my father for a minyan and he would hide and tell us to say that he wasn't home. I remember going to the *shteibel* on Simchas Torah and getting a flag with a candle, or going into their sukkah, and it was totally foreign: everything was in Yiddish. My parents and aunts and uncles spoke Yiddish, but I never learned it. It was used to talk about things that adults didn't want the kids to know. When I went into the *shul*, everyone spoke Yiddish. I didn't know what was going on. Nobody ever explained anything. Then as we got older, the rabbi would yell at us because we weren't wearing long sleeves or some equally unclear issue. It wasn't a pleasant place.

I had a couple of friends from school who were more observant. On Rosh Hashanah and Yom Kippur, I spent time at someone's house and they would do things like tear the toilet paper before the holiday or not carry a key. Again, nothing was ever explained to me, nothing really made sense and yet I wanted to be a part of it.

On holidays, we had big family dinners and occasionally we had a big Passover with a lot of relatives. But I don't remember having matzah in the house for a whole week or getting rid of things. It was never a big ritual: it was a big dinner. For Rosh Hashanah or Yom Kippur we got dressed up and we would walk on King's Highway. My parents didn't work on those days. Yet, until I was an adult, I didn't realize there were some very Jewish things they did do: they always gave charity and they helped people who were ill, my mother cooking meals. They were very caring.

⚛

I grew up with a concept of spirituality or God, basically from things I saw on television and in the movies, and they were mostly Christian. I saw things like *The Nun Story* and *The Bells of Saint Mary* and I can quote these movies verbatim. *The Song of Bernadette* was also a popular movie and I became attracted to the idea of these nuns, who were not of this earth, just so pure, so holy—perhaps because I was the bad child in the family. I was the youngest, I was the underachiever, I was the one who always acted out. I was always being reprimanded. So I admired the discipline and saintliness of these women. To see them kneeling in front of the candle was just incredible to me. I didn't understand it, but I knew there was something very special there.

We rented out an apartment in the basement of our home and different sorts of people lived down there at different times. Most of the families were gentile. Sometime during this period, I stole a rosary and a saint card from a couple that was living there. I thought that maybe having these things in my possession would help me, because I had nothing to hold on to.

When I was thirteen, one of my friends joined a girls group at the Reform synagogue in the neighborhood and asked me to go with her. We were going Wednesday nights. That was nice, we had an activity and a little learning. I learned to smoke, my first pack of cigarettes cost thirty cents.

I became entranced with the Friday night service because it was Reform and there was an organ and a choir there. One of the girls from the Hebrew school would go up and light candles. Of course, it was the wrong hour. I didn't know that back then. One of the boys from the Hebrew school would go up and make Kiddush, and all the families were there. It was the first time I heard the Shema. They would ask for *tzedakah* (charity) on Friday night; I didn't know that you weren't even supposed to give or touch money. But the Reform temple was beautiful, not like the *shul* on my block. And the rabbi was a very nice man and I felt very warm and comfortable there. So I would go regularly with my friends to Friday night services. I really liked the feeling that I got there.

☙

When I was about sixteen, I started being a candy striper at Long Island College hospital in downtown Brooklyn. I used to pass a little church on the way to the hospital and I used to go in sometimes and light a candle. I just wanted this holy life to come down and shine on me like it did in the movies. I was waiting for this to come and of course it never did.

During nursing school, I met my husband. I never looked for anybody religious. I wouldn't even know what to look for but I only dated Jewish boys. I was afraid to cross over the line. It wasn't really discussed much but there was an understanding that this wasn't something one did. My husband came from a more traditional Jewish home. His mother was kosher to some extent. He had more people in his family who either went to yeshiva or lit Shabbat candles, and his mother lit Shabbat candles occasionally. His father would get tickets for the Jewish holidays and they would all go to synagogue.

When we were dating, people didn't talk the way they do today. It wasn't a matter of what he wanted for the future, or what I wanted. We just kind of clicked. We knew we wanted to get married, we wanted a house, we wanted to have kids, but how we would bring them up or how we would include religion in our home wasn't discussed.

So we got married. We had no clear idea about how to observe anything: we got dressed up on the holidays, but we didn't go to synagogue, we didn't keep a kosher house.

⊛

I became pregnant and delivered prematurely; my son was a twin and one baby died. My mother-in-law took care of the burial, and I remember several things: one was that she had contacted the rabbi of her synagogue to pray for these babies. She mentioned that she had to pay him money, which disturbed me, like I was disturbed about people paying for tickets for the holidays. I was never able to understand that concept. I could just walk into a church and it was nice. Then, I remember they had to bury the baby and I was still in the hospital. My husband wasn't allowed to go. My mother-in-law had contacted the burial society and they buried the baby. Six months after the baby was born, we got this note saying where the baby was buried and that the coffin cost five dollars, which disturbed me terribly. But I never spoke to a rabbi about it.

We did follow all the rituals for my son. We had a *pidyon haben* (redemption of the firstborn), we had a *bris*. Because he was so premature, he had both on the same day. We didn't go any further than that.

⊛

A lot changed for us when we moved to Long Island. Now we were living in a world of non-Jews. When we first got married, there were Jewish people all around us. My landlady was Jewish and she taught me several things. Before my son came home, she made me tie a red ribbon in the crib and on the carriage and on the playpen. She taught me how to make kugel—much more than I had learned from my own mother.

But when we moved out to Long Island, Jews were rare. We moved because a friend of mine in nursing school lived a couple blocks away. They were Jewish, so that was comforting. Then I had my daughter and my husband went to the synagogue for a naming.

We began to become concerned that my son needed to have some kind of Jewish education. We went to a Conservative synagogue near us and joined. I didn't get anything spiritual out of it, but my son started going there and hated it, which I didn't realize at that time. When my husband lost his job, we had dues to pay at the synagogue and we couldn't afford them. They told us not to bother to come if we couldn't pay the dues. We asked if we could pay them at a later date or in installments and they said no. We were very turned off by that.

Meanwhile I was always struggling personally. I had started to work again full-time. We were changing the nature of our friends and I was being exposed to a lot of different people and a lot of other religious things. We were very open and carried some of the hippie years with us. We shared everything with our friends, even living communally during our summers on Fire Island. When Christmas came, we would run around with everybody, go to mass and decorate the tree. I had no problem with any of it. Other religions had no baggage for me, which was one of the things that made it all so attractive.

⚭

Somewhere in the middle of all this, I went back to college. I was very afraid to go back because I had been such a poor student, but I knew career-wise it was time to go. Once I started, I became a different person and I began to learn a great deal. I had gone to nursing school in the '60s, when the emphasis was very technical. We had just begun to get monitors and technology was becoming like the god. But when I returned to school, the concept of the holistic practice was starting to be explored. There was an understanding that the patient was a whole being and that body, mind, and spirit are all interconnected. I started studying along those paths. I already had some interest in Christianity, based on the movies of my childhood. Now I started to explore some Eastern religions. I went the vegetarian route and I went the yoga route. I also looked into learning to heal with therapeutic touch, which was a healing modality being taught in nursing school.

I was exploring all of this. I went to Washington to study with the head of the healing order of the Sufis. I learned to meditate, I learned more about spirituality than I had ever learned, being at one with the universe, a lot of Zen philosophy. I liked that because it was very loving and I wanted to be loving because I was always viewed as such a rotten child.

We still needed to get my son back into Hebrew school, so we joined another Conservative synagogue, which was very nice. There was no great pressure and the dues were easy for us to afford. We became very active there, and both my children went through Hebrew school and did their bar and bat mitzvah there. My husband was the treasurer and I started getting a little interested. The rabbi was very old and ill; he taught my son a lot about leading the service. Meanwhile, I was working from 3 to 11 Friday nights. My son was leading these services and one day he said to me, "You know, it would be nice if my mother showed up once in a while." So I started sneaking out of work to come for an hour once a week. It was interesting. I felt comfortable there.

At the same time, I was in a twelve-step program at Overeaters Anonymous (OA). There was a lot of talk about spirituality, and a higher power, but not from a Jewish focus. They said the Lord's Prayer. I wasn't sure if it was right to say it or not, but I'd done so many unorthodox non-Jewish things, it didn't matter. At times it presented problems for my husband, not that he wanted me to be any Jewish religious holy roller, but he didn't want me to fall off the deep end anywhere. I was getting bombarded with a desire for a connection, seeing a lot of paths to spirituality and watching my son feeling involved. I began to teach the Sunday morning Hebrew school nursery school group. I started to read more because I needed to know what to offer these little kids. And I began loving what I was reading, really loving it.

Then I went on an Overeaters Anonymous retreat to Shelter Island. It's a beautiful setting. It was non-religious, but it was held at a place that was run by two brothers from a Catholic order. They were very friendly and often sat and schmoozed with us. One day, I had a conversation with one of them and told him my life story. He said, "It's always very easy to go to a new faith. You are always the star when you walk into a new place and everything's new and everything's exciting." He said, "You don't have any prejudices that you have to overcome, like you do with your own faith. But the right thing to do is like the *Wizard of Oz*, to quote Dorothy, 'there's no place like home.'" He said, "To go back and overcome your issues is really the spiritual path. If that takes you someplace else after all of that, you know that is the right place to be." I thought a lot about that.

๑๖๑

A woman in OA had been discussing some of these issues with me for a while, our Jewish connection, spirituality. One day, we discovered an article in *Jewish World*, which was some give-away paper, and it said that a Jewish women study group was forming. We decided to join. It met on the only morning of the week that I was free and we started attending. I was absolutely fascinated. Here were women who lived lives, not like the nuns, but real lives that were dedicated to their belief system. I found a tremendous wealth of knowledge in this belief system. I would come home and share this with my husband who could care less. He was staying where he was and he didn't want to know anything about it.

I went away to a *shabbaton*, a weekend retreat, and spent time with the other women. There was a lot there. It took me a while to get my husband to attend. We were friendly with another couple at the Conservative *shul* and her husband became very interested, so my husband began to join me more often. I really didn't take on much to start with. My kids were concerned as to what I was getting into now. I had put them through any kick that came along: whatever it was, their mother was involved. I was very free spirited and willing to try new things, so they never knew what the next six months of their life was going to bring, who I was going to be meditating with or what incense I was going to be burning or what we were going to be eating. I always tell them that they should be thrilled I made their lives so colorful.

∞

I don't remember what the major turning point was, but I remember the study group talked about a *mikvah*. I went on a tour to Crown Heights to see the *mikvah*. I was interested in what I perceived as an act of purification. That these women went on a monthly basis had a personal ring to me that I thought I would like to try. I mentioned it to the leader of the study group. I said that I wasn't ready, but it was something that I'd like to think about.

I have a cabin up in the mountains with a lake, but I don't like going underwater. That summer, I practiced a lot, how I would go underwater. After Labor Day, I learned about the *mikvah* and what it involved. I thought I wanted to try it. I learned what I needed to know. One of the issues is separating from your husband, not having relations for seven days, which was not high on my husband's priority list. He still wasn't going along with this deal yet. But somewhere along the line, I said I'd really like to do this the right way. He said, "Well then, that's what you'll do, you'll do it the right way."

I went through this ritual but I didn't feel purified. I had been warned that this wasn't going to be something that would cleanse my life, but it did have very long-lasting effects. When I came home, my husband asked me what it was like, what it was about. It was hard to explain, but it was really connecting to the women who had come before me. Somewhere along the roots of my family, somebody did this. Somewhere this was part of their ritual in Europe. That was very powerful to me because I never felt like I belonged, and this really created a bond. So I told my husband this was something I'd like to continue, although I hadn't thought I would. I said I would like to do this right before the holidays. He said fine and it became part of our lives. We weren't kosher, we weren't anything then. It was simply something I started to do.

❧

After a while, my husband and I started becoming more observant and were progressing all the time. A Chabad house had opened near us so we were moving on that track. We were lighting Shabbat candles, we were having a Shabbat meal, we koshered the house. My husband was slowly coming along but the kids were not happy with any of this. One day my son, who at the time was a senior in high school, came home and I was wearing a *sheitel* (wig). He looked at me and said, "I can't live like this." He ran away for a couple of hours and then came back and said, "You know, I don't agree with what you're doing. You always warned me about cults. I think this is what's happening to you." I didn't have very thick hair so I used to wear it cut severely short. When one of his friends came over and saw me with my longer *sheitel*, he said, "I don't know what your mother did, but she looks terrific." So my son calmed down. I think he was concerned about what his friends would think.

Meanwhile, I was dealing with other issues with my children. My son was still involved in the synagogue, which was part of our lives. We had been there for many years. That was our home. My kids were comfortable there, played there, grew up there, and knew all the kids there. But as things started changing, I had to make decisions, too. One of the things that prompted me to move on further spiritually was that the older rabbi had died, and another rabbi had come along. He was an Orthodox man, why he ever came to a Conservative *shul* I don't know. I joke and say I'm sure the only reason was to get me and this other couple. But he came, and he was the first man I met who lived in the world, and yet he was Orthodox. He came every other weekend and stayed in the *shul* and observed Shabbes. He started to have an influence on us. We saw that there was a way to live in both worlds to some extent. My husband liked him and the kids liked him, so we hung out with him. He only stayed a year.

My son was always an A student, but my daughter was a poor student. She was never happy that I worked. She was young, but I began to dislike who she was hanging out with. I was projecting a lot of my own growing up on her. One day, we went to visit this rabbi and I told him I was concerned about my daughter and thought maybe she should go to yeshiva. We had talked about my son possibly going, but I was afraid. I was afraid that I had become too religious and I wanted my money for my good time, not to spend on tuition. But the rabbi said there's a nice girls' school. He said he could get us an interview. So we asked my daughter if she would be interested in going to this girls' school. She knew we weren't happy with her life-style. She must have been fourteen at the time. Everything in school was on Friday nights and we wanted her at the synagogue. So we took her for an interview: we scrubbed her up and took off her eye make-up, put on a skirt, and tried to make her look religious. We took her to the school, which was in a beautiful old house, and they accepted her. But they didn't have dormitories, so she had to live with a family.

That changed her entire life. As she was going through this, we were trying to be one page ahead of her, which didn't last very long before she got books ahead of us. My son went off to college. They were revolving in their own worlds and we were progressing. The Chabad house near us got stronger. After the Orthodox rabbi left another rabbi came to the Conservative *shul*. He just rubbed me the wrong way. His sermons seemed to come from *The New York Times*. I was not impressed with his family, I didn't think they were very *haimish*, very warm. I was seeing a whole different world through Chabad. Chabad is very loving and they take everybody, whoever they are, and money isn't an issue.

ֿֿֿֿ

As soon as I was exposed to Chabad, I knew that I was home. Something there spoke to me. I did a lot of different things, I went to different groups, I learned and read a lot. I also went to see the Lubavitcher Rebbe, which was a big turning point in my life. On Sundays, the rebbe would give out dollars and blessings to people. Our rabbi was taking my husband, myself, and some other people to this. Usually the men and women go separately, but because we were going first, we were going to pass him as a couple. Standing, waiting for the rebbe, I thought, okay, if this is where I'm supposed to be, if this is the path I'm supposed to keep traveling on, the rebbe is going to know what's in my head. Basically, I was wondering how to start moving my husband along in this. How do we start moving along together as a couple? We were lighting candles and we had koshered the house, but he really wasn't there.

Our turn came. I couldn't speak, because I knew I was in the presence of something very, very special. Normally I can drown my husband with words, but at that moment I was paralyzed, so my husband spoke and asked for a blessing for the family. Then the rebbe gave him a dollar. It was my turn; the rebbe gave me a dollar. I didn't know the protocol, like when you come in you don't turn your back on the rebbe. They move you through very quickly. All of a sudden I heard somebody talking. The person who was helping to escort us out said, "Turn around, the rebbe is speaking to you." The rebbe said to me, which I didn't understand at the moment, "You are the *akira habayis*," which means, you are the foundation of your home, and "it is through you that your husband will come to his spirituality." I didn't understand or know if he was talking English or Yiddish, I was just dumbfounded and stood there. I got very emotional. My rabbi's brother, another rabbi, said to me, "Did you understand what he said?" I was blubbering and I said no, so he repeated it to me. That was a major turning point. At that time, they took videos of people going through the line, so I have it on tape.

❧

From the time of my son's bar mitzvah, he had been reading the Torah on the second day of Rosh Hashanah. My husband and I were already going to Chabad more than the Conservative *shul*, so one day I said to my son, "We really need to be there." He was very upset. He asked if we were going to hear him read for Rosh Hashanah. I said, "I will always support you at that synagogue. We will pay for your tickets, whatever you need, but we can no longer go there." He was heartbroken, he said this is your *shul* and this is where we grew up. My daughter, meanwhile, was living in an Orthodox world, so she wouldn't go there anyway.

My son finally made peace with our Orthodoxy, and he started to come to our *shul*. When we began to observe Shabbes he would come for a meal, he'd come for services, and they were letting him read the Torah on the second day of Rosh Hashanah, which he still does. I think he feels more at home there than he ever did. But he's not becoming Orthodox tomorrow. Now he's married and his wife's family is at a Conservative *shul* and he goes to both. I think he's comfortable in both worlds.

My daughter married the son of one of her teachers and they had a very Orthodox wedding, one of these weddings with 375 people. My son wanted to be married by my rabbi and his wife's cantor, who was very active in her growing up. They were married by both. My rabbi's one condition was that she would go to the *mikvah*, and she agreed. This was a very difficult subject to broach because if somebody had asked me when I was getting married to go to the *mikvah*, I would have told them where to go. But I think she knew it was important to us and she went ahead with it. They were married and went through the majority of the rituals that were important to us.

I had a big issue with my son because I had stopped dancing publicly with my husband. That's probably what we miss most about our increased Orthodoxy. Sometimes we ask, is it the lobster? Is it the shrimp? Probably what we miss the most is dancing together. We like to vacation. We were in the Grand Cayman Islands, and the band was playing on the deck of the condo where we were staying. So we went to a dark spot and just danced. We dance in the house, but we won't dance together publically and we miss those kind of things. But the issue at the time was: Do I dance with my son at his wedding? I really didn't know what to do. He's very emotional, caring, and compassionate. He said, "How could you tell me no?" I didn't know what to do, so of course I went to my rabbi. He said, "Why would it even be an issue? It's your son, it's one night." We met his needs, I met my needs. It was something that I really wanted to do.

๙✛๏

I had a professional path that was going on all through this, with major decisions to be made. When the hospital offered me the position that I'm in now, as Executive Director of Nursing, I talked it over with my husband and my rabbi because I knew it was going to suck the life out of me. I went in with the thought that it was going to be temporary, and discussed it with professional people and personal people, mentors in my life. The rabbi thought it was very important that an Orthodox woman take a public position like that. So I took it on a temporary basis, and found that I loved it.

But when I went to apply for the permanent position, I had to state my requirements from the start. I go home on Friday at two o'clock. If the hospital is falling apart, that's what I do. And I don't work on the Jewish holidays. Everything else is negotiable. They held to that. They only asked one question. If the hospital had a disaster or something, would I come? I said I don't answer my phone, I will not have my beeper on; certainly if a life was in danger, I would discuss it with my rabbi. The chief executive officer of the hospital felt okay with the fact that there was always that kind of room to do what's necessary.

๙✛๏

We still don't know exactly where we should be. Although it's hard, I like living in both worlds. My husband and I are still very much drawn into the regular routine life. We like to vacation, we like to do things. We've lost a lot of friends along the way, but we've gotten new friends and community. There are people to share the events of our life. People were here when my father-in-law passed away, people were here for our kids' weddings; these people had also been on the journey, and know where you are going and what your struggles are. They're not the same kind of friends as before. We had real party friends in our lives, people who we were close to, who lived in our house and we lived in theirs and went through many life experiences with them. But none of them are Jewish, none of them were where we were spiritually. Although they are wonderful people, and some we still have contact with, we have a way of life, that's our way of life. As difficult as it is sometimes and as often as we're drawn to the other, we know this is where we belong.

We moved to be within walking distance of Chabad. That was a decision about the life we wanted to have. When my husband lost his father he made a commitment to say Kaddish; in order to do that we had to stay at the rabbi's house every Shabbes. To move into someone's home every Shabbes, when they have six children or whatever, was very difficult. We talked about it since obviously it wasn't an optimum situation. We discussed the fact that we have other parents, and they should live to 120, but somewhere in our lives we were going to go through this again. My daughter and her husband, who I adore, didn't come to us often for Shabbes because he would only *daven* with a minyan. I worried that my grandchildren wouldn't sit at my own table. If I want to be with my daughter, it has to be in her house or in the rabbi's house, where they would stay with their kids. My son is going to have children; maybe they'll come for a meal at the rabbi's house, but how will they learn if they don't come and stay with us? So we felt that we needed to move. If we made the move we knew we were going to be obligated to a community. If somebody called, we couldn't say we're not home. That would be a responsibility that would fall more on my husband than on me. If they need him for a minyan, he has to go.

As soon as we bought the house, our rabbi's two and a half-year-old daughter was taken very ill. She was brain dead and on a respirator for a long time. I was very involved with the medical issues surrounding her. We had just moved in and when she died we had people sleeping in our house. You open up your home along the way, as people opened their homes for us. That's what we've chosen to do.

I certainly don't do it perfectly; I still carry lots of guilt in my life for a lot of things. I hope I get better at it. Sometimes I'm very lazy, it's easy to get comfortable. The job has consumed my life. I came from a very balanced place with my family, my parents, my spiritual religious life, but it's very easy to get sucked into a position like this. That's the daily struggle: How do I bring my spiritual life into my work? How do I really make it a part of me so that I'm not living two separate lives? How do I blend both lives together and yet still be me?

That's one of the things I wrestle with. I don't want to be a carbon copy of the next person. I still have to do things my way. So when I light Shabbat candles and I have a beautiful picture of the rebbe above them, I still have to keep flowers on the table because in Eastern practices you always have an altar table and you always have flowers. We still burn incense because that's a part of who we are and I have to get somewhat comfortable with that. I can be practicing and I can be observant and I can be Jewish and follow everything I need to follow, but I can also be myself.

ॐ

There's a wonderful rabbi, Mannis Freedman from Minnesota, and I used to listen to his tapes. That was one of the things that helped me grow, his wonderful educational tapes. I heard him speak many times and my husband and I went on several weekends with him. He said that if you had a sense of humor before you became Orthodox or more observant, and you find that you don't have a sense of humor now, you're not doing it right. I really liked that. I struggled a long time in my life to be comfortable with who I was and I need to take that with me on this journey. I can't and won't separate the two. Sometimes that's the struggle.

13 Resonating Spiritually

Ray G.

I was born and raised in a very suburban community in New York. Essentially, my Jewish upbringing was very much influenced by the fact that I had approximately twenty-five members of my family die in the Holocaust. My father's parents and eighteen members of his family died, including his aunts, uncles, and cousins. My mother had to flee from Vienna in the middle of the night across the border to get into Czechoslovakia, because time had run out for them. The person who was supposed to escort them across the frontier never showed up. So I grew up with this image of my grandparents and my mother, she was about twenty years old, in the middle of the night with a suitcase, fleeing through the woods. This ambience, influenced by their loss, was the context for my growing up. You had to be on guard against anti-Semitism.

Ray G., the son of Holocaust survivors, is a therapist in Oregon. He struggles with incorporating his long-term connection to mindfulness, as practiced by Vietnamese Buddhist Thich Nhat Hanh, with his new reconnection to Judaism.

We went to Reform synagogue, which my parents dutifully went to on the High Holy Days, and I went to Sunday school and Hebrew school once a week. I had a bar mitzvah; my religious education, for the most part, was pretty boring. It was boring because, as the joke goes, going to the synagogue was like being introduced to Jewish aerobics: stand up and read, sit down and read, responsive reading, stand up, open the Ark doors, close the Ark doors, sit down. I knew that half the congregation was in the foyer during Rosh Hashanah services, smoking and shmoozing.

Judaism, for me, was missing any kind of meaning other than the basic procedures. The focus was on the watch—when is this going to be over? In terms of my Jewish education, there was no one who I was inspired by or who I wanted to identify with. It felt like all my peers were in a pretty similar situation, they dreaded going. Right after my bar mitzvah it was clear that there was no real obligation for me to continue. Since then, I have realized that as soon as my bar mitzvah was over my parents basically stopped going to *shul*. We've discussed it; with their thing of God died in Auschwitz, they were not really able to sustain any type of belief in a Judeo-Christian notion of God, because of their losses and the notion that if there really is a God, He would not let this happen.

For them it was extremely important to be a Jew, but it was completely secularized. My father said that it was very important for me to bring up my kids as Jewish and hopefully not to marry a non-Jew. I needed to tell my children about their legacy and I had to be vigilant so that what happened in the Holocaust and in the pogroms won't happen again—and it will happen again if you're not careful. Much of the education was fear-based with a consciousness that we are a step away from being annihilated. In some ways I took that very seriously. But I also remember, during a seder, my sister and me giggling and poking each other in the stomach as it talked about how God did this for His people and saved them, how He would always take care of His people.

We immediately went to the fact that we have no extended family because we're Jewish and they had been killed. So this always seemed incredibly hypocritical and meaningless.

❧

As an early teenager, I stopped going to the synagogue. I was at a loss in terms of a connection to something beyond myself, something more spiritual. During my late adolescence through my mid-thirties, I tried a lot of different things as a way of having transformative experiences, or high experiences, or spiritual experiences, which wound up being really cut off from a deeper spiritual meaning. Going on meditation retreats was more like a variation on tripping.

I read *Zen and the Art of Motorcycle Maintenance*, which was a very important book to me. I remember reading books like *Be Here Now* and *The Only Dance There Is* by Ram Dass and glancing through *Zen Mind, Beginner's Mind* by Suzuki Roshi. I started to get interested in all this, in a way, through the influence of the drug culture. Things intensified in 1974 when I came out to California and worked in a Jungian-based residential treatment center. I worked for fifty dollars a month and lived in a treatment home for schizophrenic and autistic adolescents. The orientation of this place was to focus on dream life, archetypes. That first summer we built tepees and lived with very psychotic kids while having a Native American experience and doing a lot of rituals. I got really turned on to looking for something beyond one's personal unconscious, some kind of a common consciousness that's shared by humanity in general.

I lived in Berkeley for a number of years and experimented with a lot of Eastern stuff. When I was in graduate school in 1975, I took a transcendental meditation course and started meditating. I studied t'ai chi and for a couple of years I practiced aikido. I was becoming interested in Eastern philosophies and that, combined with my deepening interest in psychology, seemed like a good fit. Throughout my twenties and early thirties I went on a Siddha yoga retreat, saw Ram Dass at Berkeley a number of times, and continued to study and practice t'ai chi.

☙❦❧

At one point in Berkeley I went to a Rosh Hashanah or Yom Kippur service hoping that, since I was in my mid- or late twenties, I would have a different experience from my childhood. But once again, I went away feeling very empty. It was a fairly traditional service, I don't remember if it was Reform or Conservative, but it was the same old thing to me. A lot of reading, some singing, but the sense of being touched in one's heart, where something happens or begins to happen, that was really absent. I was left cold. It's very different from today and some of the stuff that actually goes on with the rabbi we have now. He will pause and say, "Let's take a moment and be quiet and turn East to Jerusalem." He'll wrap himself in his tallis and say, "I'm going to make nookie with God now." We'd all be quiet. And I love silence.

☙❦❧

I got my M.S.W. from the University of California at Berkeley in 1977. I then went to the Pacific Graduate School of Psychology. This was a place where people who had their master's, who already practiced psychotherapy, could go back to school in the afternoons and evenings and get a degree. Interestingly enough, I did my dissertation on the interpersonal adjustment of children of Holocaust survivors. I had started to read about some variables in offspring of Holocaust survivors and I became interested because I didn't do really well in relationships beyond two years and it took me a long time to get married. So I wound up doing a comparative study with children of immigrants, children of Holocaust survivors, and children of American-born Jews. It turned out to be an interesting study, and it helped me account for some of my own weirdness and difficulties and how they might relate to my parents and their experiences and losses. So even though a lot of my interest was away from Judaism, there was still a very deep connection to it. But in the context in which I grew up it wasn't about spirituality, it was about what happened to people time and time again all through history.

☙

I wound up, to my parents' delight, marrying a Jewish woman. Nancy, for her own reasons, was also a pretty disenfranchised Jew. It was interesting to come together and figure out how we were going to be married. We ended up having a Jewish wedding and it was really neat. We found a rabbi who didn't have a congregation but used to be the rabbi for Hillel at Stanford; he was also a therapist. He did weddings, bar mitzvahs, and rituals as well as marriage and family counseling. He did a really nice ceremony outside where he actually talked about what some of these rituals meant. He talked about the huppah, he talked about the breaking of the glass, and really brought some life to these things. It was wonderful, especially because he talked about his own quest for spirituality, since he also was involved in meditating. He piqued our interest.

We came up to Oregon right after we got married. I got my Ph.D. in May of 1986, we got married in April, and we moved in July. So there were a lot of changes at once. Nancy had decided that if we were going to leave the Bay area, she didn't want to move to another large city. We had developed some opportunities in Bend, so we decided to come here. Before we moved, we asked about a Jewish community and spoke to a psychologist here who is Jewish, and learned that Bend didn't have much of a Jewish community. That didn't dissuade us.

We moved and in those first years there were informal get-togethers around the High Holy Days, but never any services per se. But over the twelve years we've been here, there have been efforts toward a more formalized community and over time that has occurred. In the last six years, a couple of different rabbis started coming. We have a diverse community here with people like myself who have been pretty far away from Judaism combined with a lot of wealthy retired people who built houses in gated golf communities. Their frame of reference is large congregations in Los Angeles, San Francisco, and Seattle and they wanted something more traditional. So there's been a lot of tension and struggle around what type of Jewish community we're going to have, and what type of spiritual leadership.

❦

A couple of years after we came here we had two children, and I started wondering, how well I could raise my kids if I was struggling spiritually about being a Jew. Was it enough for me to just go to the services, to give them the same kinds of negative experiences as I had as a kid, to encourage my children to go to Sunday school and Hebrew school and hopefully have a bar or bat mitzvah, if I was feeling pretty empty about it?

About five years ago, I started hearing about Jewish Renewal; I heard that there were a lot of people like me who had found much of their experience in Judaism fairly empty spiritually and had searched out experiences in other traditions. Those people were coming back to the fold so to speak, under this movement that stemmed from the work of Zalman Schachter-Shalomi in Philadelphia. I had actually heard about him on the radio first and got interested. I got some information and thought, wow, there's something going on here. He was talking about retreats, about deep meditation and the Kabbalah, the mystical tradition. Over the years I had gotten some books on the Kabbalah, leafed through them and thought it was kind of interesting, but had trouble relating. It's a hard thing to just read about and not be taught. Anyway, I then read Michael Lerner's book, *Jewish Renewal.* Then I read Rodger Kamenetz's *The Jew in the Lotus,* and I started getting very excited, because I have an interest in Buddhism. I wasn't interested in becoming a Buddhist, but just what they talk about: how to be a spiritual being, the practice of meditation and the concepts of compassion and right livelihood, right attitude, the work of Thich Nhat Hanh and mindfulness. Those notions make sense to me.

Lerner talked about things like Shabbat in ways that I had never really experienced it. He spoke about Shabbat in the context of a day-long retreat, and using it as an opportunity to be with God. I hadn't grown up in a culture where that's what Shabbat was about. It was also very interesting because I wanted to learn more about being and not doing. So much of my culture and so much of my own being is about having to produce, I have to excel, I have to do more, it is never enough. And then here's a ritual within our own tradition, that says this is a day of stopping. That was a lot of the attractiveness in the Buddhist traditions; on retreats and during meditation you stop, you contemplate, you reflect, you observe your thoughts and let them go. The whole idea of becoming much more aware, moment to moment, of what you're feeling and thinking is also related to my own existential psychotherapy, where you look at what's going on internally, in the moment, and you don't spend as much time looking at historical roots to your trauma. So there's some kind of interface between the spirituality and psychology. That was an eye-opener.

ঞ

About the same time I was having this experience, we started looking for a rabbi for the community. We brought in guest rabbis, and it was like going back thirty years to my childhood, and I couldn't deal with it. As part of our search we found a student rabbi in the Jewish Renewal Movement. He came with his guitar and talked about mindfulness and meditation, about having passion and retreats on weekends.

He had an incredible presence with children, a real sense of getting down on the floor and talking to them in ways I never experienced as a kid with my rabbi. We set up weekends where he would come and do a Friday night service and a Torah study on Saturday morning. Myself and a couple of other people asked if he would be willing to do something on Jewish meditation. We found out that this was one of his primary interests. So we had a number of Saturday afternoon discussions, where he would talk about the tradition of Jewish meditation. We would chant, we would even do some movement meditation; it was unbelievable. We couldn't believe this is in our own tradition! We spoke about what was lost in the secularization of the religion over the last 200 years, the effect of the Holocaust on the American Jewish community, the impact of losing something like 90 percent of the hasidic rabbis who in many ways carried some of these great mystical and spiritual traditions of Eastern Europe. In many ways, with increasing secularization, we lost a lot of what was once an integral part of the religion.

Concurrently, I was becoming more interested in mindfulness, the work of Jon Kabat-Zinn, as well as feeling a need to establish a more regular spiritual practice. It felt like my life was incredibly frenetic. I had two young children, I had a practice, I had a separate business, and I was struggling with, What about me? I was serving my clients, my children, and being angry and upset, off balance a lot. I felt like I needed something.

At about that time my wife was dealing with a chronic illness, a condition that medicine had real limitations in treating. Part of the challenge was how to learn to live and maintain a quality of life and good attitude when one is dealing with a chronic difficulty. We discovered a book *Full Catastrophe Living* by Jon Kabat-Zinn. After reading that book and seeing a special on healing and the mind, my wife went on a retreat and we started sitting together every morning. Then I went on a retreat and since that time we've gone on retreats usually twice a year to practice mindfulness, meditation. Meditation has become like eating breakfast for me. I do it every day, and it's not like I have profound, illuminating insights. It just feels like it's part of a way of living my life. It's a way to stop doing, it's the way to observe my thoughts, it's a way to be aware of my feelings, and it's a way to become centered.

So part of my struggle right now, although I think it's coming along, is that I have something that's very significant to me, but that there are parts of going on retreats that are very foreign to me. Chanting in a language that's very foreign (it's not Hebrew, it's whatever) at the same time as feeling comfortable, there it is— a piece that is uncomfortable. It's not my tradition and it doesn't feel like it's deep in my bones and my blood. It feels like a disconnection. I can sit quietly and that's real helpful, but when you get into the more intense practice, where you actually are going on retreats, and the nature retreats are Buddhist, it feels discrepant with who I am. That fuels more of the interest and path toward Judaism and Jewish Renewal.

I started experimenting with integrating various rituals into my own family and into my own life. For example, every night for the last year and a half both my wife and I say the Shema with our children. It's the last thing we do before they go to sleep at night. It's a time of quiet, it's a time of reflection. That's followed by my daughter usually thanking God for certain things.

⊙✤⊙

I struggle with the language of the liturgy. It is hard for me, with such notions of God as supreme being, as King, as Lord, as some kind of entity that's up there, omnipotent, and the cause of all that we do. As much as I try to redefine the concept of what God means to me, the liturgy and going to services reinforces notions of God that don't fit. It was much easier in the Buddhist tradition, where they don't even talk much about God. I have begun to redefine God in my own mind, despite the interference of the liturgy. It's almost like I have to keep on translating in my own mind: no, you don't have to conceive of God as a supreme being, you can begin to see God as a force in the universe, as something that is in nature, something that can't be encapsulated by the words that have previously described Him or Her. I have begun to convey that to my children and they have begun to see it that way. They see God in nature and my son in particular gets very upset about the destruction of the earth. So coming back to Judaism is part of translating my own conceptions of God and what God means; that's encouraged by the teachings in Renewal.

It makes me feel that maybe I can return home here, but to a home that's different than the way I grew up and different than the way my parents grew up. And I see in my children, the way they look forward to Sunday school and look forward to seeing the rabbi, a passion that I never experienced as a child. My son talks about how he wants to be a rabbi; my daughter looks forward to her Hebrew lessons for her bat mitzvah because she is inspired by the kind of Judaism that she is being exposed to.

We don't have a synagogue, we don't have regular services, but we have people who have come into our family's life who epitomize a spirituality, something that is deeply meaningful and very powerful. That spirituality comes in the form of songs, of stories, of a non-paternalistic, non-authoritarian relationship with the rabbi and God, and it fits. It works in a way that, up to this point, I hadn't been exposed to. If I was living in southern or northern California, or in New York, where you can go on Jewish Renewal retreats for a week, I would probably be doing that. But I don't have that available to me here, so the challenge is that I have to seek out now what works for me and what is accessible. I'm hoping what Judaism offers will become, over time, more accessible to me.

☙

Part of the tension that I experience in this diverse Jewish community is because there are a lot of Jewish folk who have been satisfied with the kind of Judaism they experienced in their adulthood. But I'm not. Some people feel that our rabbi's services are very confusing, chaotic. They're not what they are used to and that troubles them, whereas for me it's fine. I could care less whether they follow the protocols or traditional rituals of Judaism; others are concerned that if you start compromising here and compromising there pretty soon you're not going to know that it's Jewish anymore. I don't feel that way. I feel like the spiritual tradition has to be alive, has to invigorate and resonate with one's heart in such a way that one wants to continue to practice and participate.

❧

Silence. In order for me to be contemplative, in order for me to reflect on God and a spiritual connection to something beyond myself, I have to turn the radio down. I have to be with myself, I have to be quiet, I have to be still. My experience traditionally in Judaism was that there was no room for that. For me it was noise, whether in English responsive reading or listening to the rabbi, it was just non-stop talk. I know part of what we do as Jews is to talk; we like to wrestle and we like to wrestle with God and we like to have intense intellectual discussions about the Torah, the Talmud, and the meaning of this and that. But to me, this is an intellectual exercise and that doesn't take me where I need to go, to be more in touch with myself and something beyond myself. In order to do that I need quiet. I need to stop, because most of my life is talking, listening, and doing. If I go to services and I experience the same talking, listening, and doing, the Jewish aerobics stuff, then I'm not having a different experience, it's all still in my head. I have to move beyond my head for this to be a meaningful endeavor. Silence allows me do that. It gives me that space.

We had an interesting experience: we did Havdalah in someone's home, and before we ate, everybody washed their hands. The rabbi said, "When we do this ritual, let's just be quiet." So we had twenty-five people going up silently, washing their hands. It was wonderful. It got us away from the chatting. I feel like sometimes you lose touch with what's sacred. The Torah might be sacred, but for me, I can't even contemplate the Torah if all I'm doing is listening to it, just listening to the stories. They're great stories, they are our tradition and the Bible is wonderful, but it has to go beyond a cognitive, intellectual process for me in order for it to resonate on a level that is spiritually meaningful. That's what I need. And I know other people, close friends here are also looking for that.

❧

We've been planning a *shabbaton*, a weekend where we can do meditation; we would have a Shabbat of not doing, of just being and doing Jewish ritual. It'll happen here in central Oregon, and it has the potential to bring that type of experience into Judaism, where you spend more time being reflective and contemplative. As I understand it, because I'm not schooled enough in Hebrew, *davening* is supposed to promote some of that. We've done some repetitive chanting and that's been very nice, I've enjoyed that, but not having experienced *davening* I don't know whether it would encourage the same experience for me. It might. But once again you're talking and once again it's noisy.

Repetitive movement can get you into a meditative place too. I've been experimenting in my meditation, doing some prayers, adding some of the Amidah to meditation in the morning. I just bought a siddur and during meditation I'm trying to say some prayers. So I'm experimenting. I'm trying to transform the meditation into something that brings some of the Jewish tradition into my own practice. I'm working on making it work for me.

14 A Rabbi's Perspective

Gershon Winkler

I was ordained in the ultra-Orthodox tradition in Jerusalem in 1978. I was the greatest rabbi that ever lived. Now, of course, there are many. Back then when I was Orthodox, my main job was reaching out to those who were not Orthodox and making them Orthodox. So I taught at yeshivas that were geared to baalei teshuvah. I went out to campuses, sat next to the Jews for Jesus people, and while they were trying to lure them away I was luring them in. In fact, I also ended up sending one leader of Jews for Jesus to a yeshiva in Israel. And she came back to her roots.

I left that whole party line Orthodox Movement scene in 1982. I left because I felt a strong surge of doing Jewish some other way that was alive in me and that I needed to follow. So I call myself

Rabbi Gershon Winkler is the author of *Sacred Secrets: The Sanctity of Sex in Jewish Law and Lore* and *The Way of the Boundary Crosser: An Introduction to Jewish Flexidoxy*, among others. He lives in the desert of New Mexico.

flexidox instead of Orthodox. That means that I live more flexibly and when I teach my Jewish stuff to people, it's exclusively to people who have very little to no background in Judaism or have been turned off for most of their lives from anything religious in general. I've lived way out in the sticks for the last sixteen years, in very remote regions of the country; I hang out in the mountains, which is what I like. In that context, the only kind of Jews I meet are Jews who, like myself, have run away from home—except they ran away from never having had one, from being turned off by one, and I ran off to be in a new way, a different kind of way.

⚘

The most frequent reason for disenfranchisement for the majority of the people I've met has been the bar mitzvah factory assembly line. In other words, they grew up in a family where their parents exhibited no Jewish participation or interest; they were members of a Reform or Conservative institution, where there was no spirituality or at least not enough to keep them. They were raised to go to Sunday school and you couldn't wait to get out. Suddenly in their tenth or eleventh year of life, it's bar or bat mitzvah time. You're thrown into a program to learn a language that you have no interest in, that is totally meaningless to you, to read about a portion from a book, a Torah, with an ideology that you have no relationship with and never did. Just so you can get it over with at your bar or bat mitzvah and then get your checks from Uncle Harry and Aunt Rachel and you're free. After that system, kids look forward to never having to put up with that crap again, it's over and I'm free to be whoever I am. So the result is that kids grow up with no meaning, no relevance to Judaism, and no connection to it. In fact to the contrary, it's a headache to them, because their parents get really nervous about them being able to read from the Torah. They force them through this very painful ritual, just like some of the people in the islands in South Pacific do to their kids. The only difference is, to the kids in the South Pacific islands, their rite of passage is meaningful and relevant to their new stage in life. To the Jewish kid it's totally irrelevant, it's something they have to do to get their parents off their back and get Uncle Harry's check.

❦

After that, they grow up, they go to college or not, but somewhere down the line a little bell goes off inside saying I'm looking for something more meaningful in my life, some spirituality, whatever you want to call it. So they go looking for it, but they're not going to look for it in the place they grew up knowing had none. Many of these people were raised by parents who themselves were turned off in the same way. So that's really a picture of American Judaism outside the very Orthodox circles, where Judaism is a living part of life.

Another group I'm meeting more and more are people who are older, in their late sixties and seventies, who come from a different kind of turned off-ism because their parents didn't raise them with any participation. Their parents came during the early immigration from Russia, from the pogrom period, to this American haven. Here they began to assimilate and be just like the non-Jews so that they wouldn't get punished again for being Jewish. Judaism in general was totally eradicated from their lives. There was no trace of it except maybe for a Hanukah candle and a Maxwell House Coffee Haggadah for Passover. The spirituality of Judaism and any affiliation with anything Jewish was totally absent and instead was transformed into social actions, communism, socialism, all the isms. Those people are coming back to their roots at a very late age because none of that gave them what they had really been looking for. They find themselves lacking some kind of spirituality, some kind of deeper meaning to the soul part of life.

❦

The way I've been doing things is by minding my own business and hanging out in the woods. In the process of doing that, people have been drawn to things that I do. For example, once a month I go and play rabbi in Durango, Colorado, for a fledgling little Jewish community there, mostly composed of refugees from New York, Philadelphia, and that scene, people who fled anything that had to do with synagogue, temple, and Judaism and went all the way out to Durango where there is nothing going on. Some older folks there were doing Passover seders. Somebody invited me there to do a seder one time for the community. The older folks dropped out because it wasn't their version of traditional, in other words Reform traditional or Conservative traditional. I was doing it according to the way it was done in ancient times, with a lot of meaning and kabbalistic symbolism, a lot of fun and singing and joking and meaningfulness, all combined. All the emotions of the human body—that's how I do all my stuff, even Yom Kippur. So what happened was the old guard dropped off and a bunch of other people, who had been turned off from the bar or bat mitzvah factory, wanted more. I was bringing, according to them, aspects of Judaism that they never knew existed, that they never believed existed. A lot of them looked for it in other traditions, from witchcraft to theosophy to Buddhism to Native American. People went everywhere looking for spirituality.

So these Jews, living in Durango, some having been drawn to other religions, some to nothing at all, were curious and came to the seder. That was three years ago and it's been going on ever since. Now, once a month, I go over there and do a whole weekend. I do a Shabbat service that is very different from anything they'd ever known. I do a lot of singing, chanting, and teaching in between, just bringing life to the words and to the rituals, which is what I feel they need. They want to know, they want to learn, nobody ever taught them anything. It was just, This is what you do, this is what you read, all rise, all be seated, turn to page twenty-five. That's what they grew up with. Then we have an *oneg* (Shabbat gathering). The next morning we have a three-hour Torah study session, where we sit in somebody's living room, maybe thirty people or more, and we talk and study. They ask all the questions they were never able to ask their rabbis because the rabbi had no

time, he was busy planning a funeral or making an agenda for a committee meeting. So they are coming back; some people among them
are not Jewish, who were drawn to us in Durango. From a mailing
list of thirty-three there are now 187. A lot of people are finding
out that what they didn't know existed is there in their own roots.
When someone shows it to them, they'll come.

⊕

There's been a transformation for a lot of people over the years,
no matter where I lived, because all I do is teach what's there.
That's the secret. The main reason people are so removed from
their faith is ignorance, total ignorance. It's not intermarriage, it's
not anything but total ignorance. Jews in this country haven't been
taught the richness of their tradition. The teachers are not teaching, they're CEOs of temples and synagogues. Rabbis are supposed
to teach, go out there and teach, teach, teach. People are not being
taught and nothing is happening, there's no meaning, so they're
leaving.

At the same time that people are continuously being turned off
by the same old stuff, there's also a resurgence, there's also a lot
of returning, coming back to Jewish roots. Not everybody, but
a lot of people. For example, somebody, through their soul-
searching, is drawn to Buddhism. You can't reach them by just
giving them vodka and teaching them Kabbalah. You have to listen to where they are and what it is in Buddhism that drew them
and then show them that in Judaism we have that same kind of
thing. Judaism has so many different paths in it. It doesn't just
have one way to meditate, or one way to believe in God, there are
many, many ways. But the problem is that only one way has been
taught by every denomination. In other words, there's Orthodoxy
in every denomination: there's Orthodox Reform, Orthodox Conservative. If you only teach your party line, you're Orthodox. What
flexidox means to me, what I'm trying to do and what a lot of
rabbis I know are trying to do, is to not have any party line. I come
to the people and welcome them with the broadness and the

multidimensioness and multifacetedness of the Torah. There
are many paths, many teachings. There's enough in there to fit
everybody's foot, not just Cinderella's. So you see Cinderella was
a Jew. Cinderella Berger. No doubt about it. Nice Jewish girl.
Worried about getting home on time. Everything will fall apart.
All that stuff.

⌁

Jewish shamanism is teachings in our tradition about sorcery,
invoking of spirits, being very attuned to nature, speaking to the
animals, understanding the language of the trees. It's not that I
know these things, but I've been trying to recover it from layers
and layers and centuries of it being subdued. A lot of Jews are drawn
to shamanism. It's the new thing. In the '70s it was Hinduism and
the Ashrams, and then Buddhism; now the latest fad is shamanism.

Jews are just flabbergasted to discover that in the Jewish mystical tradition the farther back you go the more you discover a
whole shamanic tradition. Even the Bible itself talks about how
King Solomon knew the language of the animals and the plants.
Hillel the Elder in the first century B.C.E. communicated with the
animals and the plants. Teachers performed invocations and
brought spirits to do their bidding.

People are also drawn to Native American spirituality, to all
kinds of things that draw the Jews to the non-Jews. We have a
whole tradition in the Kabbalah about the four directions and the
sacredness of each. Some guy came to me and said, "Well I bet
you don't have colors, like the Lakota have a color for each direction. Does Judaism have that?" I said yes, and I told him the colors and he stood there with his mouth agape. He didn't believe it,
so I said again, "North is red, south is white, east is yellow, west
is black." He said, "But that is exactly the Lakota way." He saw
that the richness is in our tradition as well.

There's a lot of really heavy-duty stuff that I've been trying to
recover, study, and teach. I give workshops on Jewish shamanism and they're mobbed. It draws a lot of people who have been

turned off, who have been looking for meditative practices and, having never been exposed to it in their Jewish upbringing, sought it elsewhere. A lot of rabbis and teachers now realize through their own experience that there's a hunger that is not being dealt with. We're seeing such a variety of people that you really have to be prepared as a rabbi these days, to meet everybody or as many as you can, wherever they're coming from.

The era of the congregational one-size-fits-all is over. Our people are scattered all over the place and they're dabbling in everything because they're searching. They're searching because no one told them anything. It's up to us to expose to them what is in the books beyond the party line.

ॐ

Rabbis can be the catalyst for many Jews to come back to their roots. It's not only accessibility, it's also really listening to the individual's path. It's like we're tailors. Now the rabbi who says to a person searching, "Okay, put on these clothes," like the army that person will find another tailor. They look funny in those suits because they don't fit them. We have to measure everybody. We have to help each to find his or her path, and that's very much a Jewish tradition.

We were comprised of twelve individualistic tribes. Each tribe had its own way of praying, its own way of understanding and interpreting the Torah, its own stone on the breastplate of the the high priest. Each had its own apportionment of land because each tribe had a different persona, a different sentiment about land. Some liked the desert, some liked the mountains in the Galil, some liked to be near lakes, some liked to be near the ocean. The tribe of Naphtali liked to be near the water, the tribe of Dan liked the desert. There's a lot of teaching about individuality and the sacredness and importance of it. A one-size-has-to-fit-all theology is totally not Jewish.

Today the repercussion of the one-size-fits-all theology is exploding in our faces. We are living in an era of individualism. If we're not meeting their individual searches, we're losing them. But a lot of people who are vanishing are coming back or will come back. That's the way it's going to work and has been working. And it's not just Jewish Renewal rabbis who are bringing people back. Sometimes it's a good, accessible Reform rabbi or an ultra-Orthodox rabbi who observes every single law and some that Moses never dreamt of, but that rabbi welcomes the person, the seeker with compassion.

The bottom line is how the teacher responds to the disciples. The arrogant one can't teach, and the shy one can't learn, the Talmud says. If you want to reach out to people you have to make yourself so accessible that there will not be shyness and you have to leave your arrogance at home.

15 A Rabbi's Perspective

David Zaslow

I was born in Brooklyn, New York, in 1947. I grew up in what was, at that time, a pretty average, assimilated Jewish American home with a family's affiliation to an Orthodox synagogue. Even though we were living in a home that didn't particularly promote a Jewish environment, there was a tremendous sense of Yiddishkeit and Zionism in our home and we went through training for a bar mitzvah in an Orthodox synagogue.

When I was seventeen, eighteen years old, and it came time for the draft, I applied to be a conscientious objector. At that particular time, 1965, conscientious objection had to be based upon a belief in a supreme being. Support from pastors, rabbis, priests was very important to be able to achieve that status. But my rabbi

Based in Oregon, Rabbi David Zaslow's own story of reconnection to Judaism came after a career as a poet, educator, and children's book author and publisher. He now travels to many small communities in the region to act as the circuit rabbi.

told me it was the obligation of every Jew to fight for the United States in Vietnam. At that point, my disappointment, my sense of betrayal was so deep that I left Judaism entirely. Subsequently, I found out that his reading, or ruling on conscientious objection was actually not accurate. But the fact remained that at one of the most important turning points in my own life, during a war that was by all historical standards one we should not have been involved in or was at best questionable, I couldn't get support from my own Jewish leader, who left me spiritually afloat.

I ended up getting out on a medical exemption, based upon a previous lower back injury. But the hurt went very, very deep, and sent me on a journey that in retrospect, I believe was part of what we would call divine providence. In a way, it was decreed. I really needed to leave the safety of my ancestors for a while to find out what the world was all about.

༺༻

At nineteen, I was studying at the New School for Social Research in New York. Being the '60s, I was studying the work of Alan Watts and Krishnamurti. In addition, I started intensely studying Tibetan Buddhism, including practicing different meditations from that background. I looked into Native American theology including their relationship to who they call the Great Spirit. And I began developing my own work in the field of children's poetry.

I got my master's degree in creativity, in poetry, and turned it into a career as a full-time poet in the schools. In Oregon, I was the second full-time poet in the schools. I brought poetry to children, grades K–12, and taught them directly the spirituality of creativity, the spirituality of the poetic path, the spirituality that underlies every metaphor. I published many books either for children or teachers. These books were oriented toward making creativity accessible and real to educators and children. It culminated in a book and record project with Steve Allen and Jayne Meadows called, *Shake it Loose with Mother Goose*, which won an American Book Award in 1987.

ॐ

Yet at that particular point there was a vacancy, an emptiness in my life regarding my own spiritual path. I was a little bit Tibetan Buddhist, a little bit Hindu, a little bit Native American, a lot poet. I was utilizing the moral and philosophical approaches, certainly the world views of Native American consciousness toward the planet, and Buddhism regarding the necessity of silence and mindfulness. But I was not a practitioner of any of these, I was at the smorgasbord table where all of these were available in popular American culture.

I joined my local synagogue sixteen years ago, when my daughter was born. It was not to fulfill mitzvot and it was not because of my own connection to God. It was strictly for reasons of transmitting my culture and heritage to the next generation. One might say I went back at that lowest, entry level point that sometimes Jews use to return to Judaism. *I* may not be doing it, it may not be something that is good for me, but it has some value, and I want to pass it on to my children. There was an innate hypocrisy in that, which was that it was good enough for my kids to send them to Hebrew school but it wasn't good enough for me to practice. As I meditated and prayed privately about that dilemma or that hypocritical position, it became clear to me there was a vacancy in my life.

At that time my children's publishing business was failing. The despondency, depression, and the quest for a sense of value from that business experience brought me to a sense of the divine. I was suddenly on fire for God. But I didn't know how to channel that. I didn't know how to bring it into fruition. I only knew that my heart was yearning for a reconnection.

That's when I met Rabbi Zalman Schacter-Shalomi. I saw in Rabbi Zalman someone who was able to take the deep meaning and profound infrastructure of our prayers and bring them forward as if they were beyond what we would call modern. They were really looking toward the Judaism of the twenty-first and twenty-second century.

I began to study with Reb Zalman. I began to see personally how the influence of Eastern religious approaches to prayer and feminism were reshaping and reinvigorating all of Jewish practice in the Western world, whether acknowledged or not. Most of the time it's not. But the influence of the swamis and feminism cannot be underestimated, at least in the United States.

ଷ

The entity of the Jewish Renewal Movement is called Aleph and is located in Philadelphia. There is a mentor-based *smichah* (ordination) program. I had a local mentor, Rabbi Areyeh Hirschfield, who I met with on a regular basis and studied with and received assignments from; I worked directly under the tutelage of him and Rabbi Zalman.

It was a seven-year program, very intense. You might call it a seminary without walls. But it's even more than that because it's a direct transmission, direct teaching in a mentorship manner. The seminary system, after all, is an emulation of the Protestant Western schools of training pastors and ministers. Seminaries in Judaism are, as far as I know, only about one hundred years old. Before that, all *smichah* programs were private, in a small yeshiva, with three, ten, or forty students in a little village or town or maybe in a larger city, but ordination came from the hands of an individual, private rabbi.

In 1995 I received my ordination, and began serving the rural communities in Redding, California, and Bend, Oregon. On the west coast we call ourselves, circuit riders—have *huppah*, will travel. Redding is three hours away, Bend four hours. I still serve those communities. I'm half-time here at my post in Ashland. I'm the rabbi of the Jewish Renewal community, Havurat Shir Hadash and I serve the outlying region.

❦

More than half of the people in the congregations I serve have left Judaism for an extended period of time. If they're returning, they're returning with painful war stories. Synagogues were excluding them because of financial reasons, because they couldn't afford to buy High Holy Day tickets, or the synagogue wasn't meeting their needs in terms of their spiritual being.

People come with wounds, or during the '70s and '80s found value in practices from other religious traditions. They were looking for a synagogue that permitted them to bring the truths they had gained in these other practices into their Jewish prayer life. For example, I have many congregants who are meditators, who practice non-theistic forms of meditation such as those taught by great religious teachers like Thich Nhat Hanh, or meditative techniques that come directly from Tibetan Buddhism. They approach me and I have empathy for their position. I have a sense that there's a fulfillment in God's purpose, in them having, so to speak, been sent by God, consciously or unconsciously, to these teachers in order to come back, to bring a new enrichment, a new renewal within Judaism itself. I have congregants who have sat in silence with Quakers, or practiced with Sufis, or have a sense of planetary consciousness and pantheism that comes from the Native American tradition. Because of my own background and experiences I have more than an empathetic heart. I believe it was a divine mission from God for these brothers and sisters of mine to go elsewhere and to help bring back what we once had in Judaism. Teachers like Rabbi Aryeh Kaplan have shown us that Judaism has a profoundly rich practice in dietary discipline, meditational practices, to enhance prayer, and that these meditational practices were very much a part of Judaism but have become lost.

❦

I serve congregants that have this need. Here are the kinds of things I'm willing to do: a regular weekday morning prayer service might have in an average siddur eighty to one hundred pages of liturgy that needs to be read. Without *kavanah*, intention, these words are simply read at an incredible rate of speed, and with not a lot of intention placed on each word. What if we do the morning service by putting on a tallis and tefillin and then reducing it down to fifty words, to be able to pray each phrase many times, in a mantric style, so that the words themselves take on shape and color. It gives the worshiper time to develop some intention about the words that he or she is saying to the Holy One. This is an example of how a meditational practice, a practice of using mantras that we have learned from Eastern religions, can come into Judaism in a way that still keeps the prayers kosher but yet utilizes a different approach.

Judaism can be thought of in two ways, informational or transformational. I think many of us from the '60s, baby boomers, have had experiences in other religions, Eastern religions in particular, and often prefer a religion that is transformational.

๑๖๑

The second element I see in people's reconnecting is the influence of the divine feminine. Twenty years ago you didn't have Jews in average American synagogues, Reform or Orthodox, talking about the *Shechinah*. Now it's almost part of the normal, daily conversation: we can speak about God as the Holy One, Blessed be He, or as the *Shechinah*, one of the feminine names of God, meaning the divine presence, the holy presence of God. Prayers, the formula for blessing, are now being explored in their feminine formulas. There are different formulas for it, God as a king and God as a father are two ancient group metaphors. They're not the total truth about God, they're simply metaphors that worked for millennium, but no longer seem to work for millions of Jews around the world. We know that these are anthropomorphisms, that God is just as much mother as father; God is just as much queen or sovereign as king. So with feminism comes new language. If language is a barrier to a person, so that speaking of God in a hierarchical manner, like the language of monarchy and the patriarchs, puts people off, we need to find language that still fulfills the mitzvot, fulfills the spirit of Jewish law, but is willing to expand and explore new names for God.

The need for women to be able to address God in feminine language, whether we agree with it or not, almost doesn't matter; it exists. We're either going to ignore the call of millions of women's voices or we're going to ask ourselves what's wrong with addressing God in the feminine. My answer is, I can't find anything wrong in it. It's absolutely wonderful, it's a joy for me to, so to speak, put some new systems software into my own hard drive, to update a new version of Judaism that is still based in Torah and God and Israel.

Women are changing Judaism, bringing with them the reinvigoration, not just of Rosh Chodesh, but also how the rabbi behaves in a more egalitarian and less hierarchical fashion in the synagogue itself, and even in the way the prayer service is being conducted. Whether it be in a circle rather than in pews, whether it be in group leadership of the prayers rather than one person leading the prayers themselves, Judaism is changing.

☙❧

I know Judaism is going to survive intensively in America. Judaism is changing in the Reform Movement, the Conservative Movement, and the Orthodox Movement and certainly in Jewish Renewal by bringing in the concerns of people who want to meditate, the concerns about language and egalitarian language, and inclusiveness.

Judaism itself, the practicing of mitzvot, serving God in moral passion for moral causes, is being reinvigorated, I believe primarily, through the forces of the divine feminine, and through practices from other religions giving us a new foundation and a new way to practice. This may not be necessary for many traditional Jews, but it is being screamed for by many, many millions of Jews who have been left in the cold by traditional Jewish practices that had either no silence, no space for meditation, or no heart—lots of brains, no heart, and not much room for understanding God in a more profound, imminent, and intimate matter.

ଈଡ଼ଵ

Why are there so many messianic Jews who affiliate with organizations like Jews for Jesus? I studied this for a long time and found out that many of these Jews went to their rabbis and said something like, "Rabbi, I'm having a crisis in my life—divorce, alcoholism, drug abuse. Please teach me how to speak to God." And the rabbi would say, "Come to services tomorrow morning." And the next morning, the person who was in crisis and simply wanted to speak to God was told to open to page eighty-seven and to read the words in the book until he got to page one hundred and five. Afterwards, the person would come back to the rabbi and say, "Rabbi, I read from page eighty-seven to one hundred and five. I didn't understand what I was saying because I don't remember the Hebrew so well; please teach me how to speak to God." And the rabbi or leader of the Jewish community would say, "Let me sign you up for our basic Hebrew class on Wednesday nights." And the person would say, "Rabbi, do you understand I'm in crisis? I'm an alcoholic, drug addict, I need help, I need to talk to God right now." And the rabbi would say, "Be patient, in time, in a couple of years, you'll get your Hebrew back, and you'll be able to read from the book."

The next day, the person walks into a fundamentalist Christian church or messianic Jewish group and goes to their leader, and says, "Pastor, I want to speak to God." The pastor grabs his hands and says, "Let's talk to God right now. Lord, bless this person in his dilemma, in his crisis. Bring blessings in his life." I have had dozens of these Jews come to me and say the reason I left Judaism was not because I wanted to, but because what was available in messianic Judaism was a personal, intimate relationship to God that was not available in my corner synagogue. I was desperate and I just needed to talk to God. So my sense now, after having worked with bringing many, many Jews back from messianic Judaism or fundamentalist Christianity, is that they were getting something that is available also in Judaism, but the rabbis and leaders of Jewish communities are going to have to, for one moment, put the siddur down. Put the Hebrew down, put the study down, and take the hands of our congregants and say, "Let's talk to God on a personal level."

Modern American Judaism, in the last hundred years, has lost or given up the God of our ancestors, the God of the shtetl, the God of Golde and Reb Tevye. That God we talked to all the time, without the siddur, without the Bible. Jews coming back from Jewish Christian movements are looking for that relationship with God and frankly I'm either going to provide it or I'm not; if I provide it, then we're going to have one more Jewish soul lighting Shabbes candles, one more Jewish soul putting on tefillin and doing mitzvot. If I don't provide it, they're going to find it elsewhere. On some level, and I don't say this in a mean way, they should find it elsewhere. If we can't provide what we already have in our bank, in our storage cabinets, which is a personal relationship with God when a congregant needs it, they *should* find it elsewhere.

So when I get one of these people coming back to me, I embrace them. I grab them and hug them, I tell them I love you, it's so incredible that you found God. Let me show you that we've got the same stuff right here in Judaism. I teach them how to pray from a more intimate place. I'm not afraid to hold their hands, to have a prayer circle where we're praying for healing. The outsider comes in and says, "Look, it looks just like a Protestant prayer session." I don't care what they say, I don't care what it looks like, these are Jews, using Jewish prayer, talking to God in a personal way. And at that particular moment, the siddur is secondary to the heart.

IV   A Choice of One's Own

To be a Jew is a destiny.
—Vicki Baum

Whether one agrees that the percentage of Jews in the United States is a precarious 2 percent of the total population or remains steadfast in the belief of statistical fallibility, there can still be no doubt that the United States is overwhelmingly Christian. Thus, it is remarkable that Judaism, a religion that does not advocate proselytization, is still able to draw more than 5,000 Jews by choice a year. Without active soliciting, one out of every thirty-five Jews has converted to Judaism from another faith.

For most, the choice is viewed as one of the most pivotal and life changing that they will ever make. The reasons are as varied as the people who make them: the wishes of a Jewish spouse, the desire to give children a unified religious upbringing, an attraction to the sense of Jewish community; or more inexplicable and intangible reasons, such as the pull of a forgotten Jewish ancestor, the sense that one has a Jewish soul, or the quest for a satisfying spirituality.

16 From Violence to Peace

Theodore P.

My dad was a career army officer so I was the first American born in Japan after World War II. Typical of an army brat, I moved around a lot, attending thirteen schools in twelve years to get my high school diploma. My father, the son of a Baptist minister of German descent, had undergone a lot of discrimination in World War I, to the point that he changed the spelling of his last name. That was the problem: he was a very angry, bitter man.

My background was religiously scattered. I would probably have identified myself as a fundamentalist Christian. When we visited my parents' home state I was shuffled off to church, mainly because my mom's sisters went to church. I got some religious education there, but mostly I went off on my own, even by fifth

---

Theodore P. is a psychiatrist living with his family in the south. Born into a fundamentalist Christian home, his violent childhood and upbringing resulted in his quest for meaning. Today he works with sufferers of post-traumatic stress disorder.

grade, practicing a lot more than my family. When we were stationed overseas in Germany, there were some good army chaplains that had youth programs with clubs, outings, movies, and things like that. I joined with some friends and I remember even about sixth grade my family would sleep in on Sunday morning and I would get up and go to church. I was the family oddball in that regard.

ॐ

I kind of lapsed, so to speak, when I was in seventh grade and we weren't living on an army base. There really wasn't much access. Until tenth grade there was pretty minimal religious activity by me and of course none by my family. Then some friends took me to a Billy Graham youth rally and the evangelist scared me to death. I was going to die on the spot and I was going to hell. He did a very good job of convincing me of that. I was hyperventilating, so I went down and I joined up. In the Baptist tradition, you get yourself saved, meaning that I talked to one of the ministers and made a public profession on the spot. I got five minutes instruction about what I had to do to be Christian and to be safe from going to hell. I memorized one verse from the Bible, made a public profession of faith that Jesus died for my sins and saved me from hell, and I accepted his death for my sins. Bingo, I was a Baptist. So I was "saved" when I was fifteen. That was the first time I joined any religious organization.

My family kept moving and I never really settled in. I was also beginning to ask annoying questions when I was attending church and going to youth groups. I was reading things about Buddhism, reincarnation, reading all the terrible stuff about evolution and creationism and I kept asking questions. If we aren't allowed to drink, how come Jesus turned water into wine? If the earth is only 5,000 years old, why do we have 2 ½-million-year-old fossils? If we started in the Garden of Eden, why are there fossils in Africa? I tended to be quite pesky.

◈

There were many problems in my childhood including a dad that was a combat veteran of World War II and Korea who had a very serious problem with alcohol. It was a very violent home. As I see the pattern now, I had a scorching case of post-traumatic stress disorder—I guess more so when I was extremely young, cooling off a bit when I got older, but still your typical emotionally distant alcoholic family.

My dad and at least two or three of his older brothers were extremely active in the Ku Klux Klan. As a small child I witnessed a couple of KKK killings or other violence with my dad involved. Once, when I was about eight and a half, a couple of my uncles took me to a Klan meeting. I think it was just supposed to be good old boys drinking beer, talking stupid stuff. I think the whole game at the time was guys just got together and drank beer and had a weenie roast, like being in the moose lodge or something like that. But at this particular one, some individuals from outside the local chapter showed up with a young Jewish boy, probably about three years old, that they had kidnaped. As I recall, the kid's parents made the mistake of moving into one of these sunshine counties; you know, don't let the sun set on you, which means that if you're black, Jewish, Catholic, or whatever, you don't stay in the county after sunset. You can come in to work but God help you if you live there, they'll teach you a lesson, which is what happened here.

My uncles were rather severely drunk, and for whatever reason, probably the fact that my father was a major player in the Klan and also in the German American Bund Nazi organization before World War II, I was volunteered. They took the boy up on a hillside away from the main group and put the child down on a rock and the intention was to have me kill the boy with a large Nazi dagger. What a lot of people don't realize about the Klan unless you get intimately close to it, as unfortunately I was, is that in a twisted way it is a religious organization. Some of their activities and killings are sacrificial. They follow a lot of Norse mythology, worshiping the old Norse god Odin. They call it Klankraft. They burn crosses, they say they're Christian. But the deep dark secret is at the higher levels they adhere to very intense pagan beliefs and practices, which is what Hitler did. He was always obsessed with the Valkyries, Wagner, and all that stuff. He was into a lot of necromancy and astrology and the Klan just picked up where he left off after World War II.

Anyhow I was selected for the honor of killing this child. My uncles were as drunk as monkeys. As I best recall, one of them was actively throwing up and the other two probably weren't capable of much beyond walking. This was an honor since my daddy was big in the Klan. Because he was the fair-haired boy with all he did in the war, they gave me, his son, a great honor.

I refused to do any killing and ended up throwing my body over the child. The guys at the top of the hill didn't like that. By the time they were done with me, they had cracked a vertebrae in my back with a rock and I was taken down the hill, beaten, and gang raped. After that, staying sane in and of itself was an adventure. The next morning, Mom figured out I'd been in some kind of a mess and had been taken to the doctor, who sewed everything up nicely and didn't keep any charts—like in Pat Conroy's novel *The Prince of Tides*, where the prison escapees break into the house, beat and rape everybody, and they kill the guys, then mom makes supper and says we're never going to talk about this again.

Conroy knew what these people were like. I'm sure my father figured out what happened because he was the one who took me to the doctor. I still remember the doctor giving my dad a totally disgusted look and Dad making some remark about not discussing this. Of course if you wanted to live in that area at that point, you kept quiet. My dad handed him a nice crispy one hundred dollar bill, which was a whole hell of a lot of money at the time, since doctor visits were generally going for about three to four dollars.

My dad knew, but we never talked about it. I wouldn't be surprised if some vengeance was extracted against some individuals involved in the abuse of me.

I still have the scars but the trip to the doctor was the end of the discussion. My mom was given this cock and bull story about me falling off the tent I was playing on and she either believed it or just wanted to believe it, but that was the end of it. It was over.

I carried that with me for many years, which relentlessly drove me as far as trying to find something in my church, in religious observance. I was looking for something that would give me a sense of escape from my depression, anxiety; something that would help me to be at peace with myself. The Christian experience certainly promised that, but for me anyway, it didn't provide it.

☙

I did my first year of college in 1965 and the first Sunday I decided I was going to church. I went down to the end of the campus where they had an Episcopal church. There was a nice little service, and the priest announced that they were having a wine and cheese party afterwards for all the new incoming people of the college. I joined up. This was great stuff after being a Baptist. I was kind of a hell-raiser in those days. I discovered beer, wine, and poker all in one year and got a 0.6 grade point average.

Then I married my college sweetheart, way too young. That only lasted a few years. She was a Methodist and a very regular churchgoer. I continued in the Episcopal church and went through the process of converting, including several months of newcomers' class. I was baptized officially in that church and became a member. That was right around age twenty and until five years ago that was my religious affiliation.

I was rather active in the church. I was a once- or twice-a-week churchgoer and for quite a few years a Sunday school teacher. Right before I converted, I was licensed as a lay minister and one of the things I was doing was assisting the priest in distributing communion and things like that. Interestingly, most of the people I talk to who have converted come from a background of being more active than normal Christians before their conversion.

❧

I eventually did very well academically in college, then went to medical school and did a post doctorate in psychiatry. One of my ways of dealing with everything was becoming the world's greatest overachieving workaholic. It worked. But anybody could be a psychiatrist, so I double trained. I worked both in emergency room medicine and psychiatry, did more than anybody else.

About five and a half years ago my mother died from cancer and that was a major blow. I guess it is for anybody. Dad had been closet drinking, hiding bottles in the home, saying that he quit, but the minute Mom's funeral was over it came out in the open. I'd already moved about four hours driving time away from the the rest of the family so at that point I really ceased having any-more contact.

At that point, a lot of things were boiling around. It was a bad time for medicine with HMOs and things like that, so there was job-related stress. But the upshot of all this was that I went to counseling for a period of time and got some very good advice. I started to plug into this adult children of alcoholics program, which was the first time I had a chance to talk to people who had been on the receiving end of the same kind of violence and the abuse that I had. I began to process what had happened to me. What Al Anon did for me more than anything else was lead me into the concept of the old AA "higher power." Even though it's a religiously based program, our group kept it pretty generic. We were a mixture of various flavors of Christians, Buddhists, and a few Unitarians, which was kind of crazy for the area.

But this started the process of looking at my involvement with the Christian church. I was where I was because some evangelist scared the holy hell out of me. And it wasn't working for me be-cause I was approaching God as being the same kind of violent, abusive, throw-people-in-the-pit-of-hell individual that my human father was. Didn't work. I was floundering. Yet I was terrified to look elsewhere because even though I was versed in other religious traditions, I couldn't imagine looking anywhere beyond a so-called Bible-based Christianity. The minute I started thinking in that direction, the fear button hit and I could smell the old sulfur and brimstone.

This led to months and months of agony and then things started to happen. As we look back, we start to see patterns that we don't see when we're in the middle of it. But in the course of my clinical practice of psychiatry, I had a chance to work with a very nice elderly Jewish couple and they, especially the wife, really impressed me. Looking into Judaism was something I would never have thought of because Jews don't believe in Jesus and in the back of my mind there's this hell, fire, and brimstone. I guess God won't throw these two people in hell because they're nice Jews, but boy, they're taking a chance. They're taking a big risk and I hope it comes out all right for them.

At this point, I was working for the U.S. Veterans Administration. About once a month I had to make a long drive to service one of the satellite psychiatry clinics. This involved going down a long winding country road with little rolling hills that was just about an exact duplicate of the road I went back down that night with the Klan. It doesn't take Sigmund Freud to figure out what that did to me sitting in my car. The whole time I was on that road, in spite of fighting it, it was flashback city, panic attacks. It was a miserable experience. And of course, I kept doing it and doing it because I was going to fight this thing and it wasn't going to happen next time. I guess it was like being a Vietnam vet, that when a helicopter goes overhead, wow, wild stuff. But there was one time I was going down this road and the fear and the panic started crawling in as usual. The flashbacks started coming and I was in my big old Buick station wagon and I just grabbed for a tape to stuff in, anything to play to have noise in the car. It's a pretty isolated road. I ended up grabbing one of my daughter's Amy Grant tapes.

I had never been a contemporary Christian God rock type person. I hated that kind of music. But I shoved the tape in, cranked it up, and it was right at the point in the song "El Shaddei," a very beautiful song, and she sang something about loving, "El Shaddei, El Shaddei, Eloheinu Adonai." It was the first I'd ever heard the true name in Hebrew. Just blew my doors off. Amazing experience. I was on that road for another forty minutes and I probably cried for half an hour going down that road playing the tape over and over again. I had an incredible sense of an actual comforting presence of God in the car. Of course I had to sit back and analyze this. I am a psychiatrist, right? So I talked myself into backing off, but I kept getting more and more interested in the Jewish thing, and more and more conflicted because this was not Christian.

๛

The final tip over: we were planning a family vacation and I always like to get of couple of big books to read. Sitting there on the bookshelf, not real typical in the Bible Belt, was Joseph Telushkin's book, *Jewish Literacy.* Like a magnetic attraction, I felt a very strong sense of being drawn to buy the book. In the course of a one-week vacation I read the book cover to cover twice. I had a mental conversation with it; it made sense. For me this seemed logical, for me this was a spiritually comfortable place. It felt like the old John Denver song, coming home to a place you've never been before.

I read the book, did more reading, and talked to a couple of Jewish friends in the counseling center where I worked. They were convinced that I was crazy, a *goy* (non-Jew) even wanting to look into this. But they were nice and referred me to some other books and it finally led to my getting up the nerve to go down to a Jewish worship service. We have a Reform temple here in town. I went and met the rabbi. I told him I was looking into Judaism and thinking about converting. Like all rabbis, he asked: why I want to do this. In the course of just a couple of meetings, he got the whole story, including the KKK incidents, and his response was, what can I say, that's quite a story.

The rest was like hitting the ground running and not looking back because our rabbi is not full-time. He just comes on Fridays and most of my instruction was him supervising what I did, recommending reading, asking questions, telling me to explore this and that. He was very strict about going through the process of what he calls living a Jewish life for a year before finalizing any kind of conversion. Basically I was self-taught, checking in with him every week or two to make sure I wasn't teaching myself anything too weird.

෧෫෨

My parents were dead, which cut down on their reaction to my conversion. My second wife was dumbfounded for a while. She had been raised Roman Catholic and was attending the Episcopal church with me. She was also realizing that what she and I had been doing for religious observance for nearly twenty years of marriage wasn't working for her either. I wouldn't call my attraction to Judaism a source of conflict between us; rather a source of confusion. On one hand there was—not so much anti-Semitism —but just this thing that Jews aren't Christians. On the other hand, she was seeing what was happening to me mentally, emotionally, and personally. I was experiencing a lot of peace and stability, and a lot of things just started falling in place in my life. It was a very confusing time. But after some initial, "My God, what's happening here?" she was pretty supportive, especially when she found out that this wasn't going to involve any pressure on her to convert. She wound up going back to the Roman Catholic church and found her spiritual needs there, and is very happy with that. It's a very good place for her.

෧෫෨

One of the ironies of life is that I'm pretty much in the same position in Judaism as I was in Christianity. When our rabbi is not there we still try to have services and discuss the Torah. They're not quite sure what to call me. It's really kind of an irony, the UAHC (Union of American Hebrew Congregations) is not really doing the rabbinic assistant anymore like they use to, but if I had to stick a label on myself that's what it would be.

We have about 200 members and any given Friday night service we make a minyan, sometimes just barely. We follow the Reform liturgy. My wife has gotten into attending with me, and a couple times a month I go with her. Her priest is a pretty spiritual Catholic guy and has his head screwed on pretty straight. He's very accepting of me, Jews in general, the Jewish community. He started out as a Martin Buber-type guy, reading the Kabbalah in Aramaic, so he's cool.

Life is calmer. I have a lot more of a sense of the world, myself, and the people around me. A typically Jewish thing, I evolved away from a big emphasis on belief to being pretty laid-back about actual detailed theology. I see my overall expression of who I am with God as being an action-oriented thing. I define myself based on the work I do, with the temple and the congregation, trying to be a good father to my kids, and my work with Vietnam vets, who are a very difficult population, a truly needy group. I'm doing very dirty work that other people don't want to do and I'm proud to be there.

One of the nicest conversations I had was with a very huge, very red neck Vietnam vet, ex paratrooper, big guy. A couple of years ago he was signing up for the clinic and as I was talking to him he looked over and said, "Oh, so I hear you're Jewish." I thought, I don't know this guy, something's going to get real interesting here. I said, "Well yeah, we don't go into much religious stuff in therapy, but yes to answer your question, I am." And he started crying. And when he got done, I asked him what had him so upset, and he said he wasn't upset, he was just happy because the doctor who had been doing the Vietnam vets program years before was a Jew and a psychiatrist, and "you and him were the only two people in the world who had ever given a damn about me." So I guess that's how I define myself at this point in my life.

17 Meant to Be

Anne B.

I was pretty much raised in a non-religious home. My father was born Jewish, but never raised to be Jewish. In fact, I really didn't find out he was Jewish until I was thirteen years old. That just happened by chance when some letter came in the mail from Israel and he casually said, "Oh yes, I'm Jewish, you didn't know?" I said, "No, I didn't know, nobody told me." It was weird. My mother's mother had been a devout southern Baptist until my mother's brother died of an ear infection when he was seven. At that time my grandmother completely renounced Christianity. So my mother really didn't have much religious upbringing to give to any of her children.

We celebrated Christmas and Easter but it was done in a very secular fashion. We enjoyed them more from a charming tradi-

---

Anne B., art teacher and mother of three, chose Judaism more than thirteen years ago. In the process, she learned much about her own Jewish ancestry and gained a deeper understanding of herself.

tions standpoint rather then a religious nature. I've since come to realize that as a child I was looking for something religious and spiritual—I was always a little unsatisfied. In fact, I would look for a little clarity from my mother, asking her what religion we were. My mother was very vague. Once I really tried to pin her down, and she said, "Well, um, Protestant." But another time I asked her and she said, "Presbyterian, we like the hymns." So it was confusing.

I was frustrated that there wasn't something there. I remember wanting to know some prayers, to say a prayer at night. My mother tried to tell me a prayer she remembered, like "now I lay me down to sleep" and "if I die before I wake," which is a real charmer. So I said this every night and then I would say God bless everybody and I would go through this litany of people, which would be exhausting.

The one thing we did that was nice was we said grace every night before dinner. The way we said it was again pretty secular, like, "God is great, God is good, now we thank Him for our food." One time I said I know what color God is, because I thought the prayer was "God is gray," which seemed to make sense. So I was always a little unclear. I remember in third grade a teacher asked who knows what a minister is, and I enthusiastically raised my hand and said, "He's the man in church who's always shouting at everybody, he's very angry and I never know why he's so angry." So these were the limits I knew about religion.

❦

When I was eleven, a friend who was involved in the Methodist church encouraged me to take Sunday school classes with her and join their choir. Primarily because I always liked music, I joined. I remember that at some point they gave me a Bible with my name printed on it and that was very exciting to me. My parents, on the other hand, were not thrilled to come to church to hear me sing. The minister even came to our house to get them to join the church and my parents just wanted me to stop the whole thing.

One day, after the Sunday school teacher's lesson, she asked if there were any questions. I thought, wow, now I can ask the burning question I've had in my heart all these years, so I said, "How do you know there's really a God?" She looked at me with horror and said, "If you have to ask that, I don't know what you're doing here." I was so ashamed! I was a child who was always very good, I would never do anything wrong on purpose, very anxious never to displease anyone. I was mortified that this woman acted as though I was trying to be fresh, and saying something bad. At that point, I felt that this wasn't for me. I really think that caused me to leave that church.

When I was thirteen, I decided that I should choose what religion I was going to be. So every Sunday I would ride my bike and try out different churches. I did try a synagogue once but it was closed, it was Sunday and I didn't know that I was supposed to go there on Saturday! I wasn't adventurous enough or I didn't even think to try a mosque or something like that. After a while, I abandoned the search. I just decided that it didn't really matter, that I would just sort of have my own beliefs.

Unfortunately, I also grew up without even the most basic religious knowledge. It was embarrassing sometimes. When the opera *Jesus Christ Superstar* came out, my brother and I tried to figure it all out: now this guy Jesus is obviously a really big deal, so let's see if we can really listen carefully to the lyrics so we can figure out who he was, what the whole deal was. We were really trying to piece together the whole story because we knew nothing.

ॐ

By the time I got to college, when people would ask me what my religion is I would say, "It's like my major, undeclared." At this point I felt that people would peg you by your religion and by what your father did, but I really felt I didn't need to classify myself for other people's convenience, so that they could either like or dislike me based on that. The only good thing, or at least one good thing, about growing up without any religion was that

I also grew up without any religious prejudice of any kind. I never heard any religious bigotry at all.

During my college years, people from the Lubavitch community would come and build a sukkah every year on our campus. I always thought that the whole sukkah thing looked off the wall. I couldn't imagine what this thing was, it looked really strange. But I remember my husband Howard, who I met in my freshman year, was quite charmed by it. He didn't think it was weird at all, even though I don't know that he had ever seen one before. He was happy to go inside and say a *berachah*. I found that very curious.

I knew Howard was Jewish, but it had no meaning for me whatsoever. I was only eighteen when I met him and I dated him all through college. Just after I graduated, I turned twenty-two and got married. We were married outside, there was a beautiful mansion on our campus with gardens and a gazebo, which sort of made his mother feel like it was *huppah*-like. I knew his parents wanted me to convert and they suggested I take this short two-week course. I said I'd look into conversion but I told them that I had too much respect for their religion, which I knew absolutely nothing about, to even consider doing such a thing after a two-week course. So we had the mayor marry us, and there was no religious clergy at all. We also got married on a Sunday so it wouldn't be against the Sabbath. We were willing to agree to that kind of thing but I really couldn't do much more.

ଊଡ଼ଡ଼

I had said I'd look into conversion, but I didn't really know what that meant. I was also really busy because I was getting certified to teach, I had a degree in art but I didn't have certification to teach. I had an intense year doing student teaching and getting certified. I was also working part-time, and I just didn't have a minute to think about it.

Three years later when I was pregnant with Matthew the whole situation of my conversion became even more important to my in-laws. I asked Howard how he felt about all this, and he said he would like it but only if it was something that I felt comfortable with and wanted to do. We really hadn't figured out or thought through what we were going to do in terms of raising children.

I agreed to take Jewish classes but I again told my in-laws that I wouldn't do anything unless I really believed in it. Howard and I took a six-month class together. Each week was a three-hour class. Unfortunately the teacher was terrible and the class was long and tedious. But he did assign reading, and that was very interesting. I started to get a sense that this is really beautiful; I had no idea that this was what Judaism was all about. At this point, of course, I had been to a number of things with Howard's family, from Passover seders to breakfast on Yom Kippur, which was really nothing more than a dinner. Maybe at the seder there was a five-minute service with a seder plate. There was no sense of not eating things that were not kosher for Passover. I didn't know about that yet. I just knew you were supposed to eat matzah.

We also went occasionally to Howard's grandmother's house. She kept a very traditionally observant Conservative Jewish home. But at Shabbat dinner at her house there wasn't a real sense of what Shabbat was about. She would simply invite us over and feed us. I guess she did some prayers but I don't remember those. What I do remember is that his grandmother didn't have a place set for herself because she literally did nothing but run back and forth with inordinate amounts of food. I had never seen or heard of the idea of two main courses, an enormous thing of soup to be refilled. I found it all very interesting, but then again I wasn't getting a huge sense of what Judaism was about.

⊙⊱⊙

I went to services with Howard and his father, his mother never went. Howard would go a couple of times a year, maybe at the High Holy Days and Passover, and I would go with them. I found it interesting to read the prayer book. They belonged to a Reform synagogue and I liked what I was reading. I finally had this feeling, even though the class was so poorly presented and I still had never seen anything in practice, but I had a sense. So I said it really sounds like a beautiful religion and I see the depth of the heritage there, and for that reason I would certainly like my children to be brought up Jewish. But I also felt that this is not something I wanted to do for myself, at least not at this time. And I didn't see it necessarily happening.

Everyone was sort of okay with that. I knew it meant that if it was a boy we would have to have a *bris* and that was fine with me. But I needed my in-laws to handle the details. I'd never been to one, I didn't know anything about it. My mother-in-law said, "Oh no, it's a horrible thing, I would never ask you to do that." So unfortunately, Matthew never had a *bris*. She arranged a naming ceremony about a month after he was born. Later, it made me sad that he hadn't had a *bris*. He also could have had a Pidyon Haben because he was the first child. But we didn't have that either although she sort of brought it up, but she never pursued it.

◎❦◎

Soon we began to explore a couple of synagogues, but we often felt, certainly at the High Holy Days, that bringing a child in there was an unforgivable sin. If that child makes a peep, you will be banned. Nobody actually said that, but they would give us these horrible, glaring looks. Well, how are we supposed to raise our child to be Jewish if we're not allowed to bring him to a synagogue until he's grown-up and ready to sit perfectly still? We were so turned off by that, we didn't return.

When Matthew was nine months old, I did ask Howard if he knew how to bless candles, if he could teach me that blessing. Just by memory he taught me how to say the blessings over the candles, and without knowing any Hebrew or being able to read any Hebrew, I phonetically memorized it. I started blessing candles and we started more and more having Shabbat dinners on Friday nights, just the three of us. It was a very quiet little thing. I didn't know about Shabbat candles and I thought Jewish people must be rich because they have to buy a pair of tapers every week. I didn't know about the big package you could buy.

So we started doing these Shabbat dinners, and by the time Matthew was about eleven months old, religion had started slowly becoming more important to us. When he was about eighteen months, we moved to a house in Caldwell, New Jersey, our first house. I remember looking in the papers and saying, "You know Howard, there's a synagogue in town. Do you want to check it out?" He always seemed very vague about the whole thing, but I pushed it and we went. I remember being very nervous because I didn't know why I was pushing him into this; this is his religion, if he's not into it, why am I bothering? I was very anxious because when I married Howard I really didn't understand that it was a big deal for someone who's Jewish to marry someone who's not Jewish. I had never known that this was a problem. Five years later, I definitely knew this with a big deal. This wasn't the way it's supposed to be and I was worried. Were people going to start hissing at me or pointing fingers or whispering because they're going to know that I'm not Jewish? They're going to see that I'm the only one in the synagogue who doesn't know how to follow the Hebrew. These were the things that concerned me.

I always loved sewing, so I had made Matthew an adorable little suit for services; gray flannel shorts, white button-down shirt and bow tie, and a little tiny navy blue blazer. The people at the synagogue were incredibly welcoming to us. They couldn't believe how cute Matthew was, they were all over him. The rabbi's wife came over and introduced herself to us. I met so many people who were nice and genuine. For the first time I was seeing Judaism as it really is and I was seeing people who were genuinely observing, joyously observing Judaism. They weren't doing this with a sense of guilt or I have to or I ought to—it was heartfelt. They were really into it, and I was just fascinated and drawn in.

It was easy to go there again. We went a month later, then we started going every couple of weeks and before long we were going virtually every week. We started to get invitations to Shabbat lunch, to a Passover seder, and it was incredibly nice. I was able to see Jewish observance and how it translates to the home, which I had never seen before; what a happy wonderful thing it was and how spiritual it was. I was just fascinated by the various ways to approach it. It fed me from a spiritual sense, it fed me from an intellectual sense, there was so much to read about and be fascinated by. It fed me from a simply social sense in that I was meeting so many lovely, friendly people. It was like a whole new world opening up. It was incredible. We had moved in February and by September I was thinking that this is what I wanted for myself and my family.

❦

I talked to the rabbi and he wanted to get me into a class. He also wanted us to join the synagogue, which we did. He handled it all very well, gently nudging us in the direction. I told him I would really like to learn more but I previously had a rather disappointing experience with study. He assured me that he had a teacher that was very good. The teacher was great and the group of couples he led met in different homes instead of the synagogue, so it was a little more cozy. We liked a lot of the other couples and felt some connection. Different people were there for different reasons. I also kept telling the rabbi that I wasn't saying I definitely wanted to convert. I was just saying I wanted to look into it. To me, this was such an important decision. I couldn't say that I was going to do it until I had a chance to properly study and learn more and go through the cycle of holidays, to try everything on for size.

So I did that and we studied and studied. During the year-long class, we met for a few hours every week and I really found myself feeling more and more like this was what I wanted. By the time I was pregnant with my eldest daughter, I knew I wanted to convert. The rabbi suggested that I convert even before the class was over, so that my daughter could be born Jewish. I was due in

June, but I was so enormous that everyone was terrified that I'd be a couple of months early. So I was converted in April.

☙

As I was nearing conversion, it was feeling more and more right to me. I was also studying with the cantor, which I had started in September of the previous year because I really wanted to learn to read Hebrew. It bothered me that I couldn't follow the prayers, and even though the rabbi had assured me that I was not the only person, by any means, who couldn't follow the prayers, I didn't want to feel like it was this empty thing. I wanted everything about this to be genuine for me. So I started studying Hebrew with the cantor. He had an adult bar/bat mitzvah class, which was wonderful. He was very interesting so it was enjoyable and rewarding to study with him. By Passover I was able to read Hebrew very brokenly and slowly, like a first grader, but being able to read was a great feeling. I loved learning what some of the different prayers meant. It still bothers me that I can't understand enough to pray in Hebrew, so I will always go back and forth between the Hebrew and the English.

By this time I had looked very closely at the prayer books. I remembered thinking that in the past, in churches, I couldn't bring myself to say the things. But I felt right about most everything I was seeing in the synagogue prayer books. I felt so comfortable with the prayers. More and more I really had the sense that this was my spiritual home.

I didn't feel it right away, but certainly now, I feel that my synagogue is the first place that I truly belonged. As a high school student, I was one of those kids who felt left out or that they don't belong to a group. I was definitely one of those loner types and I thought I would never be involved in any kind of a group. It was so amazing to me, and it felt so right, and the people felt right, and I couldn't believe that people seemed to accept and like me for who I was. I was really grateful for that.

A lot of congregants from the temple were very supportive of my studies and my conversion. People were totally helpful and open. Nobody ever made me feel like I should know this. It was never wrong to ask a question

That was one of the things about Judaism that I really loved—my questions were welcome. I was never made to feel bad for asking questions, and for me this was a really big issue from my childhood experience. To me, religious study is all about questions and what I love about Judaism is that it is all about questions and searching out. I loved that Judaism could be approached from so many different angles. Our rabbi consistently talks about what he calls head Jews, who relate through their intellect; hand Jews, who relate through their deeds; and heart Jews, who relate through a deep gut level. I really saw myself as all three. It was fascinating to find an endless amount to learn in Judaism. There's always more to it, always more to pursue.

ଚ୨ତ

I felt really Jewish and committed Jewishly when I converted but I feel much more so now. For example, when I converted, if somebody had asked me if God forbid something happened to Howard would I still be Jewish? or, if I were to remarry would I need to have a Jewish mate? I don't know if I felt that strongly. I didn't feel it as strongly then as I do now. Certainly not with the sense of a Jewish spouse as being imperative. Now it's totally in my core.

It's so clear to me that I was meant, destined to be Jewish, whether through a far-off Jewish ancestor's soul touching mine in some way, or just something in my past. There is some indication that I may be related to a highly regarded rabbi from way back, and my sister also converted. Whether it was something that came to me on my own, I don't know, I just feel so strongly that I was meant to be Jewish. I have heard that in the Midrash there is mention of people who weren't born Jewish having a Jewish soul. I believe that is true about me.

Now my life is totally entwined within Judaism. My whole life revolves around the Jewish holidays and very gradually, since I've converted, I've added to our observances. We've been building a sukkah for eleven years. We've become more observant of Shabbat, although we were already fairly observant by the time I converted. I really make an effort to do special Shabbat dinners. For a long time I was making *hallah* every week. I still make it a lot, especially during the winter months. I always make the table really beautiful, and we invite people over frequently, people who are Jewish and those who are not. The kids feel very proud when they're having some school friend over who's not Jewish, and I explain what we're doing.

We koshered our kitchen about five years ago and that again came from a very deep, gut feeling. I'd actually wanted to do it sooner, but whenever I brought it up to Howard he wasn't interested. But six years ago when I brought it up he agreed. So we did that and it felt really right. I was filled with a great sense that we had purified our kitchen in a profound way.

Then I felt I should be purified, too. I wanted to go to the *mikvah*. Unfortunately, I first went on my own. I should have talked to somebody about it first because I wound up feeling very uncomfortable, like I was doing it wrong. It made me really sad, and I came home and cried. It was frustrating. I was turned off by the experience, but still somewhat drawn to it. But within a year I was able to return; I told the *mikvah* woman that this was something I wanted to do, that I wasn't sure that I was comfortable with it, and asked if she could tell me how to do it. She did and she was very nice. I felt so much better and really thanked her for enabling me to do this mitzvah. I have to say that it's become a very special part of our marriage and our observance. We both really like it.

Something that always bothered me was that we weren't married under the *huppah*. I had nudged Howard about it for years that I wanted to be remarried under the *huppah*. I said well, maybe for our tenth anniversary, but that came and went, and then the

fifteenth. By our twentieth we were going to be dealing with college tuition. So for our eighteenth anniversary, I said it's *Chai*,
which stands for life, it's perfect. So we got remarried under the
huppah. It was a small ceremony, just with my sister's family and
our kids, the rabbi, the cantor, and Howard and me. We did it in
the little chapel of our temple and it was really special and felt
just great.

❀

I did have an adult bat mitzvah two years after I started with
the cantor. The year after I converted, I had an adult bar/bat
mitzvah ceremony. It was a group ceremony with the twelve
other people in my class. My dad, who doesn't like traveling,
came and that meant a lot to me. It was a wonderful feeling to
know that if I didn't look up from the prayer book I could follow the entire service and know what we were doing and where
we were.

The Hebrew school then asked me if I would teach the kin-
dergarten Sunday school. I felt so honored that I knew enough
to do that! Having completed the conversion class and the study
with the cantor, I needed something to hold onto to keep me
growing Jewishly. I felt at that point that I just couldn't leave
my study. It was really important that they asked me at that time.
I don't know if they knew how important it was to me, in terms
of Jewish growth, because it put me on a path of continuous
study.

I did that for about five years. It was adorable and I loved that
the rabbi would come in, and we did a thing called Ask the Rabbi.
Of course, one of the most common questions was how you know
there's a God when you can't see or hear Him. It was so great
to hear the rabbi's answer because he would always start out
by saying that's a great question. I loved that. It made me
feel so proud to be Jewish, it made me feel so right about my
decision.

I've come to realize that I'm a very spiritual person and I probably have become more spiritual over the years. I really need the kind of interaction, the kind of dialog, the kind of reading matter that I've found in Judaism. It brings me so much on many deep levels that fascinate me. I've always been a happy person with a happy nature but I really don't know that I could have been truly happy if I hadn't found Judaism.

18 Finding a Framework

Yona V.

I grew up in a Catholic family in Holland. My parents were very Catholic. For a long time my mother had been involved in a Catholic organization called Women of Nazareth. She was going to lead a life of celibacy and become a nun. She must have had some doubts because she answered an ad of my father's and they got married shortly thereafter. They were very committed to their religion. In Holland, for instance, there are fifteen political parties and a lot of them were based on religion; my parents would always vote for the Catholic party, no matter what the agenda was. That was their life.

However, my mother told me that in the past, I'm not sure how many generations ago, both her family and my father's family had

---

The paintings of visual artist Yona V., born in the Netherlands, can be seen in galleries in Europe and the United States, in private residences, and in countless music videos. Throughout her life she was drawn to Judaism until she could no longer resist the connection.

converted to Catholicism. As a matter of fact, one of the families converted twice, so I have no idea what the original religion was or what the next was, but eventually, they both ended up being Catholic. Several years ago a friend told me that my last name, which actually means painter in old Dutch, was a Jewish as well as gentile name. It wouldn't surprise me if there was a Jewish component in my father's family.

I've been through holy communion, confirmation, the whole thing, but I gave that up as a teenager. My life didn't have anything in common with the Catholic church. I was interested in the values that it stood for, to be a good person and to help other people and that never changed, but the religious surface of the church didn't mean anything for me. As a teenager, you go your own way.

ᐕ

I was twenty when I went to art school. When I was there, I met a friend who mentioned someone in Amsterdam who was Jewish. It was a very casual conversation, I'll be going to Amsterdam next week and I'll be meeting my friend so and so. He didn't even say that his friend was Jewish, just by the name I could tell this person was Jewish. All of a sudden, out of the blue, I thought, I want to be Jewish. It sounds totally ridiculous, especially coming from someone like me. I am a very level-headed person, not prone to weird things like this, but for some reason, it must have sparked something that was already in me, although I had no idea when that started. Of course, when you grow up in Europe, you hear a lot about World War II and how the Jewish people suffered, but that had nothing to do with it. It was a totally independent feeling. The reason I mention this is because that kind of really strange, emotional reaction came back later and that's what eventually got me to convert to Judaism. But that was the first inkling there was something going on.

I kept that feeling with me. Every once in a while he would mention his friend and I would think wouldn't it be great to be

Jewish. You have to understand, I didn't know anything about Judaism, I didn't know anything about the Torah. I didn't even know Jews had a Torah. I knew zip.

Then I graduated from art school and this friend and I both came to New York. He was going to stay for a couple of months, but I knew I was going to stay. The feeling of wanting to be Jewish intensified. Since nobody knew me in the United States, when people asked me where I was from, the first half year I actually lied. I said I'm Dutch and I'm half Jewish, or some days I would say I'm a quarter Jewish, not realizing at the time that there is no such thing, you're either Jewish or you're not. Those intricacies were completely lost on me. After a while, I started to feel bad because I was meeting people who really were Jewish and I thought, I just can't lie to people. So I gave it up and I completely forgot about the whole thing. I had a lot of friends, Jewish and non-Jewish, and the whole thing of wanting to be Jewish sank to the background.

ዕᙵᖚ

Then, ten years ago, I got into an accident and I couldn't walk. For three months I was in a wheelchair. For nine months I was on crutches. I had a lot of free time on my hands. Even before the accident, I realized that there was something wrong in my life. Things just weren't working right. I wasn't happy. I was stuck, but I didn't know what to do about it. Then, having this accident and being in a wheelchair, friends of mine told me about a healing workshop that might be very interesting. So they schlepped me there and that was the first time, the first beginning of looking into some spirituality in my life. This had nothing to do with Judaism. This was more of a New Age kind of thing.

I started to read books and to think about the concept of a divine creator and the meaning of it all—the kind of things that you could easily live for years and not think about, as you were caught up in your daily living. But now I was forced to think about those things and that started me searching in different directions. I started to meditate a lot; whatever seemed spiritual, I tried. I went to a couple of Buddhist places, but nothing really caught on. I kind of just drifted along.

⊙╬⊙

About five years ago I was in a relationship with a man who is Jewish and he started to explore his Jewish roots a bit. He asked if I would mind lighting candles on Friday night. He said, "That's the only thing I do. I light candles on Friday night and I go to synagogue twice a year." I loved the idea of lighting candles on Friday night, so I said sure! That was it. We didn't observe Shabbat, we didn't even know what you were supposed to do on Shabbat. That's all we did, we lit those candles and then went on with our lives.

Then he invited me to join him at a Rosh Hashanah service and I agreed. I went not so much because I was interested in Judaism, but really from a cultural point of view. I thought this might be interesting, just as an observer. We went there, it was a Reform temple, and to my enormous surprise, after ten minutes, I was completely engrossed in the service. I wasn't an observer, I was participating. I was moved by the melodies. I was fascinated by the text, the English text.

There was also another moment that reminded me of that instant in Holland when I was pulled by Judaism: we stepped into this temple and saw all the men wearing prayer shawls and *kippot*; my friend, about as secular as can be, all of a sudden took something out of his back pocket and put it on his head. It was the first time I saw him with a *kippah.* Then it hit me that he really is Jewish and all these people here are really Jewish. It was a very emotional moment. Again, I didn't know what it was based on. I was so moved by the view of all these people I practically cried on the spot. It did something to me. This usually very numb person just got emotional by the sight of these Jews. So we went through the whole service. My friend had warned me in the beginning that it will get very boring because it's very long, the whole day. The longest time I had spent in a place of worship was an hour, because that's Catholicism. I thought, I'm not sure if I can get through a whole day of services. But frankly, I was completely moved by the whole thing. The time flew by.

வ்௰

After that, we went to the Yom Kippur service. From then on, we decided to try some Friday night or Saturday service. We liked them very much. Then he started to go to a Conservative *shul*. I wasn't really keen on going Conservative because I was totally ignorant about what Conservative meant. In my eye, this was getting much too religious for me. But I went once on a Friday night. Everything was in Hebrew, they didn't have transliterations, and I never had heard the melodies before. I thought, I don't know what we're doing here, I want to go back to the other place, a Reform temple where everything is in English and I've gotten to know some people a little bit and everything is user-friendly. I didn't feel any connection in the Conservative *shul*. So I said, "I'm never setting foot in this place again."

Famous last words. My boyfriend started going to a learner's minyan there and he loved it. He went for months. I said I'm not going, this is not for me. I'll stay at the Reform temple. So Friday nights we went to the Reform temple and Saturday mornings he would go to the Conservative *shul* and I stayed home. He started to read books about Judaism, it lit a fire in him, and his enthusiasm was infectious. I started reading his books. Finally he said, "You have to come. There are a lot of people in your position, they don't know much." I decided to try it again and that time I was welcomed warmly.

வ்௰

I started going to the Conservative temple and I joined in at one of the sessions of the learner's minyan. The rabbi who was teaching was fantastic. I noticed that people were asking questions, the same type of questions that I would have asked if I were in the class. Afterwards, people talked to me. A couple of women were in the conversion process and they said, "If you ever think about converting, please call us. We'd love to talk to you." All the people were so friendly. So I thought, I'll try it. I brought some transliterations so I could at least follow along with the service.

I started to read a lot more books and then, finally, I realized I wanted to convert. It started to mean a lot and I thought I should just take the plunge. I was practically living a Jewish life already, I should just go ahead and do it. I needed to think about which *shul* to choose because someone had told me you need to have a connection with the rabbi you're doing the conversion with because you'll be speaking to this person about personal issues. They said to choose it for the people who go to the *shul*, but also keep in mind the rabbi you want to convert with. That for me was a no-brainer at all because the rabbi I had met at the Conservative synagogue was so fantastic. I saw how he conducted himself and how he talked to people and I thought this is someone I can really relate to. I could not imagine that I would ever have personal issues to deal with; I thought you just go in there and convert. I think about that now and laugh.

֍

I started the process and studied for about nine months or so. Toward the end, the relationship that I had with this man disintegrated and we broke up, and I still hadn't converted. I started to wonder if part of me actually wanted to convert because of him. Everybody assumed that was the case. I had always thought I was doing it because of me. But all of a sudden I was not so sure if this was really for me or not. First of all, I couldn't go back to the synagogue I was attending because he went there and I felt we couldn't be in the same room. Even though it wasn't a hostile breakup, it was painful nevertheless. As a matter of fact, for a while, I couldn't go into any synagogue because I felt that I had discovered Judaism because of him more or less. Any service reminded me of him and it was just not pleasant. So I took a break for a while.

Then, friends of mine invited me to Europe for a month in the summer. I thought great, I'll be away from it all, I'll be able to clear my head, and we'll see what happens with this Judaism thing. I arrived in Geneva, where my friends live, thinking I wouldn't be surprised if this whole thing fizzled out. There's no connection anymore with this man and I'll see by the end of the summer how I'll feel. I'll know for sure.

I arrived on a Friday and the first thing I did was ask my friends if there is a synagogue nearby, just in case I wanted to go. They looked it up and yes indeed there was one. I ended up sleeping the entire Saturday because of jet lag, so I missed the whole thing. But that Sunday morning, from the moment I woke up, I felt the urge to go to that synagogue. Even though I knew there was not going to be services, I felt an emotional pull like I wanted to be in a place with something Jewish. I walked to the synagogue and circled it a couple of times, just to kind of sniff the smell. I felt this is something weird, something irrational, not me.

I gave in because everything about Judaism seems weird and irrational. I have just learned to go with the flow. When I returned to my friends' house, I said I know this is strange for you, but I just realized that I cannot just eat regular food anymore. I'm not ready to go completely kosher, but I really need to separate my meat and dairy. If you don't want to cook like that, it's fine. I'll find stuff to eat. They said just tell us how to cook and we'll prepare whatever you can eat. The meat and all they cooked wasn't kosher, but it was a beginning, like a first step toward the kosher life.

After a week, I went on the train to Holland to visit my family. I wasn't sure what was going to happen. But I noticed that on this Friday afternoon, alone in a train car, I found myself singing Shabbat songs. There was no one in the car, so I could sing loud; I was singing "Shabbat Shalom" and whatever other song came to mind. By the time we got into Antwerp, I saw the Star of David near a train station and my heart just jumped. I was so excited; I thought, oh my goodness, I think this is for real, I don't think there's any way to return from this. I just felt this is the way to go. I reacted so strongly to these very minimal hints of Judaism. I guess this is meant to be.

❦

I visited with my two sisters. I told them I was interested in Judaism and they were very helpful. They started cooking differently for me. Everybody in Europe, at that time at least, was extremely accommodating and puzzled. They thought, why would anybody choose religion, let alone something obscure like Judaism? The people I know don't know many Jewish people, and certainly don't know anyone who is an observant Jew, especially in Holland. There was an enormous rate of intermarriage after the war and most Jewish people are only culturally Jewish. I was there for a month. I would go to Amsterdam specifically for the weekend, not realizing there was a synagogue right near my sister's home. I didn't know about it.

❦

In the fall and winter after I returned from Europe, I finally realized I should go through with my conversion. I went to my synagogue and told the rabbi that I was ready to go back to the conversion process and to set a date. I converted that spring.

That day was fantastic because twenty-five of our friends took off from their jobs to come to the synagogue for the last part of the ritual. The first part of course was in a *mikvah.* We had a big lunch and everyone hugged me and it was a fantastic day. It made me feel like I had finally come home. Even though some of my friends weren't Jewish, everyone was very happy and wanted to celebrate this very special day with me.

❦

I had been preparing up until the moment I actually koshered my home because I knew it was going to be difficult. I did everything: I bought kosher meat and cooked kosher stuff, except that my kitchen hadn't been koshered. So really I wasn't eating kosher, but I had done everything to practice. I wanted to have dinners for Hanukah, so I finally koshered my home and I've been keeping kosher ever since.

No doubt, it's been difficult. I've made mistakes that I end up throwing in a box. Eventually I rekoshered everything again because I realized I made so many mistakes with utensils, I redid everything to be on the safe side. It's not as hard for me to keep kosher in the home as it is outside the home. You open yourself up to a lot of criticism and that's hard, but you do it and that's it.

ഐ

Right after my conversion I thought I probably won't read anything Jewish for a while, because it was such a cram course. But I noticed that the actual day of my conversion was a turning point for me and propelled me toward much greater observance than I had planned on. Right away, I read something about modesty and dress. I used to wear a lot of miniskirts and all of a sudden I thought, let me just put them aside for a while, let me buy a couple of longer skirts. I still wear a lot of pants, but I just thought, let me get some of the real short miniskirts out of the way. I thought I was going to take my very own sweet time doing things, and instead I found myself hungry for learning more and really becoming observant much faster than I had anticipated.

Then I had an upsetting experience. I wanted to study in a program with some friends of mine from my synagogue. They asked me to join them to study the Torah portion every week. I spoke to the rabbi who was leading it and he pulled me aside the next day and said "You cannot attend, you're not Jewish." I said, "What do you mean?" He said, "We don't recognize your conversion. We have an Orthodox program." I was stunned. In fact, I was crying like a baby. This was the first time I realized that maybe this conversion wasn't valid in some people's eyes. It never occurred to me and it was such a blow to me, I was completely devastated by it.

I have decided to go ahead with an Orthodox conversion because I can't deal with the fact that I'm not being recognized as Jewish. Part of me thought that I would to be able to rise above that and just let it be other people's problem. I realized that I can't, it just bothers me so much that half the Jewish population doesn't consider me Jewish.

❧

I'm an artist, so there isn't really a nine to five structure to my life at all. I actually welcome the organization that Judaism gives me because it helps me function better as a human being.

With Judaism, there is an emphasis on balancing the heavenly life and the earthly life. It makes me value this person, the day, whatever you do. You're supposed to think about your actions because you say blessings over them: for example, before eating. Or the first thing when you wake up you have to wash your hands and say a blessing and it goes like that all throughout the day. So for me there's a dual function. On one hand, every time I say a blessing it connects me with God or creator or however you want to call it, and at the same time, it brings me back to earth. I have to focus on this right now; now I have to wash my hands and say this. It's like a reaching. In a way that's what you do the whole day, you reach in and you reach up at the same time, for what you eat and how you get dressed and what you smell. It's a very structured way of keeping in contact with your creator and staying balanced. Judaism very much provides a framework for my life.

19 Lightning Bolts

Marianna N.

I converted on December twenty-second, right before the Christmas holiday. Two years of intense studying lead to that point. But looking back, it's been a lifetime on this road. That's what I actually wrote in one of the essay questions I had to answer for the *bet din* (Jewish court). I really examined what it was that brought me to the decision to convert.

I grew up Presbyterian and went to church every Sunday, yet it never really held anything special for me. There were some friends there, my parents seemed to like to go, but there was never a spiritual connection. In most of my adult life, I have been pursuing some kind of spiritual work. My husband, Scott, jokes that, since for a while I was looking into paganism, I finally became

---

Marianna N., an accomplished bookbinder, has recently taken a job as the Coordinator for the Department of Radio and Television for the Jewish Theological Seminary. Married with a young son, she explored many ideologies before finding her home.

Jewish because it's a lot more acceptable and hands-on than being a pagan. Of course, with today's hindsight, what I was looking for wasn't paganism. Paganism didn't fill me up and that's
what I was looking for. So I've been through quite a journey to
get to this point.

❧

I am a fourth generation apart from Jewish heritage. My great-
great-grandfather, Albert Strauss, was a German Jew who came
over in the 1800s, clearly before the war, and was associated with
the *Our Crowd* kind of people. Although he wasn't the rich Lord
& Taylor Strauss or any of those, he did associate with those
people. So he's my closest connection, historically speaking, to
Judaism.

My grandmother, my father's mother, had been pretty much
raised as an agnostic. She converted to Christianity as an adult,
and became very devout in her forties. In hearing the stories my
mother told me about her, she had similar experiences to what I
have been going through, like this awakening I'm feeling. There
was also a big family joke that five minutes into a conversation
with her, the conversation would turn to God and Christianity.
So I've been a little wary of that because it's not a joke for me, it's
a real connection.

❧

In the first six months after I moved to New York, a friend that
I had just made invited me to a meeting of the National Buddhist
Society of America. American Buddhists. It looked very interesting. They chanted three times a day to a scroll they had up on the
wall and there was something very attractive about it. Yet, at the
same time, I was repulsed by it because I saw people getting together in groups and chanting for Cadillacs—very materialistic,
which really turned me off. At that point of my personal development, I was very wary of being sucked into some groupie thing,
which was my sense of it.

I tried chanting for about two or three weeks. There was a little booklet, a transliteration, very similar to what I eventually carried at the synagogue but different liturgy obviously. It was about getting into a rhythmic, ongoing, droning meditation. Again, that was a very short-lived thing.

From there, I didn't do anything for a while. Then I started to get very into Goddess. There's a lot written up on Goddess, Wiccan. Did I want to be a witch? No, I didn't think I wanted to be a witch, but I really started to get a sense of the four elements, earth, fire, water, air. For about a year, I did some very serious reading. It was all by myself. I was not ready to get back into some group, but I accumulated books. My shelf is chock-full of Goddess books and rituals and I would practice just acknowledging the four elements and drawing a circle and just creating a cone of energy for myself.

After that died down, I didn't do anything. I continued work on myself in therapy and other external work. There was a lot of growth and development going on, not so much spiritual but more personal productivity. The spiritual element came and went, but it all seemed to coalesce for me inside of Judaism.

ॐ

When my husband and I started getting involved, there was very little discussion about religion. At that point, religion was not at all a part of either of our lives. I never went to church, he never went to synagogue, but I knew he was Jewish. Actually, the first time I met his family was when they invited me over for Passover. That was my introduction to his family, which is a little ironic because his family is pretty much nonobservant.

When we decided to get married we first began to discuss how our marriage would work. I asked him about children. I said, "How do you want to raise them?" He said, "I don't know, I just want to raise them." It didn't even occur to him. I said, "Well, I'm not very religious and you're not either. I guess we could have a Christmas tree and a menorah for the holidays." But that was about as far as the conversation went.

At our marriage ceremony we concentrated on having a ceremony that would acknowledge who we are for each other and also to have a really nice party to acknowledge our friends and family. There was a little bit of a nod toward Judaism in our ceremony because Scott did break the glass, but that was pretty much it. Actually, when I was talking to the rabbi who was leading my conversion class, he asked about our marriage ceremony. I said we broke the glass. He said everybody does that, it doesn't mean anything. I didn't know that. So that was the extent of Judaism in our marriage ceremony.

⊚✝⊚

I actually realized that I wanted to convert to Judaism when a friend of ours had a baby girl. We went to her baby naming. I already had a six-month-old son, Max, so I had gone through the extraordinary experience of childbirth. That alone was a spiritual experience for me. We were hanging out, fifty or so people, and I started talking with the new grandfather. I told some joke with Yiddish in it, and I said, "Hey, not bad for a *shiksa*, (non-Jewish woman)" because everybody was laughing. The grandfather looked at me and said, "You're a *shiksa*? I could've sworn you were Jewish!" He launched into this story about a woman he had known who was gentile. When she was told that she couldn't be buried next to her husband when they died she was horrified. What do you mean I can't be buried next to my husband? she said. What do I have to do to be buried next to my husband? They said you have to be Jewish. She said okay, sign me up, make me Jewish. I want to be buried next to my husband.

That was nothing short of a lightning bolt that went off for me. It really had nothing to do with being buried next to Scott, although that would be nice, but somehow all the things that I had been working on, thinking about, and writing just came together in a flash. I knew at that moment what was next for me. It was really a very clear message. After that party, we walked back home. I asked Scott what he would think if I converted. Scott was not a very religious man. He was bar mitzvahed pretty much by the skin of his teeth, not even a three-time-a-year Jew. He said all right. I always come out with these bold statements and he is such a wonderful man that he will just support me through most of it.

That's what started me on a serious path. Then we were invited to attend a Purim celebration at a synagogue. I didn't know about Purim from anything. We walked in, Scott, myself, and Max, who by this time was about thirteen months old. People were climbing the walls of the synagogue, celebrating, it was like a mad house. I was thinking, what did I just walk into?

Max was not phased by any of it. I thought he would freak but he was comfortable sitting on top of people's shoulders that he didn't even know. He was being passed around and having a good time. Then he boldly walked up on to the *bimah*. They were reading from the Megillah at that point, and he walked straight up to the rabbi. The rabbi looked at him, picked him up, and Max watched as they read. It was like he led the way. He was right at home and then I knew that I had found the place in which I wanted to worship.

☙❧

After that, I started to attend services. The first service after Purim that I attended was a Friday night Shabbat service. Again, I had no idea what to expect. I think I had been in the synagogue only four or five times before that, for a bat mitzvah or some other family event. Things were moving so quickly and all in Hebrew! I was used to a preacher who would give a little bit of the sermon and tell you what was going on, but this service just overwhelmed me. I was completely lost and I realized there was so much for me to learn and do to even begin to get to the point of being called a Jew. I wasn't even bothering to look at the Hebrew because it looked like gobbledy-gook to me, I was reading the English translation. There was one point, I don't even remember where it was in the service, but it said something about either God is watching us or some reference to our connection with God. I felt such a moment of love, I guess that's the only word to describe it. Emotions came up and I started to cry. It was another little lightning bolt. I guess it's been a series of flashes and lightning bolts for me.

I've just really followed my heart since then. I did this whole journey on instinct and what feels right and wherever I see love present, I go to it. And that works.

◈◈◈

I went to college in Missouri where I studied theater. I house-sat a couple of times for a woman on the theater faculty who was also the Hillel advisor at the school. She kept kosher and I was completely terrified about doing anything wrong in her household. The only thing I ate there was peanut butter and jelly sandwiches. But she was one of the key points that I referred to in my essay of people and moments that have influenced me in my choice to become Jewish. I didn't have that much contact with her, but I had enough obviously for her to trust me to watch her house for a week.

I remember seeing pictures on her walls of people dancing, celebrating—there was a presence of joy in her house. I didn't equate it to any religion, it was just who she was. In realizing that she had this impact on me, I called her about six weeks before I converted. I went to great lengths to find her because she's no longer at the school. She had moved, remarried, and had a different name. I finally located her in Kansas City. I called and left a message.

She called me back and she had so much to provide me. She didn't remember who I was, but she said, "I honestly don't remember who you are, but it was a very dark point in my life and you sound like a nice girl, so I would like to talk with you." We talked for about an hour on the phone. She was thrilled for me and she told me she converted many years ago, when she first got married. What I remembered about her is how she had thoroughly integrated Jewishness into her life. A few weeks after our conversation, she sent me this incredible packet: photographs of herself and her family and of things that she had written. It was an incredible support for me, to see how she's taken Judaism into her life and the contribution she makes with it.

ॐ

When Max was born, I didn't know that I was going to convert. That had not yet occurred to me. But when I decided to convert, I knew I was going to be converting Max as well. I decided I was going to raise Jewish children, there was no question about that. Scott was fine with that. The question was how to convert Max. I wasn't sure if I should convert him first, and a year and a half later, after I did all my studies, be converted myself. I spoke to a *mohel* (ritual circumciser) about it. He said we should all do it together, so we'll all be Jewish together.

In December we went to the *mikvah* with a *mohel* who was part of the *bet din.* I took my dip first, and got dressed. Then Max had a little pin prick in the penis because three people have to witness that they saw blood. One drop of blood was all that was needed. After that he went down to the mikvah.

It was chaos. I didn't know whether it was registering for Max or not. He was not quite three and couldn't tell what it was, but I just kept explaining to him what was happening.

My mother and her husband of seven years, an ordained minister, came to New York from Vermont for my conversion. They have been so supportive of the choice that I have made. My mother was a little sad, but also instantly supportive because she saw that this was not an act of rebellion; this was not the youngest daughter lashing out or anything. Larger than the sadness was her real joy at my discovering a sense of a spiritual self. That's something that we never really discussed before. She's always been very moved by God and religion, which is something I never really understood until now. It provided another level of communication with my mother that I didn't have before.

❦

We'll go up to Vermont to see my mom on a Friday afternoon and get there in time for sunset and we'll light candles. I'll bring a *hallah* with me and we'll say the blessings. They really love to participate in that, so it's interesting. My older sister, on the other hand, has had a very difficult time with my conversion. It's been quite surprising to hear the different anti-Semitic words that come out of her mouth, that I don't even think she realizes are anti-Semitic. I've been a little timid in pointing that out to her, which may be something I need to work on.

When I first started this process, I asked her what she thought of my converting. She said, "I think it's a little weird. We're going to have different holidays now and we're going to have a different schedule." That was hard, that's the hardest that it has been as far as dealing with the outside world.

❦

Today my connection to Judaism is really strong. I actually had a special moment today. I've been teaching bookbinding at a private school and I had to go there to drop off some reports. I was waiting for the bus to head back downtown and I'd been rushing all morning, going and going. I walked across Fifth Avenue and it was going to be about a ten-minute wait for the bus. I looked out into Central Park and saw this incredible thick green foliage right before my eyes. I just stopped for a moment and then I said the Shema, just looking into this deep greenery. I was overcome by such a wonderful feeling of peace and quiet. New York City melted away for a moment and I was just there with the trees and with the greenness. That never occurred before I keyed into a spiritual practice. There are moments that I stop and just thank God for what I have and who I am and where I am. Something comes back, like a feeling of expansion, into me.

We don't officially keep kosher, we haven't gotten to that point yet, but we have successfully separated meat and diary in all of our meals. That's something that occurred very naturally for me, which my husband, bless his heart, has really followed. When I was told about the laws of *kashrut,* and when I began to get a deeper understanding of what they were and why they were, it was just a natural occurrence to stop eating ham and cheese sandwiches. I don't eat shellfish or shrimp anymore. It's evident in our kitchen.

It's not anything that I *have* to do. My decision was coming from a different place, not that I really should do this. When I was looking into paganism, there were rituals that I would do because you're supposed to do this, and there was no wind beneath my wings in that one. It has not been a burden, but rather moment by moment, little steps of enlightenment, some heavy words to use, but it's just been like that.

We have mezzuzahs up on all of our doors. There's a mezzuzah on Max's room. That was one of the big things I did when he converted; he demanded to have the mezzuzah moved down to a level where he could touch it. It didn't occur to me to put one at his height. So we moved it down. Now one of his favorite things to do is to go around and touch all of the mezzuzahs and kiss them. It has turned into a game for him, which is nice.

I'm starting to teach Max a little about *kashrut* and the food he's been eating. He doesn't even think about it, so I'm trying to point that out to him. I say that we can read from the Torah, we can carry the Torah around, we weren't officially allowed to do that before because we weren't Jewish. So it's starting to slowly sink in for him. He'll play little games, roll up a rug and throw it up on his shoulder and march around our apartment and pretend that he's marching the Torah around.

§

It all came together in a way recently, when I read from the Torah for the first time. It was an amazing event. I had been part of a study group at my synagogue. They have a group every year for about eight or nine months and at the completion of study, they have a graduation. The rabbi said we're opening up the learner's minyan to anyone who's Jewish and for anyone who would like to read from the Torah, we'd love to have you. I raised my hand and I said I'd like to read from the Torah. I had never done this before and I had no idea what it will entail. The rabbi was thrilled.

We got right to work and I studied for four months. I read seven or eight lines from the Lech Lecha. That was another thing that I share with Max, now he sees his mom reading from the Torah and thinks that's pretty cool. It's just been one opportunity after another.

⚬✛⚬

I love to get into deep inquiries of what is it to be human and why we do the things that we do. There is that inquiry inside of Judaism; to take readings from the Torah and applying them to today. It takes a lot of work, but that's one of the greatest gifts my conversion has given me. I have an opportunity for life-long learning. I've come to appreciate the value of continuing my education. When I got out of college I said I'm never going back to school. I couldn't wait to get out of it. I have come full circle and realize I want to be studying. With Judaism, it's a life-long time of study and new challenges; what will be next and how do you share it and what can you learn from the opportunity? The idea of all that questioning and learning helps guide me on a path that I know is right for me.

20 A Completely One-Person Decision

Claire H.

I was brought up, with my five siblings, in a Roman Catholic household. We were all churchgoers and very serious about the faith. I had twelve years of teaching with the nuns and after that I went to work and didn't return to higher education until much later in life. By that time, my ideas about things had changed.

I think that I was always interested in Judaism, not that I thought it out as a subject, but I would read things in the paper and be interested. I suppose my mother's interest, limited as it was, probably supported my being able to look around a bit. She listened to Temple Emanuel services on Friday night. I remember when we were living in New Jersey, coming home from working in New York, she would have it on at night. I would ask her why she was listening. She said that the rabbi is very interesting and has some

---

Claire H. is retired from her thirty-year service as an executive assistant at the United Nations. Holder of a master's in Jewish Studies, her intellectual interest in Judaism evolved into a life-affirming commitment.

different things to say. Then, since it was Friday night, we would have our fish chowder, replete with matzahs. Actual matzah! Looking back, I think it's kind of interesting. It was just such a coincidence.

Much later, about a year before my father's death, which was in 1967, he told my mother and my sister that his mother had been Jewish. He remembered her lighting candles on Friday night. Sometimes my father would be away on Friday night, I don't remember this, but my mother told me she said maybe he was sitting in one of the synagogues. She didn't know. She never asked him. When my father told her about his Jewish mother, my mother was rather upset, since she said it would have made no difference to her. She looked on it as a lack of confidence in her on my father's part. Be that as it may, we never had a chance to talk to my father about this.

ᐧᖵᐧ

The result of my becoming Jewish started really a long time ago and I would categorize it, to begin with, as an intellectual curiosity. Growing up in an observant churchgoing house, I was used to a certain discipline and identity. But I began to feel that I wasn't learning enough about God. I wanted to know more about Him. And where I was did not seem to be giving me any satisfying answers.

This is all in looking back. Years after this initial murmuring, I met a friend in the UN who was brought up in Algeria, a French Jew. I somehow found myself attracted to Jewish people, Jewish history. She and I spoke a great deal. She had many interesting stories. She suggested to me to read history, Jewish history, Max Dimont books. I did, and I was absolutely entranced with the history. I thought with Jews having gone through all of this, the Crusades, the different problems posed for survival, for the Jewish people to be so connected with their God, this is really worth exploring. So I did my reading and I remember one thing she told me about her father: she said that when he was dying, he was saying the Shema, and as she told me that story, the tears started to roll down her cheeks and I found my eyes welling up. All of this was saying something to me.

᭦᳝᭦

I met my first husband, Bernie, in 1970. I had not been very assiduous in following Catholicism. I went to church occasionally and that was about it. Then I met Bernie, who was Jewish, and of course the way I felt about him encouraged my feelings toward Judaism, although he was not religiously inclined. I really was more active in my faith, but I was on the edge of leaving and I didn't know it. When you do things for many years, you just think that's what you're supposed to do. Anyway, little by little I began to learn more about the Jewish people, flesh and blood, not just from the history books. I met Bernie's family, and saw who they were and how they related to one another and the importance of family, which was true of my family, but different. I began to see it as a general characteristic among Jews, which I heartedly embraced. I didn't feel that my siblings were absolutely acceptable just because they were family, whereas Bernie felt that it's important, they're family, and we just have to overlook some of their foibles. I liked that Jewish ethic very much.

᭦᳝᭦

Bernie and I were married by a rabbi. Bernie had said to me, "Since you're more active in your religion, if you want to be married by a priest, that's fine with me." So I went along with that, only because I felt some obligation, I suppose. I spoke to a monsignor up at the Catholic Center and explained the situation. Bernie was divorced, he is Jewish and I'm Catholic. He said, "All right, I'll be glad to meet Bernie and talk to him." So I went up to the center with Bernie. I figured the atmosphere was really quite different, I'll try to ease him into it with the crucifixes on the wall and all, which of course was really quite natural. The monsignor patted me on the shoulder as he and Bernie were going in. He said,

"Don't worry, I'll take good care of him," and I thought oh, my God. What an immature sense! The upshot of that interview was the monsignor was very interested if Bernie was sure that he was a Jew. There's poor Bernie, sitting there saying, "Of course I am a Jew."

So, what about his first marriage? Bernie said he was married by a rabbi. The monsignor said, "Well, we'll have to check that out and we'll have to call your former wife." When Bernie told me that, I decided this is not for us. Who is he to go and inquire about the wife, ascertaining all this! What are they? It was a marriage, a valid marriage, who is this superior in Rome to say no it wasn't. So I said to Bernie this is it, we are going to be married by a rabbi. I wrote to the monsignor and told him that we were withdrawing the petition. We would not continue this and so forth. I got a letter back from him saying, "I can only presume this was your husband-to-be's decision."

By that time, I was thoroughly disgusted. I was trying to do what I thought I should do. Bernie and I sought a rabbi who would marry us, under the circumstances that I was Catholic and he divorced. A Reform rabbi did perform this service. We were married under the *huppah*.

⚛

A few years later I was converted. At first, I put it this way to the rabbi. I said I'd like to know a bit more about Judaism. His ears perked up. "You're interested in converting." I said no, I just want to know more about Judaism. Well, as it turned out, I converted. I wasn't really aware, but the rabbi could see it. At first I was rather shocked by the depth of what I was going through.

I suppose I should have seen it. I went to church once in a while, probably out of duty. Then sometimes on Friday nights, Bernie and I would go to the synagogue. I realized after a while I just couldn't continue this way. You cannot live on both sides. I was so strongly attracted to Judaism that I decided that's what I was going to do. That was the road I wanted to travel. And I did. I couldn't wait to convert. Why was I wasting any more time? All along the way, the rabbi would say, "Claire, are you sure you really want to do this?" I said, "Rabbi, why do you think I would sit here?" But apparently this is what had to be said and I think it's a good idea.

Ever since then I've said it's great to be a Jew. The afternoon of my conversion I looked out the window, we were having a friendly gathering and there was a rainbow in the sky. Didn't need any more confirmation.

๑๎๏

I was about fifty-two or fifty-three at the time. I didn't marry until late, about forty-eight, and then I converted when I was about fifty-two. It started out as probably an intellectual decision. I could see that in Judaism the intellect is more involved. It isn't just a rote thing, you're thinking about what you are saying. And the fact that one could question God: Why are you doing this? Why is this important? You could discuss issues. Judaism is acknowledging that God is one, which was a little bit difficult for me, although I had no problem with it after thinking about it. In Christianity, you have the Trinity, three gods in one. Of course Judaism does not accept that, there's only one God.

The idea that there was a great deal of intellectual independence really made me feel more like a person, not always subservient. I could talk with people about different ideas and always found myself coming back to the same belief, that there is one God, whereas in Christianity you're dealing with so many things that are impossible to believe. Judaism has none of that. I could see that in the beginning I was trying to see some similarity. Now, wine is a part of a Jewish service, but it's not like in Catholicism. It's not the body and blood of Christ. I just could not see that anymore.

For me, Judaism is more vital; you can grow. You can grow as a person and find out more about yourself through the ideas of Judaism. It's a very rich and living organism. You are not just praying to someone who is sitting up there and that's about it. No interchange of ideas.

So I was converted. There was no outside pressure. My husband never asked me to convert, but he was delighted when I told him that I was going to. It was a completely one-person decision, mine. I wasn't pleasing anyone, I was pleasing only myself. I didn't worry about what my family would say. I was already more than an adult. It wasn't as though I had done this as a teenager or just getting ready to be married. It was Claire who made the decision completely. It was very liberating.

❧

I went to the *mikvah* and then went to the Reform synagogue, where I was converted, for the second part of the conversion. Even the Conservative rabbi recognizes this as a proper conversion, especially since I went to the *mikvah*. It's very interesting, one does not have to go to the *mikvah*, but I chose to because this is the way it's done and that's it. So I did.

I took a course, and for Reform, it was about three months. It's shorter than the Conservative or the Orthodox, which is at least a year, but later on, I continued my studies. Bernie and I went to the Reform synagogue for a while and that's where I decided I wasn't learning enough. I had to make a change. I came upon a Conservative synagogue near us, stopped in one Friday night, and thought this really is what I want. I spoke with Bernie and he said, "Claire, whatever you want. That's fine with me."

❧

I felt I had to tell my family what I had done. Bernie asked why, this is a very personal thing. You don't have to discuss it. But that's the way I was. So I told my mother. My mother and I were very close. She's gone now but she said, "Well, Claire, if that's what you want, that's fine." She said, "I don't understand, of course," and I told her that I didn't expect her to, but she never turned her back on me. She was not a judgmental person. She was glad that I was happy. She liked Bernie very much and he liked her. In fact, Bernie's sister invited my mother up to a Passover seder and my mother was very interested. I guess we were both alike in many ways, interested in what is it like over there. We did not have closed minds.

❧

I decided that I wanted to experience putting on the tallis, the prayer shawl. The first time I did it, the feeling of being wrapped up in Judaism was extremely moving. From the tallis evolved another mitzvah that I decided to keep. At a certain time in the Shema you gather up the four ends, the fringes on the four corners. The first two times you kiss the fringe in recognition, the third time you look at the fringe to remind yourself of all the mitzvot you have to do. It was at that point that I decided to kosher the kitchen. That was a big undertaking—hottest day in August, but it was wonderful.

The next evolvement was deciding to put on tefillin. I decided to do it after Bernie died, on his second *yahrtzite*. It not only brought me closer to Judaism, the active part, but also made me feel closer to Bernie, which was wonderful. It's such a lovely and meaningful way to feel closer.

❧

About three years after Bernie died, I started to go out a little bit with Manny, who I met in the temple. That developed into a flourishing friendship. We married last year.

We go to temple together always. I also belong to a *havurah*. We meet once a month in the home of one of the participants. That actually gives the person a chance to participate actively in the liturgy. There will always be someone to lead the liturgy, to talk about the Torah portion of the week. It's wonderful to have a chance to participate. That's another thing about Judaism: to lead services, you do not have to be ordained, it just has to be a Jew who is knowledgeable. That's very democratic and that appeals to me. So even I can lead the service.

❦

I was about forty-five when I finished college. Then I decided, after I had converted, that I would like to continue learning more about Judaism, and perhaps I would be able to teach. Even though I was too old to have children, I thought I can at least teach and pass on Judaism to children. I went back to school; I went to Touro College. When I was just finishing my course work, Bernie had died. It took me a couple of years to go back to finish so I could obtain my degree . But I did, a master's in Jewish Studies, which focused more on the history of Judaism.

Now Manny and I live in Florida four months of the year. I find that I have to be doing something, not just being passive. I was told that there is an endowed Jewish chair at the Florida Atlantic University, which I'm going to look into. I want to find out more about the Jewish program so I can continue with my study.

I've also become interested in Jewish women's organizations. My experience coming out of my conversion was that I realized that I was a Jew in name only. I was told that one had to go through at least the four cycles of the year, and participate in all the Jewish holidays: Passover, Shavuot, Yom Kippur, Rosh Hashanah. It is so true. The more I went through this and participated, the more I felt I was becoming more Jewish, understanding more. You really begin to grow then and become part of the community. Becoming involved with Hadasah was a reinforcement and filled the need of participating in Jewish life.

❦

I believe and feel quite securely that reaching for Judaism and accepting it was the culmination of years of living and exploring, and the great awareness that there was plenty of room for growth.

Personal growth too, not just spiritual growth—for example, I like Klezmer music. It's just another aspect of a Jewish life-style. There's so much warmth and pathos in it.

In Judaism, one is always living with past history. It's always there. You're living and remembering through different seasons of the year. But Judaism is a living belief. The others I see as dead. It's good to be in a living community that values life. Even Jews who have been through terrible things, the Holocaust for example, still treasure life. The emphasis is not on the life hereafter. It's right here and now and living properly. It's life that's important.

21 A Rabbi's Perspective

Stephen C. Lerner

Most people who convert do so in relationships. There's a certain percentage who are individuals, and of that group some have a Jewish point of origin, a father, grandfather who has helped them or who pushes them to convert. That is especially the case for people from Hispanic countries or from Central European backgrounds. But most convert in relationships, usually before marriage. Some are already happily married and that tilts them forward. For example, I just had two start with me yesterday who are married for a few years. Sometimes I've had people married thirty, forty years, which is even more interesting. Generally, you don't have someone convert unless it is in some way important to the Jewish spouse or partner. He or she makes it clear to the

Rabbi Stephen C. Lerner is the founder and director of the Center for Conversion to Judaism, where he has performed more than 800 conversions. He is also the rabbi of Congregation Kanfei Shahar in Teaneck, New Jersey.

other person that, at the very least, that person should look into Judaism. In some cases it's convert or else.

Most of the Jews who are requesting that their partner convert are what the modern sociologists call sacred survival Jews. They have warm Jewish identities but very little Jewish practice. They want their partner to become Jewish but they're quite ambivalent about how much Judaism they'd like the person to practice and how much they'd like to practice with the person.

What happens in this process, since the Jewish partner has to participate, is that the two people are really looking at the river called Judaism from opposite banks. The Jewish partner is looking at it as a peoplehood identity and their partner, the potential Jew, is looking at it as a religion with values and practices. They're often talking different languages about supposedly the same thing. Each needs to broaden their understanding of Judaism to encompass the other bank.

⊙†⊙

There's a small but growing number of people, couples, where the Jewish spouse is personally, massively committed, observant; a Sabbath-observing Jew, a child of a rabbi for example. In one case, a man with Orthodox ordination, still considered Orthodox and quite observant, was keeping company with a woman who wasn't born Jewish. That's different than in past years. It would have been inconceivable for a person from this background, twenty, thirty years ago, to entertain the possibility that such a marriage could work out.

This is both bad and good—bad because it means that the wariness of dating people who aren't Jewish is weakening, even among those who are most committed. What is good is that they're committed enough to want their spouse, their friend to convert.

⊙†⊙

The number of conversions seems constant over the last years, but there are more programs so it may well be that there are more people converting. Now there are more competing kinds of programs. Studies have shown that there may be more conversions, but compared to the percentage of intermarriages, it's not keeping pace. That's the change I've seen. It's a not so subtle shift. People who would never have thought of even dating a non-Jew are now willing to consider marrying the partner if they would convert. A very lukewarm person thirty or forty years ago who couldn't have imagined marrying someone without a conversion is going to be less apt to push for a conversion today because there are so many intermarriages.

⚶

A tremendous number of the singles—more than half who come to see me—never complete the program. It's much harder to do it as a single if you're going to be serious about it. A number of them are just searching for something, fishing around for something to give their life meaning. I'm very wary of singles. Some of the finest people I've converted are obviously singles but I'm very careful. I indicate to them that they're going to have to do much more because they have no partner to reinforce them.

⚶

The gender ratio is probably three or four to one, women over men. Traditionally in relationships it was the husband who said to the wife, take my name, follow me to my job. So the fact that we have a growing number of proudly assertive Jewish women who are asking their husbands to take their religion is notable.

Among the singles, it's overwhelmingly women who are converting. We do have a growing number of men and they have an extra hurdle: they have to get circumcised or have a symbolic circumcision. The symbolic circumcision is about two seconds of pain and, I tell many people, three weeks of sleepless nights beforehand worrying about it. Even so, some people will not do it. It's nothing, but that doesn't stop some people from saying absolutely not. That's very rare but I've had it happen. People are just nervous about it because nobody likes their penis played with in this manner.

☙❦❧

Although I don't have statistics, I believe the level of involvement or commitment after conversion is pretty high. Certainly the majority of converts that I am still in contact with have remained committed. Anecdotally, I was up spending a Shabbes with a colleague of mine in Westchester and his kids go to Solomon Schechter Day school there. I looked through the list of children attending and I readily recognized five families that I converted. On the other hand, there are clearly some who, if a marriage didn't take or whatever, may have reverted to their past religion.

The major challenge to the people who converted is to become integrated into a meaningful synagogue and to make sure that the Jewish partner does not undermine the significance of the conversion and the enthusiasm of the one who converts. Of course the biggest problem is to help them develop a sense of connection to the Jewish people.

This dimension of Judaism is the part that's weakest. I spend a good deal of time trying to develop in them some sense of ethnic connection. There is simply no parallel in their past religion and it's certainly the part that often speaks to their Jewish partner most powerfully. It's something they need to work on. You can't be a Jew if you like God and Jewish commandments and have no feeling for the Jewish people or for Israel or things like that. That's a crucial dimension that must be addressed.

☙❦❧

The role of the rabbinate today is crucial for those who have converted as well as those who have been born Jewish. The classic rabbi of a few generations ago was much more removed from their people. He was a cathedral rabbi. The big thing was that he wore a black robe and gave a sermon. He did not involve himself with kids. The really classy ones might be fine Jewish scholars and I have great respect for that area of concentration. But the idea that you need to warm up kids and deal with teenagers was very rare years ago. I think the newer rabbis are much more informal, they're much more interested in interacting and being programmers and *ruach* leaders, leaders of good Jewish spirit.

I know the little kids from my *shul* love me because I always give them candy. A little boy woke up this past Saturday and his mother was there, but he immediately started running to me. I guess he figured I had candy for him. The mother was amazed. Here's a twenty-month-old kid just running right to me and he hadn't seen me for a few weeks. We had a connection. I don't think that kind of connection could have taken place in most synagogues years ago.

I think that's a big change. As one of my avocations, for years, I've been writing off and on the honorary degree citations for the Jewish Theological Seminary. Every two years they give out Doctors of Divinity degrees to rabbis who have lasted twenty-five years and haven't murdered anybody, who have stayed in the *shul* and haven't gone into engineering or the stock market or something. I wrote forty of these citations and it was amazing how many of the rabbis said the same thing: they like working with people. They like to be with them in their times of joy and sorrow.

❖

I have made my life teaching people Judaism. That's what I've done for 80 percent of the last twenty years. Now my son is going to be a rabbi and he's graduating the seminary this year. He probably had a little deception because, since I've specialized in conversions since about 1981, I have had very few meetings, very few boards to answer to. I do what I want to do.

He's going to go into a *shul* and have to deal much more with committees, board meetings, and a formal kind of apparatus. But I'm glad that I inspired him to be a rabbi. I like what I do. My son and my daughter, who's also planning to be a rabbi, saw me doing what I'm supposed to be doing as a rabbi: teaching Judaism. Teaching people about Judaism brings me a good feeling, and I have fun doing it.

V   Faith Into Art

Art is that chalice into which we
pour the wine of transcendence.
—Stanley Kunitz

From the first words of Genesis, the connection between faith and the act of creating has been immortalized. The conception of art has always been perceived as divinely driven, the spark of the transcendent being an imperative for creation. And so it is that music and art are for many a spiritual avenue, an opportunity to connect with their Jewish roots.

Artists and musicians create out of a passion and that passion is for many mirrored in their faith. This connection has a profound resonance. The heightened interest on the part of the Jewish community has enabled the growth of a market in Jewish art, music, and literature

The cynical or wary may say that the accumulation of Jewish art is nothing more than another avenue of acquisition for the wealthy. Even worse if the art is used as a substitute for Jewish living. Yet the purchase of many of the objects being produced—including *ketubot* (marriage contracts), menorahs, *yads* (Torah pointers), Havdalah sets, and kiddush cups, as well as pieces derived from biblical stories and themes—may well signify a desire to proudly exhibit religious identity through practical, exquisite objects d'art.

Musicians and artists often talk about the symbiotic relationship between faith and art. Study and prayer engender inspiration, which produces images and melodies, thus creating prayer. A creative circle. The artist with faith creates a life of seemingly disparate parts and produces an organic whole.

22 Reflection of Life

Irene H.

Although I grew up in a home where our Judaism was more gastronomic and ethnically based than connected to any real observance, I can recall early sparks of the *pintele yid*, a potentially religious Jew, inside me.

Growing up in Brooklyn, I was involved in what seemed like a very typical kind of Judaism. The entire block was an extended family. Our neighbors in east Flatbush were a mix of secular and Orthodox Jews. But my friends were all secular and I felt distanced from my Orthodox neighbors.

My parents were kosher but that is absolutely all. We didn't go to synagogue but we observed every holiday with a feast. Yet, they identified very strongly as Jewish. I grew up with Jewish expressions, with Yiddish in the house, and from one grand-

---

Irene H., former public school art teacher, turned to pottery over seventeen years ago. Today she produces an internationally known, individualistic line of ceremonial Judaica based on the evolving needs of her family, friends, and the larger Jewish community around her.

mother, a lot of Jewish cursing. But there was not an intelligence to our Judaism. We were left with the remnants of the superstitious part of Judaism, but not an intelligence. And there was no Hebrew schooling, nothing.

When I was ten, I asked my parents to give me Hebrew school lessons. My father said that I was just a female, it wasn't necessary. My mother, however, directed me to the Eastern Parkway Jewish Center in Brooklyn, where free lessons were available on a weekly basis. On my own, I traveled there by bus six or seven times before dropping out because the classes had no structure, and I seemed not to be learning anything.

The subway near our house was located up a hill. When I would come out of the subway and go down the hill, I would pass a synagogue letting out. I remember on one holiday, it must have been Rosh Hashanah, the streets were filled with Jewish people coming out of synagogues. I think there was an egg roll in my mouth as I was coming downhill. I tried to avoid eye contact. I could imagine the unspoken question: Aren't you a Jewish girl? So why weren't you in synagogue today? I felt so isolated, I didn't know what I was. I wasn't Jewish and it was a terrible feeling, a feeling of separation. I was probably fifteen at the time.

I think I've always been a very spiritual person. But when I was growing up, it was not cool. People were atheist, that was the cool thing to do. In my Jewish neighborhood in Brooklyn, other than the Orthodox, everybody was atheist. Nobody was spiritual.

My grandparents were immigrants. My grandmother came as a fifteen-year-old girl, without her parents, and immediately went to work sewing in a sweatshop. She couldn't read at all, in either Hebrew or Yiddish. I don't remember her ever lighting a candle. They simply worked hard to make a living and to survive. I try to figure why there was no Judaism with them when they came, but she kept kosher. And she would announce when it was Sukkot. We knew when it was, but we didn't know what it meant.

It was really kind of sad, but also somewhat ironic. As a result of getting only an unintelligent Judaism, I spent my entire twenties, once I was out of college, guitar in hand, all over the globe, trying to find some sort of spiritual me that was out there. Of course it wasn't out there. It was my Judaism, which was within me, which was part of me all along.

֍

Growing up, a lot of little Yiddish words became sprinkled into my English. I didn't know that there was a word for pancakes, I only knew latke. Then I went to school at Indiana University. I worked in a little restaurant, waitressing tables. The kitchen help, local to that area, didn't understand a word I said. I said half a sentence, and there would be little Yiddish words here and there; it was funny. I spent a lot of time learning how to not say *eppes* (something).

After college, I wasn't Jewish. If people asked who I was, my background, I was Irene, just a woman with a guitar singing "Imagine" (the Beatles were popular back then), trying to find a place that was spiritually right for me. I spent a long time living on my own in California. As a public school teacher, I was given the opportunity to observe Rosh Hashanah. When my father asked if I was going to take off, I told him I was not. He became upset and said that as I was Jewish, I should definitely not be teaching on the holiday. Straight arrow then as I am now, I took the time off and went to a synagogue where the rabbi was known to give charismatic sermons. He did and I returned on several occasions and on subsequent Rosh Hashanah holidays. I always went alone, a woman in her early thirties. As I look back, I cannot remember being greeted by anyone.

֍

A chance meeting brought me together with my husband Morrie. Morrie was raised in an Orthodox home and was always connected to his Judaism. However, when we met, he did not belong to a synagogue, was not kosher, and Saturdays were a day like any other. After we married and moved to Long Island, Morrie wanted us to join a synagogue. We started to search for a place that I would be comfortable with and we joined a Reform synagogue. I was one of those people that when the rabbi said we should light candles, it wasn't very long before we were lighting candles on Friday. And it just kind of increased and increased.

I guess we were members of the North Country Reform Temple for about six years and more and more observant of traditions. At the same time, I fell in love with pottery and was teaching pottery classes. One day I made a seder plate and brought it to the Jewish Museum. That was the first Jewish ceremonial object I ever made. Thankfully, they liked it. They gave me all sorts of suggestions, including, since I had done it in English, to do it in Hebrew. So I went home and started practicing Hebrew lettering. After our daughter was born, I started making Judaic things at home. I used the suggestions from the Jewish Museum and created four different Judaic objects, brought them back to the Jewish Museum, and they bought all of them. That got me started in making Judaica.

I took a maternity leave and started working while taking care of my baby. Little by little, my business started growing. We had been regularly attending the Reform synagogue for over six years every Friday, always very seriously. When we did something, we did it very big; no halfway stuff. Then a second daughter was born and I took another two years maternity leave, and added more ceremonial objects to my line. At the suggestion of one of the synagogues I sold to, I went to the biennial conference of the Women's League for Conservative Judaism. I think I was probably the only exhibitor who got up at seven in the morning, before everything opened, and went to services. I was completely blown away by the Conservative service, as I had never been in the Reform service, where everything was shorter. I had no idea there was all this wonderful stuff and I just completely loved it. There was just so much more to it. I had no idea. Where we would do a paragraph at the Reform synagogue, there would be pages in the Conservative service. I just enjoyed the service very much.

When my older daughter was three and the younger one was a month old, we went to Israel for a month in the summer. When we came back, the three-year-old kept asking what day it was. On Shabbat she would ask, "Why aren't we in synagogue?" The Reform synagogue we belonged to only had services on Friday nights. And actually, on Friday night, although they didn't discourage bringing children, people made so many faces that when you brought a child it was clearly not encouraged. So we started going to services at a Conservative synagogue that had been a customer of mine in the area. After a year we joined that synagogue and we've been there ever since, and active. Both my kids go to Hebrew high school now. Judaism is an integral part of our lives.

◈

At this point, my faith and my art are so interwoven. I have always been an artist. My paints and sketch pads shared every journey with me. It was only natural that my art would become an expression of my life as a Jewish woman. I've taught for seventeen years and now I have been a potter for seventeen years. And in the last five or six years, suddenly, everything I'm doing has clicked. I'm a teacher. In my pottery, I'm teaching. On all of my pieces, the children that I create perform mitzvot. I have a *tzedakah* box, and on the top is a child with sweet stuff, baskets of food in it's arms. On my bat mitzvah candles, there is a little girl, a bat mitzvah girl, in her white dress holding a siddur and a kiddush cup. We belong to an egalitarian synagogue, we make *yads* for girls. Once people receive my gifts, they not only use them, but they explain the customs.

◈

I'm researching and studying all the time. I spend all day thinking about my ceremonial art. They are an expression of how I'm living. I guess how I live every day in my life, Jewishly, comes out in my pieces. If you saw them, you would see that the children have grown as my kids have grown. I now make a Havdalah set that is a computer, it's a computer spice box. My kids weren't using *yads* ten year ago, now I'm doing *yads*, very feminine *yads*. Ten years ago, I was making Shabbat toys, tiny little clay Shabbat sets, my kids would play with on the floor. So if you look at my pieces, you look at a reflection of my life and the lives of my friends. Someone at the Jewish Board of Education in Rhode Island needed a traveling Havdalah set as a gift for a kid going away to school. So now I make traveling Havdalah sets for kids going off. My Shabbat candle has a kid with a T-shirt that says "Shabbat" reclining in between the candle holders, with books all scattered around. The siddurs are always open because my children are always learning. Their dreidels always land on *gimmel*.

I do contemporary people living Jewishly on my pieces. Even while I'm in the synagogue, I'm always looking for ideas. Whenever I paint a face, it's the face of my rabbi, or my cantor, or the friends of my kids. My art and faith is all just a great big merge. I go from one thing to the other, it's very natural. My work is a coming together of what I've learned as an artist, a teacher, and a Jewish woman. I could never again be a "passive" Jew and my pieces aren't passive. They reach out to embrace the owner. They say use me, enjoy me, practice, and celebrate your Judaism.

ֿ◦֍◦

I keep studying and growing. It's funny, but when I look around I see that there's not enough to fulfill all the Jewish themes. For example, every year we have a sukkah, and now I'm really into making sukkah ornaments out of clay. I thought, that's the last time I'm going into a Christmas store looking for something, looking for some paper maché fruit to hang. I know it's time there were sukkah ornaments.

We are now practicing Conservative Jews, actively participating in services. Judaism has made sense of my life and placed what I do in a context that has meaning for me. I feel a connection to everything that has come before and an active participant in what will follow. My life has a rhythm and a flow that feels right and makes sense to me.

23 Carrying It to Completion

Jo H.

I was born in Minnesota and raised in Seattle, Washington. My father came from a very Orthodox family. He was one of ten children. He married my mother, who also came from an Orthodox family, but she knew nothing about her religious background at all, except that she had a grandfather who was a rabbi. I went to Sunday school as a child but I don't remember much of it after all these years. The thing I did remember were the Hebrew characters. I don't know why that stuck.

My father would go to services at the Orthodox synagogue in Seattle, but he raised us Reform because of mother. My mother's family came from Denver and they were very socially prominent people. Their social life was more important than their religious

Jo H. is a potter in her seventies residing in Arizona. Her art has been showcased in The Israel Connection Gallery as well as the Georgia Pacific Collection. Her newly plumbed affinity for the creation of Judaica has brought her life a wave of meaning.

life so she didn't get much of a Jewish background when she was being raised. When she was ninety, she asked me if I could tell her a little bit about the Jewish faith, because she knew nothing. At the same time, I didn't know very much either, so I went to the temple in Portland, Oregon, and got her some books to read. That was her first real introduction to Judaism.

෴

We used to have wonderful joyous Passover seders for the whole family. My dad's brothers and sisters would come with their kids and the house was simply full of people. My mother did like to cook, so she learned to cook the dishes for the seder. That was mainly the biggest celebration that we had in our home. Hanukah in our home was not a big deal.

We also had a Christmas tree at Christmastime and we lived a few doors down from the rabbi. One Christmas I was sick and I remember one evening the tree was all lit up and my mother saw the rabbi coming down the street. She yelled at my dad, "Quick, Robert, the rabbi's coming" and dad grabbed the Christmas tree, lights and all, and ran to the basement with it. When the rabbi came to the door, he said, "Hello, Robert, what did you do with the Hanukah bush?"

෴

I went to Portland and got interested in art. I married, had two children, and they skipped Sunday school whenever they could. I didn't find that out until later. Neither one of my children married into the Jewish faith, but my daughter is more interested than my son. I have a little Hanukah service in my home and I read a lot of material on Judaism and what's going on in Israel, but my art has been more of a teacher than anything else. Now that I'm seventy-two years old, I guess I'm more curious about my background. The fact is my faith has grown with my art.

I was involved with art before I got married, but only after did I start my formal training. I took classes at Portland Art Museum and I showed my work in Oregon and Washington. When I moved to Arizona, because of an auto accident, I had to give up my paintings and my wood block prints. I turned to working with clay. Carving the clay, which is softer to work with, wasn't so difficult on my wrists. I studied with a woman, took ceramics, and developed my own style of art. It's been an exciting experience for me.

๑♦๑

My work with Jewish themes started with clay. Before that, my paintings were basically abstract. I studied formal sketching, but I went to abstract. I think that brought me into a feeling of how to do my Hebrew characters when I came to my pottery. For me, there's this same feeling of the abstract in it.

The first things I did in pottery did not have a Jewish theme. They were more of the Native Indian theme that we have in Arizona. I won several awards for that work, but it wasn't satisfying. When I got a chance to show with Jewish galleries, I started developing. That's how it began. I was asked if I could do something along the lines of interpreting the Jewish faith in some way in clay. I tried first with little hasidic figures because they're so distinctive, but I didn't feel that mine were as good as others I had seen. So then I went to pottery and started looking up translations of Hebrew in a book I had given my mother. I carved Hebrew from the scriptures and, of course, then I had to find out what I was saying. The translations helped me to grow.

After a while a gallery in Phoenix said they didn't want a quote from the scriptures, they just wanted the characters on the pot and anything else I wanted to do with them. I am now doing sixteen- or eighteen-inch-tall pots with a tallis on them and I can't make them fast enough. I'm getting calls all the time, "Can you bring some more in?"

๑♦๑

I'm studying and learning. While I do the pots, I listen to Klezmer music. The feelings in the music take my work and help carry it along to completion. I think it shows in the finished piece. I was shocked one day to realize that while I was creating I was praying. I guess I do it automatically.

The whole endeavor has turned out to be financially very successful, but more importantly, I'm enthralled with what I'm doing now. In the past, being a Jew was not a priority. Now my artwork has become the force behind my understanding that I am part and an extension of my faith. I'm developing, I'm still learning and I hope I continue till the day I die.

24 Each Feeds the Other

Judy S.

I grew up in rural New York State, sixty miles north of the city, where we were, in fact, about the only Jews in our school district. We were the anomaly because we did take Jewish holidays off. My sister, who's six years older than I, was probably the first Jew any of those kids had seen, and they thought she had green horns and wouldn't play with her. There was a lot of difficulty in that arena. It wasn't like that in the city six miles away, but we weren't really associated with that area, except that it was where my father worked. That was where we joined the Orthodox synagogue and my brother got his bar mitzvah training.

My mother was born in Russia. She kept a kosher home and observed Shabbes. On Shabbes she would light candles. Rosh

Judy S., winner of an Individual Artist grant from the Connecticut Commission on the Arts, has exhibited at the Museum of Yeshiva University and Chesterwood Museum, among others.

As an artist, sculptor, and teacher of both art and Jewish traditions, she is committed to bringing life to the images that grow out of her Jewish study.

Hashanah and Yom Kippur we didn't go to school, and for Rosh
Hashanah we always took the two days off. We didn't take off for
Passover or Shavuot. We had a home where if milk was used for
meat or meat was used for milk, the forks and knives got planted
into the ground for three days until they were clean. That's a very
colorful memory for me.

We didn't go to temple often because my mother didn't drive
on Saturdays. My father was as Orthodox as my mother, but my
father, for work reasons, would drive. He sometimes worked on
Saturdays, but not usually. If we were going to see family, we
might take a ride into the city. We didn't go to synagogue very
much, but I do remember being attached to some of the liturgy
from a very early age. I would just melt when I heard the Ve'
Ahavta. I grew up with a Jewish identity but I didn't get Jewish
training. I went to religious school for about three weeks at the
school where my brother was attending. I can't remember exactly
why I stopped. It was just very awkward; I wasn't sure they liked
girls. At the time it was rather unusual for girls to be getting
a religious education. As it was an Orthodox synagogue, there
weren't going to be girls getting a bat mitzvah.

⚭

There was no Hillel at the college I went to, Tufts, but there
were more Jewish people than I had ever seen in one place. I
wasn't very active Jewishly there. I arranged a major for myself
in medical sociology whereby I was able to take courses down
at the medical school. I did independent research there in psychiatry and medical sociology, which was then a brand-new
course. In my senior year, since I was also interested in art, I
arranged one of the first art exhibits that Tufts University ever
had. I did an independent study on a particular artist and then
brought his work to the university and set up an art gallery. That
turned out to be the forerunner of what is now their gallery. I
didn't know that had actually happened until I exhibited at Tufts
last year.

❦

I worked in the area of medical sociology for a couple of years in Boston and then went out to San Francisco. I essentially wandered around. I was a street artist, I made jewelry and sold it on the streets. Eventually I got my own place. One day I painted a six-foot rainbow on my kitchen wall. I looked at it and said that's it, that's what it's about.

I started painting rainbows for people, and this was a long time before the recent resurgence of rainbow stuff. I did some designs for people, everything was hand done; rainbow business cards, rainbow menus for a place in Los Angeles. I knew nothing about graphic design at that point and how costly it would be to print something in rainbow colors. Because I had done everything by hand, I didn't know anything about the technology. I did and still do a lot of work by hand.

During my five years in San Francisco, I took off and hitchhiked through Europe. At one point in Zurich I wanted to get to someplace warm. Since it wasn't far from Israel, and I had always wanted to go, I went. I tagged along with someone I met on the plane and got placed on a kibbutz, where I stayed for five months. It wasn't a religious kibbutz, but it still felt good to be in Israel. There was something about being in Israel that warmed me in ways I could not even express.

❦

I eventually came back east and got married. I started making note cards by hand printing. From 1974 to 1981 I made and sold about 5,000 hand-printed note cards. Many of them were on rainbow themes, no words. They sold out immediately from Boston to California. One of my great regrets is that I did not have the courage to get them manufactured.

In 1979, I got my first grant from the Connecticut Commission on the Arts to do potato printing. That resulted in some exhibitions. Then I did a little bit of pottery and after my third child was born in 1981 I decided to get a studio outside the house. That's really when I became a sculptor.

Soon after, I began working with fabric and materials I found in the wild. I started to do more sculpture. I did my original set of ceremonial rods, which are about reverence for whatever is in nature. I had stood out in the woods and said, "God, you did a great job." I had said that a couple of times very spontaneously and I wanted to see how I could show reverence for all that was created. The ceremonial rods were the initial piece, made of a wild bamboo that I have to dry for a period of time.

⊙✝⊙

In 1983 I had an adult bat mitzvah. I was really hungry for my Jewishness. There was a synagogue that I heard about and I joined. It was a Reform synagogue and what I got out of it was how important it was for me to be touched in this way. We had always done Shabbes and the holidays, but I became much more involved. I wanted to learn Torah, so I studied with a group of women for about five years. We also began a Rosh Chodesh group. Each one of us would take responsibility for a certain month and we'd work together to create a program for the group. We are blessed in New Haven to have the Yale Hillel.

I started to have resources of which I could ask questions. As we would read Torah, I would have visions of things that I wanted to translate into art. I did a set of rods on the seven days of creation, a set of rods on the tribes of Israel. I found texts that interested me that I wanted to work with, so I started doing some text pieces. I began naming some of my other artwork with Hebrew ideas, Judaic ideas. I was reading and studying a lot on my own, and I would go to different people and say, "I'm working on this idea, do you have some sources that I could go to?" I learned about sources by asking questions and from people being very generous in sharing their knowledge.

I would tend to read not just Torah text, but the *midrash* (story) behind it. That's how we would study—we would go to lots of different sources. Then I got hold of the book *The Legends of the Jews*, by Louis Ginzberg. That had so many rich resources in it that, if I were curious about something, I searched out some of his sources to get the nuances.

Around this time, I received a second Connecticut Commission grant to do outdoor pieces exploring human emotions through art and sculpture. I also proposed something for the Memorial Foundation for Jewish Culture. I proposed two pieces, the tribes piece and also a large piece that I've done called "Seventh Heaven" from Jewish perspectives. When I was doing research on the seven days of creation, it talked about the seven levels of heaven. Seventh heaven was the highest one where the souls of the unborn and the souls of the very righteous reside. Around the same time as I was reading that, I discovered my grandparents' Russian *ketubah* from 1899. It contained a cryptic translation where my grandfather promised to take care of the souls that were yet to come down to them from heaven. The joining of those two ideas had me imagine and envision what seventh heaven looked like. I pursued that and actually built a piece called Seventh Heaven. It's about 13 feet tall and it is built like a tallis. It is made of gold and silver mylar, thousands and thousands of strands of it. Tucked inside the strands are referential objects as to what might be in seventh heaven: angels, bells, mirrors, and the Hebrew letters *lamed* and *vav*.

☙

For five years I taught at the Hebrew high school. I created a curriculum of experimental Jewish art to learn about Jewish concepts and Torah through art. I have actually adapted and taught some of it to adults. The response has been incredible. I actually help people get to the Modeh Ani, the source of creativity within themselves, to tap into it and be nonjudgmental about it, so that it opens up avenues for approaching issues and problems in one's life. I've also taught for several years at the Jewish healing conference in Boston on facing the unknown through art.

I was doing a lot of sculpture and getting a lot of acclaim, but I needed to do something more. As each of my children had a bat mitzvah coming up, in 1990 I started doing pieces of text from her Torah portion, from the service, and then something about each child from the Haftarah, for the walls of the synagogue. Those pieces then became a body of work. We had three bat mitzvahs, so I did seven pieces for each of those. People really fell in love and were very moved by them, so I started doing more. I now have reproduced two of them, the Shehechianu and the Modeh Ani. Then I started doing some selling shows and the text pieces seem to move people. People would stand in front of my booth and tears would come to their eyes, which told me that something was happening to them when they saw my work.

❦

The connection between my faith and my art is a tricky thing. I end up creating for a not very commercial market, but rather a more specific one. Many people have come to my booth and said, "You know, you make us think." It's not like I'm handing people just a mazel tov card. I really want them to engage, because I'm engaged with it. There are things that need to be said, or ideas that I think are so important that I want to get out in the world. When I get captivated or stopped by an idea in a prayer book then I know that there's something there for me and maybe there's something there for someone else.

Some of the morning prayers, for example, I think are so amazing. I wake up and say thank you for the return of my soul to me. Thank you. That whole emphasis on gratitude, on knowing you're not alone, knowing that every day is a gift. I don't exercise that every single day, I have to work and remind myself. Life is very bumpy and the connection to one's faith is a source of strength through the bumpiness. We're all human, we're all trying to make sense of this world, and we're all trying to make sense of the different paths in achieving that goal. For me, I'm lucky that my art and my faith are each a source that feed the other.

25 A Way of Building a Life

Renee and Howard V.

Renee: I was born in Poland. My parents are Holocaust survivors who moved to Israel, where I lived for nine years. We came to the states in 1958. My parents are observant Jews, Orthodox, especially my mother. But when we came to the United States, I went to public school and Hebrew school every day except Friday and Saturday. It was pretty rigorous.

I hated it at the time. I was fairly unhappy living in an observant home, caught between two worlds. My mother was on one side and me, my friends, the television, and the whole world were on the other. We lived in Brooklyn, in a Jewish neighborhood, but it was very secular in many ways. Everybody was Jewish, but my parents kept Shabbes and that was really unusual in the late '50s, early '60s. At that time, people went to synagogue on holi-

---

Renee and Howard V. work together in the creation of handcrafted Judaic pieces as well as a Jewishly committed life.

days, but being as observant as my parents was not that common, at least among my Jewish friends. It was a battle and the Jewish aspect of our life at times appeared very negative. As I grew up, I tried to remove myself as much as possible from it. When I went to college, I wasn't looking not to be Jewish, but I wasn't looking to be Jewish.

I went to Brooklyn College. At the time, it didn't seem like I had many choices. My parents, my mother would not hear of me going away. She would not have accepted that at all. Then I met Howard.

Howard: I grew up in an assimilated middle-class family in Brooklyn. My family was fairly secular. Some traditions were observed, but I talk about them now with more nostalgia than memory of there being a religious meaning.

I grew up in an extended family. We lived in a home with my grandparents in one apartment, my uncle and aunt and their kids in another, and my family lived in another apartment. When we did go to temple, we went to an Orthodox synagogue. My father never went and my mother went mostly on the High Holy Days. My grandmother went to the Orthodox synagogue, which is why we went there. I don't think my grandfather ever went in his life.

I went to Hebrew school as did my two sisters. It was a one-room schoolhouse; primitive and rowdy. If anything was learned, aside from bar mitzvah lessons, it was amazing. But I kind of liked it. I had a good feeling about Jewish ritual and learning. When I was young, King Solomon and King David were like heroes to me. So despite the fact that my father or my grandfather never went to synagogue, I somehow had good feelings about temple. I didn't continue much after my bar mitzvah, but I enjoyed going on the holidays with an old uncle who used to visit from Boston. When he stopped going, I think I was about sixteen, I was at that adolescent stage where I said this doesn't make any sense and I stopped going.

I guess I had some connection to it in my heart because I eventually looked more seriously for spiritual nourishment in the countercultural movement of the '60s. There seemed so much to choose from at the time. People were in the streets, chanting and meditating. I actually started doing a little of this and that, and then felt that I had to look into what I left behind. I somehow felt either a loyalty to my Jewish upbringing or that there must be something there that I didn't know about. I looked at it in a more mystical plane, since that was the head I was in during my late teens and early twenties. I looked into Shlomo Carlbach, went to a few Purim celebrations, played some music with him. I became interested, but didn't really know what to do with it at that point. I guess that's the point where I met Renee.

ᗌᕽᗍ

Howard: Renee and I went out a couple of years before we decided to get married. I was trying to learn more and more about Judaism, trying to educate myself at that point. I was trying to decide, because it is a hard decision to make as a young man, whether to get married or not. I think feeling part of the Jewish tradition helped me to decide to get married, which we did in 1970.

Renee: Since that time, we've been exploring, I think initially through Howard's exploration and his intense need and interest to discover Judaism on a level he could deal with. I went along. I was very happy to go on the journey with him at that particular time. Up to a point.

Howard: When we got married I was teaching speech and theater courses at Brooklyn College and Renee got a job at a senior citizens center as an arts program director. The director and the social worker of that center were Orthodox women.

Renee: They were really the first women I associated with who were Orthodox, other than my mother and her friends, and they had a marvelous point of view. They were modern women and had a very positive and energetic attitude toward everything: Judaism, their families, their work. They made a great impression on me. I worked with them for about four years and that opened me up. It was like a first step, a window I should say, to seeing Judaism as a positive experience that I could incorporate in my life, not just you can't do this or you can't do that. I began to see it as an influence in one's life in a positive way, making you a certain kind of person, giving you a certain kind of life. That was the beginning.

◈

Howard: After teaching and working in theater projects I joined a dance company and became a professional dancer for seven years. Renee, who knew various art media like painting, began getting involved in learning ceramics and pottery. We had acquired somewhat of a consciousness and commitment to Judaism, but at this point it wasn't fully developed. Renee started creating a line of pottery. When I wasn't dancing, during the off-season, we did craft shows. She was doing regular pottery: teapots and dinnerware, and a little bit of experimental stuff, like wall pieces. She was getting good.

After a while we moved into a loft in a factory building in Brooklyn, where there was hardly anybody else living there. There were just factories—we were kind of pioneers in the Park Slope area in those early days. Our landlord was a hasid. We were always running into committed Jewish people. The whole complex was owned by this group. The landlord would come up and he'd see Jewish books on my shelf and we would talk.

Everywhere we went, I would try to find a synagogue and connect with people. I never really did. But when we moved into that loft, there was a synagogue a few blocks from us and, as I did every time I moved someplace, I went inside and checked it out. There were just a few old men there. I could see it had been a magnificent synagogue at one time. It must have had hundreds of people. Now there were a few old men, with maybe one or two younger guys. The rabbi walked from Borough Park, about two-and-a-half miles away, to be there on Shabbat. Going there gave me an actual sense that I was really needed. My presence helped keep this place alive. It was important for me to go. That was the first time I really had that feeling.

The rabbi was totally accepting of who we were. If I didn't come for Shabbes or if they needed a minyan during the week, he would come and bang on our downstairs door. I thought it was great. In a sense, it gave me that feeling of being needed. I began to respond to that. At the same time Renee had made a few pieces of Judaica, one or two pieces for ourselves. We had heard about somebody asking for photographs of anybody doing Judaica; we sent some and they were published in a book. All of a sudden, when the book came out, we started getting inquiries from around the country: send us your brochure, send us your catalog. I took some photographs, which I started sending, and before we knew it there were orders from all over wanting Judaica.

Renee: That time it was the beginning of the handcrafted Judaica revolution. About a year or two later, we had our first child. The Judaica part of my work became bigger and bigger and I had less time for other things; then I became pregnant again. I left my senior center job and devoted more time to filling the orders we were getting.

Howard: I eventually had to stop dancing when our daughter was born, to make some money and to somehow make this whole thing work from our Bohemian life-style. We became an established family and decided to try and turn this into a full-time business and sell the work.

One thing leads to another. During this time we were doing craft shows with our Judaica and we started to run into other people who were doing Judaica. There weren't a whole lot of people. There are many more today. We ran into people like the hasidic artist Mikhail Muchnich. We became friendly with him; he was in Crown Heights and we were in Park Slope. He and his wife were so friendly, they invited us to their house for sukkot and for Hanukah.

Renee: It was an interesting, eye-opening experience for us, especially me. My parents were not *frailach* (happy), they had been through a lot. They were not so joyous in their observance. They were observant because that's who they were. So for us to participate in activities with people who had such joy in their connection to their faith, it was like seeing another way of being Jewish, of celebrating Judaism, our culture, our religion, which was very positive for me. I was moving in that direction.

ᘓᆃᘐ

Howard: All the time we were growing Judaically but around this time an interesting thing happened that made me really examine myself and how I connected with the Jewish faith. The synagogue in Park Slope was undergoing change. There started to be an influx of people into the neighborhood but they were not interested in the traditional Orthodox Judaism that had been the heart of the Park Slope Jewish Center. They started exploring different rabbis. Who did we want as a rabbi? What did we want? It was an interesting time for me because I hadn't really been aware of other forms of Judaism. I learned from each person who came.

Rabbis were hired, so I started taking classes in a very concentrated way, which I had never done before. But there was a tremendous split between the old people and the newer people. I, of course, having been with the older people from the beginning, stayed with them. Although I would've thought my life-style was more like the new people, it was an interesting dilemma. It was wrenching internally, but it also made me learn something about myself and the kind of Jewish connection I wanted. What I discovered was that I am more communally oriented. Just like I enjoyed being a part of a dance company, I work well with groups. Renee is very self-contained.

It's not that she doesn't need anybody, she gets along well with everybody. It's just that she could be happy sitting by herself for hours doing her thing, whereas I function better in a group where every person counts, you're contributing your part to make it all work. I didn't feel quite the same way with the new people. I felt

I was needed by those old people. I was helping the whole system survive, something that had survived that way for thousands and thousands of years.

◦✛◦

Renee: We eventually moved out into the country. The first three years after my daughter was born we actually were successful in building up enough stores and galleries and places that wanted to carry our work that we could sustain ourselves, so we moved. We weren't really sure who we were Judaically at the time but we knew we wanted a synagogue in the area, at least one, and somewhat of a Jewish community.

Howard: We wound up in a place with three synagogues and another one in the town nearby. After we moved, I started to explore. Again, where do we go? Where do I fit in? One synagogue I went to was very eclectic, more loose, more experimental in its services. There were a lot of people there whose background was like my own and I went there for a while. But then I thought, what am I going to learn from this? I felt the whole time that I needed to learn the basics, the old, the traditions before I could go on to any alternative; I had to know what it was an alternative to.

Renee: We were learning a lot just doing the Judaic work. We did a lot of research and read a lot. For each piece, we went to the smallest detail about the *halachah* (Jewish law). Each piece has been a part of the learning process. Looking into historical and archeological books and trying to get inspiration certainly connects us much more closely to our whole history, our tradition and people. I see a fourteenth-century menorah that somebody made long ago and it inspires me.

Howard: I tried out a number of synagogues and I still didn't feel that I was home. I was reluctant, because I wasn't really totally observant, to go the Orthodox synagogue. But I said what the heck, and I went anyway, and I found a very warm reception there. Again, I guess it's a sense of being needed. . . .

Renee: . . . and a community that was very involved.

Howard: I had a sense of it being important that I come, a sense of really being welcomed there. At that time, they had started with a new rabbi. I started going and learning from the more traditional aspect. That has been a continuing process and we stayed there, now over ten years. I'm the *gabia* (person who coordinates the service) of the *shul* today. We have come a long way.

We've both been learning the whole time, through work and classes I've taken and different programs. It's not a big synagogue. In fact, it's very small and it gives the feeling that every person counts. There's a sense of community, a sense of responsibility to the community, a sense of obligation, and a sense of doing what you can do to keep this alive.

⚛︎

Renee: My theory of Judaism has changed. I see that instead of Judaism being a negative, a "don't" religion, it's positive: being a community, being responsible, being all the things that I guess my mother knew subconsciously, but we had to discover on our own. It's not just a religion of don't, it's a way of building a life.

Howard: Our own practices are still evolving. We're still learning, we're still struggling with certain mitzvot, but we see it as a growing task. There are certain rabbis who have been very accepting; if you don't do this yet, so you'll do it next month or next year. We're on a certain path. Certainly the work keeps us involved, but even beyond the Jewish rituals and learning, we read a lot, I go to classes, we discuss a lot, we work together all the time. A lot of what we talk about is Judaism.

Renee: In the business, we create together. I'm at the potter's wheel, but Howard has participated in a lot of designing and creating pieces. I put it together, but he also makes certain parts.

Howard: I make certain pieces, I do preparation, I make blazes, I run the kiln.

Renee: He helped develop a lot of pieces with me, but I'm the one who eventually executes.

Howard: I'm the shipping department.

Renee: We're together all the time. I don't think a day goes by without talking about some kind of Jewish subject, whether it's for the kids or for work or whether it's society or politics, how Judaism would look at certain issues. We're here together, creating a Jewish life.

26 A Finely Woven Tapestry

Wendy R.

I was born in Chicago, Illinois, in a cab on the way to the hospital. I was purported to have the loudest pair of lungs that the hospital had ever heard. I came into the world saying, "attend to me." I was very determined, at least that's what I kept hearing.

The Judaism that was in my house growing up was absent Judaism. My parents weren't surrounded by a community they could reach out to as a place of support, solace, comfort, or tradition. Though my father's father was deeply involved with the synagogue, he had died at a young age, thirty-eight, from Parkinson's disease. Up until that time, however, he was very active—

Wendy R. is an artist and weaver living in the Berkshires. Her one-woman show at the Wang Center for the Arts in Boston featured her work on the Jewish matriarchs. In 1993, her work was chosen to be part of the White House permanent collection during the Year of the Craftsman. The intelligent perspective reflected in her work is surpassed only by the compassion.

president of a *shul*, loved Judaism, and that pervaded my father's early years. My father had two brothers who were very devout, but not my father. After his father died, my father rejected Judaism. There were many reasons, one that I know concern's my grandfather's *shul*.

My grandfather had very little money when he became ill, so his *shul* took up a huge collection. They brought it over and presented it and did it in a very nice and ceremonious way. No one felt lessened by it. The president of the temple said This is on behalf of the synagogue. Two weeks later, my grandparents got a visit from members of the governing committee. One of the members said to my grandmother, "Celia, we hope you understood why we wanted to give this to you and we honor you and we cherish you and we hope the $5,000 wasn't too little." My grandmother just froze. She had received $2,500. The president of the temple had taken the other $2,500 for himself. My grandfather's feelings of high regard toward Judaism were smashed. He couldn't speak because of the Parkinson's, he couldn't walk, but my grandparents were so angry at the temple. After that, they just closed that whole area of their lives. No one said anything. I asked my father, didn't Grandma say anything and he said no, she was too proud. But my dad, that's where his bitterness came from. He didn't want to have anything to do with organized religion.

That was a huge theft, a huge amount of money at the time. I once asked my father why he thought they collected such a large amount. He said because my grandfather did an incredible amount of work for the *shul*. He had been very dedicated, and that's why in fact they accepted the money, because they could see it wasn't charity.

So my father rejected that Judaism, but regained it in his later years, just before he passed on. It was a real *teshuvah* and he and I connected to it very deeply. It was wonderful.

❧

So Judaism wasn't evident in our home. The sense of Jewish culture or religion came through my grandmother and my father's brother, Uncle Dave, and his wife, who was very religious.

I remember my Uncle Dave went to a storefront *shul.* One time, I must have been very little girl, he took me to High Holy Day services with the men. I remember them praying and the sounds of the Hebrew and the smells; it was terrifying and exciting at the same time. I wanted to do it and of course they explained that I couldn't. I didn't understand why so I started crying, because I was very emotional. It didn't matter what it was: joy or sorrow. I'm still like that today.

I have memories of looking out the window and seeing a man and wanting to know who he was because he had a yarmulke on and carried a prayer bag and he was all dressed up as he walked to *shul* on Saturday. The Conservative *shul* was down the road from us and I loved it, I loved the architecture. It was very beautiful, Byzantine, but I had never been in it. So I asked my mother about this man, what he was doing, and my mother said, "He is a very good son and very religious and he follows the teachings." I had no idea what that meant.

At that time, people hid their Jewishness to some extent even though our neighborhood was ethnically diverse. There were Jewish people and Italian people, Swedish, German, Irish, all kinds of European people, and some black people on the fringes of the neighborhood. Everyone seemed comfortable with Judaism, but it wasn't decorous, it wasn't what you aspired to. In fact, you were trying to do as much as you could to assimilate.

At a certain point, my mother thought I probably should get a good Jewish education. They weren't doing bat mitzvahs at the time, but there was a big new Reform congregation with a new Reform rabbi and my mother thought I should go to Sunday school and get confirmed. I thought I'd be interested in it, so I went. It was the antithesis of my uncle's rich, dark, colorful, mysterious, somewhat joyful, very intense experience. It was pristine and white, with no color in it. The only thing that had a spiritual sense was the Ark. It was made of really rich, red oak and it was carved with the *seraphim* (angels). They had angels in this place, but everything else was so austere. All the prayers were formal and everything was in English. There was a choir way up above and an organ. The rabbi was in black robes and he had horrible hairy hands, and he was really big. But I went to the school and tried it out and I was very bored with it. Then one day at Sunday school the rabbi said something to me that I must have found insulting, because I spit. Not surprisingly, I wasn't allowed to go back to religious school anymore. I don't remember what he said but it was horrible to me. I was twelve. That got me in trouble and I never went back. A lot of people in the neighborhood talked about it, of course, because I wasn't that kind of girl. I didn't go around fighting with people.

I don't remember why that happened, but I do remember that there was no mention of God, there was no connection to God. God was not alive in that temple, in the classes, in my child mind. That's the feeling I had and that was my major sense of Judaism throughout that period. I must have known from my grandma or had a sense that there was some joy and *ruach* in Judaism, but I felt it wasn't in that place.

☙❧

One summer, when I was in my twenties, I went to a crafts community on Mount Desert Island in Maine. It has a gorgeous landscape. There was an outdoor arts community and I had a little booth there with some looms in it. I was weaving. That summer I was away from everyone I knew. I had gone up there for rejuvenation of some kind because I had been having a difficult personal time.

When I went to Maine, I didn't want to be bothered with much. I wanted to weave and walk on the beach and I didn't want to deal with anything. I was cracked open and I didn't have an anchor. I didn't have a sense of how I could get through. I just knew I didn't want to keep going through those difficult times. A friend of mine, a Christian Scientist, says that trials can be proof of God's care. It's like a rug: if you take one of those old-fashioned beaters and you keep beating it, what does it do? It softens the rug, it cleans out the dust and the dirt, and that's what these trials do, they soften your heart. Heart is the seed of wisdom in Judaism, so in some way my heart was softened.

I was alone there, my husband was in Washington, DC. And a couple of things happened that summer. First, I met a clammer and lobster fisherman named Skippy. He had been a chauffeur for a wealthy Jewish couple in New York for five years but came back to the island and was self-educated, very, very bright. On his way walking early in the morning, he would pass me because I loved to weave during the sunrise. The first time he watched me and didn't say a word. The second day he came by and said: "Are you a Hebrew?" I laughed and said yes. The third day he came by and said: "Oh Hebrew woman weaving at your web," and every day after that, he gave me some information about Judaism. He had asked me some question about Judaism and I had said I really have nothing to do with it.

This guy was probably a reincarnation of a lost Jewish soul. He would tell me stories, some of them were hasidic stories, but most of them were simply little stories about Jewish people he had met. They weren't philosophy or anything. He was just so colorful that I started to get interested and really began listening. I spent mornings listening to this Irish guy named Skippy tell me stories of my tradition.

৶ৎ

The second thing happened about three weeks after I had arrived at the island. I was looking out of my booth and weaving away and I saw a very short man in a black suit with black *peyot* (side curls), and a yarmulke, real schlumpy, walking right toward me, kind of zig-zaggy, but making a beeline to me. This is Maine, way up there, what's he doing there? Is this a hallucination? I had no idea, but he came up to me and didn't say anything. He just looked at my loom and the things I created and we started to talk. I said hello and where you from; he said he's from Bangor, Maine. He spoke to me about the Jewish community there, "We're from Brooklyn, we came up a year ago, there's a bunch of us. We have a *shul*. Why don't you come? For the summer, we decided that every Wednesday night we'd have a lecture on Maimonides. One of our rabbinical students is here and he's going to be presenting it. Why don't you come? And if you can't do that why don't you come to Shabbat?" So of course, I said thank you, that's very nice, and somehow I was pushed. Talk about feeling the hand of God.

I didn't have a car up there and I had a dog, a Husky. I was staying at a house with people who were part of the crafts community and had cars but nobody was going to Bangor, Maine. It was off the island, forty miles away. But one Friday a friend of someone I knew came by and said they were going to Bangor. I said I have my dog, and they said that's okay. So I went, without calling or anything. I went to that *shul* and I waited for the rabbi I had talked to, thinking he was the rabbi. He wasn't, the fellow was a little assistant person. The real rabbi called me in and we introduced ourselves and he invited me home for Shabbat and a meal. I went. We ended up with a deal for the next six weeks. I went Wednesdays and Fridays. I was to teach him everything I knew about feminism if he would teach me everything he knew or thought I should know about Judaism. That happened for six weeks. I never understood it. Sometimes when I thought about it or talked about it, I've thought when people walk into the stream, take the step into the stream, it takes you.

I never saw the little guy again. He was one of the strangest fellows. He never went to any of the Wednesday night classes and I was invited to the rabbi's every Friday night. The rabbi's grandmother and mother were there, he had two kids, but I never saw the little guy. Also strange is that I got rides every week! One time I couldn't get back because I had my dog with me. Even the bus driver let me bring this big Husky on the bus and dropped us off! Even that happened. And I met a composer who was also returning to Judaism, so I would stay over and talk about this fascinating thing that was happening to us.

◈✦◈

At the time, I was weaving wall hangings and shawls, no Judaica, nothing with Jewish content whatsoever. If anything, I was interested in the spirituality that emanated from the Native American tradition, because weaving in this country is very tied to that tradition. The way in which they approached their weaving really resonated with me, as the way I both wanted to and did approach my weaving. It's not your ego that's creating it; you are expressing a larger whole and it's a gift given to you, it's a way of prayer. That has continued to be a theme of mine. It's really soul talk between you and God. The doing of it and the product is like a soul offering to God; you're revealing certain truths that are inviolate in the universe, never to be destroyed, and you uncover it through your work.

The Jewish tradition has all of those elements about creating. Right in Exodus, when the tribe is walking through the desert God calls upon Betzalel and says he is a skilled craftsman. He is to call upon an assistant to work with him, not to work alone, and he is to create the *mishkan* (the Temple) in the wilderness. He is to gather not only skilled craftsmen, but those who are open-hearted, wise, and of great understanding. They call on weavers and silversmiths, and people who work with forges and bellows and they all work in concert together. When I read that my heart just soared because it showed me that in my tradition there is a blueprint, a positive acknowledgment as to how we should create and this is in fact proscribed. It is honored that we have creators, it's called *hiddur mitzvah*, the act of beautification, the good deed of making and creating beauty in the world. One of the things I saw as a corollary was that there's an opposite way of creating; they're supposed to be creating beauty in the wilderness after they've listened to God—in conjunction with God. Almost immediately after that we have the Golden Calf. Moses is up there and down below is an absence of God. When you create with absence of God, look what happens: it becomes hard and solidified and not life-giving at all. For me that was a wonderful statement about how to create in the world, a lesson of what not to do. You can create that way and of course you get a beautiful Golden Calf, but it's before God and nothing comes from it, it stops right there. But when you create in conjunction with God and community and you are really listening, and that has a continuation—until I get challenged.

When I get challenged, like experiencing a death or a divorce, I often think I lose that thread and that faith. What I've noticed though is that my best work has always come after a huge descent; a descent into darkness, a descent into not knowing. I've thought of it as being thrown into the threshing machine and the chafe and the wheat and the husks are separated. We are in life to get those husks taken from us, so we can go in the right direction. I always forget it, but I've noticed that my weaving allows me to reconnect to it. It is prayer to me and normative prayer has that same quality for various people. If you pray, you start to find the reconnection again. That's what weaving does, when I'm creating a series. If I feel that I'm without faith, I'm not hearing, I'm not being guided. If I simply try to listen, and do, then I start to understand. That's in Torah, too. Rather than trying to put this whole thing together, wondering why did this happen to me, if I just do, then out of it comes intelligence, form, understanding, purpose. I get it. In the Torah, God says at Sinai: "You will do and then you will understand." Often in the creative process that is true.

☙❧

At some point, after a number of different places, I moved back to Chicago. A group was interested in forming a *havurah* and I got a phone call inviting me. We were sitting around and the discussion was focused on why people go to synagogue. I was very quiet, listening. I was the only single woman there. I didn't even know why I was there. Everyone was talking. They were saying things like history, community, education, values, good deeds, social political action, continuity, and even because my grandmother was Jewish. At this very first meeting they had, Rabbi Arnold Wolf, who has since become a mentor, friend, guide, lovely person to me, was there. Suddenly I found words leaping out of my mouth. I said, "But Rabbi, where is God in all of this?" And he looked at me and said, "Don't you know God is controversial? I never talk about God."

There was total silence. I started arguing with him. We had the biggest fight, I was outraged. I said, "How dare you, you're a rabbi! So what if it's controversial, you're supposed to be a leader! Rabbi means teacher." I had six weeks of study, I knew everything. He was tough, he was not backing down, he was throwing more on the fire. Little did I know he loves this stuff, but I kept going. I said we have to do something about this, if people are afraid to talk about God we should do something.

At the time I was reading *God in Search of Man* by Abraham Joshua Heschel. I had just gotten to the section on nature and how that's a pathway—you find God in awe, and that's where I found God. I started talking to the rabbi about that and he stopped and came over to me. He took my head in both his hands and kissed me on the forehead and said, "Let's do a class together, that's what we'll do." Everyone was quaking in their boots because they didn't know where this was going, but that's exactly what we did. We decided to do a class called God in Search of Man and forty people showed up. We thought two would come. It was the most incredible experience for everybody involved. The pain, the agony, the disillusionment they had because they could not speak to or have a relationship with God. It was a source of deep sorrow to them. And even if they had it for years through their aunt or grandma like I did, they felt uncomfortable with it. It was too intimate, like it was a secret and no one could talk about it. Now it was like coming out of the closet. And Abraham Joshua Heschel is such a fine writer, so beautiful, each one of us did a talk on various chapters that we read. I did one on nature and God and that was a real *teshuvah.* But I still didn't have any language. I didn't know Hebrew, it was very impenetrable to me, and I wasn't sure about the prayers; they still felt artificial and not right.

ঙ৾৽

The experience of birth opened me up further to the sense of awe in God's creation. It also led me to want to have a certain connection with tradition. So when my family moved to the Berkshires, I actually got very involved in a synagogue formally, for the first time in my adult life. That was great because there was a new rabbi and his wife and we got to be great friends very quickly. One day he called me and said, "I'd like you to be president of the sisterhood." I burst out laughing. To me, that image was 180 degrees from who I was. He said, "Wait, let me talk to you about what you could possibly do in this role. Let's brainstorm."

We discussed how we could bring spirituality, creativity, and strength to women. I was in the feminist movement, I was doing women's conferences and art, so I decided to do it. It was really incredible. We rewrote all the prayers, before that became popular. I started learning Hebrew, I had a bat mitzvah, I led services, I studied Torah, and slowly I started to see how this was wonderful. I just loved it.

ঙ৾৽

I still wasn't putting the weaving and the Judaism together. The weaving was separate, very separate. Then my husband told me he wanted to get a divorce and I stopped weaving for about five years. I could not weave. It was horrible to me.

Before that I did one major Jewish piece, a Holocaust piece. It's called *An Interrupted Life,* and it's based on a book by Etty Hillesum, who was a poet, writer, and artist who volunteered to go into the concentration camps in the Netherlands. From all the interviews and literature I've read, she really was a light in the camps. I really identified with her spirit. So when I was doing the first woman's show at the museum, I was weaving on linen, which is very hard to weave on. It stretches and if you loose the tension, you can't weave on it. In frustration I cut it off the loom and threw it on the floor and I looked at it, and it looked like a prayer shawl and a death shroud. I don't know where that came from, it felt very flow-through, so I made it into a piece. That was the first Jewish piece that I had done.

But then when my divorce came, I could not do anything for the longest time. The older rabbi at my temple has said, "Wendy, I think you were being steeped in your Judaism. That's what was happening. You were learning." I did. I kept going to classes. I read a lot. He said, "You were like tea, it gets steeped, so it'll taste better." I didn't think so! I thought I would never create again.

But I started back, slowly. What did it for me was my daughter's bat mitzvah. I put a warp on the loom and I said I'm going to try to weave her tallis. For me to do that today it would be nothing, a blink, but then it was the hugest thing. With great pain, I did it. Once that happened, it was like a block was gone. It was wonderful. And from that moment my work was only Judaically based. It was easy.

෴

After the tallis for my daughter, I started to play a little bit with fabric, wrapping it. When I did that, it looked like a Torah to me. I started to see where fiber could become sculptural and have forms that were evocative. I was in Torah studies and hearing stories and doing a lot of Midrash with them, and I was getting great insights. I was being fed in that way. I did a piece called *In the Beginning*. It was just a simple tapestry with a landscape and it had fiery threads and the tree and it sold immediately.

My other work was appreciated but not like this. The woman who bought it came to my studio and I saw what this piece did to this woman. It touched her on a deep level. She was a collector. It wasn't from the acquisitive side of her, she found God in it. I saw that happening. That was incredible to me. That the way I felt, the way I processed my work, she also experienced right in my studio. And that has happened over and over again. Especially with the exhibits, particularly because I'm talking and listening and speaking and asking questions.

People have limited views of how they should be a Jew or what a Jew is: you can only do it this way, and because I don't do it this way I cannot be a Jew. It's almost self-abusive. But I say, "Oh but that's a way. You garden, you see God's hand in that too." When I did this I realized I could find my relationship. In Judaism even when you struggle and you feel you don't have a relationship, that's part of it too.

๑๋๐

My father, may he rest in peace, passed on December 8, 1996. The November before, due to my father's ailing heart and Lou Gehrig's disease, we were faced with moving him from a hospital to a nursing care center. My mother stayed at my father's side constantly and was filled with despair, so it was I alone who needed to decide which nursing home. He went to one that is a bit shabby around the edges, but I chose it because it is warm, loving, and *haimish*, though I feared he would reject it as he has rejected Judaism all these years.

The next day, after a sleepless night, I took my two daughters and we walked into the nursing home. In the small, cramped waiting room on the ground floor, there was my father in his wheelchair, surrounded by other residents and a lay person conducting a Shabbat service. My father turned to me, smiled, and said, "Sing *Shalom Aleichem* with them." I asked the conductor of the service if I could. I did. They all joined in. I looked at my father, he smiled, he cried, he sang. The tear is repaired. He has done his *teshuvah*. He has returned with joy and we understand; my mother, my daughters and I all smiled and cried and sang with him. All our voices filled the place and eased the pain and wove God into our lives again.

That makes me think that the fabric of our Jewish heritage, tradition, spirituality, soul is a finely woven tapestry. It may unravel at points, have holes torn into the surface, become faint over time, but it will continue to be rewoven anew in every generation, even if there is only a thread. For that thread will be like Rachel's blood red thread that will give birth again.

27 A Rabbi's Perspective

Shefa Gold

I recently wrote an article about the positive impact that my experience in other traditions has had on my Jewish practice. I think Judaism, throughout the ages, has had influences coming in. That's what makes it so rich, the interactions between different religions. Often people don't see how that has happened. But when you're talking about a time in Judaism when things get somehow enriched, when there is a renewal, it often happens because of an interaction with another system, or having to answer certain questions of the times.

❦

Rabbi Shefa Gold has focused extensively on the effect of music, especially chants, on Jewish prayer, as highlighted in her recordings, *Tzuri* and *Chanscendence*.

A frequent lecturer at Metivta, Aleph's Kallah, and Elat Chayyim, she currently resides in New Mexico.

I grew up in New Jersey in a Conservative Jewish home. My father came from an Orthodox background, my mother was an atheist, so they compromised with Conservative Judaism. I went to Hebrew school, which was pretty awful, but I think from a very young age, I had in me a deep sense of Jewish identity. When I think about what that identity was made of, it was really an awareness of suffering in the world, a noble responsibility of being Jewish and having that awareness. It wasn't something greatly joyous, it was a burden, but a noble burden to carry to be a Jew.

༄

Hebrew school wasn't a real positive experience, it was just something you had to do. It wasn't a place where you could do any good questioning without being ostracized. It wasn't a place like synagogue, which, when I went with my father as a little girl, was a very positive experience. It almost felt like I had some kind of special status. But once I reached my bat mitzvah, there was a demotion. I was demoted as a special being because once you were no longer a little girl, you couldn't be where it was happening. You couldn't go up on the *bimah.*

Once you were bat mitzvahed, you found out you were second class. It was even difficult being bat mitzvahed because I wanted to read from the Torah and they wouldn't let me. So I received a double message. When I tried to confront it, the role of women in Judaism, the answer that I got was that Jews really respect women more, women are holier than men. Yet what I saw in front of me was not that. The party line was that women were holier than men, which was why they didn't have to do all the mitzvot because they were already closer to God. But that's not how I was treated. I think double messages like that are really crazy-making.

I was, at a pretty young age, aware of what was going on in Israel and I had questions about the way that Palestinians were being treated, questions that were not acceptable to have. I had also some kind of mystical relationship with the land of Israel and I went there when I was fourteen. I really felt the connection with the land.

❧

My identity, my spiritual identity, was primarily as an artist. That's who I was, somewhere on the fringe. Once I got older, I didn't really know how to be Jewish. There wasn't a place for me to be both heart and mind, it didn't seem possible. But it wasn't something that I ever abandoned, because I knew that it was in me.

I married someone non-Jewish when I was twenty-four. He had an incredible attraction to Judaism. He really brought me back to Judaism in a lot of ways because I could see it through his eyes; he wasn't burdened with a lot of the baggage that I carried. So things happened that were different than what people think happen in mixed marriages. His fascination with Judaism awakened me to its beauty. It was a gift. He eventually converted.

We traveled all over the world, both doing our different art forms, I as a composer and writer and he as an actor. We had a real adventurous life. I got a master's degree in philosophy. Part of my thesis was a play that was a dialog with Martin Buber. To do research for that play, I went to Israel to study. In Israel I mostly hung out with the artists, not with the religious people. I supported myself as a musician, playing guitar.

❧

We eventually found our way to California. In California I performed this play about Martin Buber, sometimes in the Jewish community, sometimes in the Christian community, sometimes in university settings. I met a couple of rabbis there who knew Zalman Schachter-Shalomi; after the performance they called up Zalman, who was in Philadelphia about to do the first Jewish Renewal gathering. This was in 1984. These rabbis said, "You've got to invite these people to come." So we drove out to Philadelphia from California.

That was an amazing experience, meeting all these kindred souls from all over. We met the Aquarian Minyan from Berkeley, which we hadn't connected with when we were in California. The Aquarian Minyan opened my eyes to the idea that you could be joyous as a Jew. They have a very jubilant, creative style of worship that really attracted me. I began getting involved with them and eventually started leading services.

֍

My path was moving me more and more toward rabbinic work. I wasn't a rabbi but people were looking to me for guidance. I was working with dying people as a hospice worker, I was traveling around performing, and the music that I was writing was becoming more spiritually oriented in response to the liturgy that I was using. I was also studying in other traditions as well. I was studying very intensely in Sufism. I had a teacher in California who was teaching me how to perceive energy. He used the disciplines that had been developed in Sufism, which is rooted in Islam, in order to work with a group and meditate and change one's state of consciousness. I became his main student and helped him lead groups.

I was also very involved in Native American teachings and exploring my own connection to the great spirits through the land. Everywhere I traveled, I went to places that were holy to Native Americans so that I could experience connecting into the different energies of different places. I had also been involved with the practice of sweat lodges, learning about it and doing it for a number of years. I also worked at a place in California called the Milia Foundation, which was a nexus between spiritual and psychological teachings. I didn't get paid for my work but I was allowed to go to whatever workshops I wanted. I was exposed to many different spiritual teachers and people who were working both in psychology and spirituality. It was an exciting time of learning and exploring. And of course at the same time I was hanging out with the Aquarian Minyan and learning the joy of being Jewish.

෨෦

At a certain point in working with my Sufi teacher, he said, "Now you have to go and become a rabbi." I said no way. I didn't see established Judaism as having any room for me. He had a vision of me studying Talmud. It seemed totally wrong to me at the time.

A while after that, my marriage ended and I was in a car accident. I was injured pretty badly and took about a year to heal. My healing time was a very inward, focused time, an opening up of my relationship with God. Beyond any of the forms I had been studying, I was able to connect with God's presence in me. During that time, I also had a number of visions that helped to clarify that I was being called into some kind of service. But I didn't know how to fulfill that. In one of those visions I was out in the desert with a group of ancient women who were dancing around me. They represented a very ancient women's spiritual path. They said that their wisdom had been swallowed up by Judaism, that the ancient religions were taken inside of Judaism. The only way to get to that ancient primal wisdom was through Judaism. I wouldn't be able to reach them any other way.

I had a lot of other wonderful dreams and visions that made me realize that my Sufi teacher was right after all. I applied to rabbinical school. At the time, my Hebrew was not very good and my body was still in pain from the car accident. I had an interview at the Reconstructionist rabbinical college and had a lot of faith that this was going to be, that I would get in, that this was my path, and this was how I was going to serve.

෨෦

It took me eight years to get through rabbinical school. It was a six-year program, but I felt that rabbinical school wasn't a complete rabbinical training. It was like a left-brain training. There were other things in terms of spiritual leadership that I needed to learn but I couldn't get at rabbinical school. I did cycles of two years on and then one year off. During the off years, I explored areas that weren't being covered in the rabbinical school. I also received *smicha*, ordination, from Reb Zalman Schachter, so I did both routes at the same time.

⚛︎

I moved my home base to New Mexico. When I wasn't in school I lived on top of a mountain there. I studied a lot about the process of retreat. This hadn't been well developed in Judaism, but I felt was a necessary practice that needed to be in any spiritual tradition. So I studied the practice of hermitage in different spiritual traditions, until I could develop a way to do that Jewishly.

⚛︎

In my rabbinate, I have been teaching and traveling to a lot of different communities. Part of what I've been doing is developing ways that work for me in terms of connecting with God and praying, spiritual practice, so that I keep growing in my relationship with God and as a person. My ability to be present and the techniques that I develop are definitely influenced by things that I've learned in other spiritual traditions. In Judaism, sometimes there are traditions we don't quite know about in terms of meditation and spiritual practice but we have a lot of hints. The gaps need to be filled in with our own creativity.

I've been developing the art of chant, the repetition of a sacred phrase. I look at the prayer service and see so much you have to say, that it doesn't work for me. There is so much that I have to stay on the surface and what I want is to go deep. I had the intuition that different sacred phrases were doorways that I could enter to bring me to a deep place, an opening into the seventy different meanings that are in each of the words. The way I've been doing that is by taking different phrases and turning them into meditative practices. These allow me to enter in through their doorway. For example, the very first phrase in the liturgy, *modeh ani lefanecha,* which says I gratefully acknowledge you, is a waking up and thanking. So I began by taking that phrase and finding the kind of melody, the kind of rhythm that would allow me to enter into a different space, to open up a sense of gratefulness. In the practice of chants, you repeat that phrase a lot, more then you would be comfortable doing in your normal, rational mind. It helps you to shift your consciousness and open your heart. From doing that, insights or different kinds of expansion happen inside.

If you have done the chant for a while, the practice is to move into the silence after the chant and to let that silence unfold. It is a very powerful practice. I take certain phrases from each part of the prayer service and use those phrases to fulfill the function of that part of the service so that I can move through the service as a transformational process. I don't use all the words, only certain words, and really work on the *kavanah,* the intention.

୶୦

I released tapes and started groups around the country of people who were interested in chanting. There are a lot of different uses of chants, one of which is to build the energy of a group. A chant can do different things in terms of connecting people with one another and building energy. The energy can then be used for healing, for clear seeing, for exploration of the heart, or for opening yourself up. As a leader I try to look and see what the potential of this energy is. I use Hebrew phrases and Hebrew words, which I think are so rich. For instance, when I say *modeh ani lefanecha,* inside the word *lefanecha* is the Hebrew word for face. When I do that chant, the intention is to affirm that wherever I look I will see the face of God. When I open my eyes, the face of God will be there in all its disguises. The idea of doing chanting is also to plant certain ideas inside me that will be helpful to me at times when I get forgetful. Something about melody can go beyond ideas. It can open us up and plant things inside us much more deeply. There are times when I'll wake up with a melody in my head and know that the idea attached to it is something that I need to remember.

What I want spiritual practice to do is to bring us into a state of constant remembrance of God's presence, because there are so many things that distract us and make us forgetful and close us down. These are some tools in keeping our heart open.

Select Bibliography

Abrahamson, A. (1998). Debate rises over Jewish census. *Los Angeles Times,* July 25, p. 4.

Abrams, E. (1997). *Faith or Fear: How Jews Can Survive in Christian America.* New York: The Free Press.

Aron, I., Rossel, S. L., and Rossel S., eds. (1998). *A Congregation of Learners: Transforming the Synagogue Into a Learning Community.* New York: UAHC.

Bauer, A. (1991). *Black Becomes a Rainbow.* New York: Philipp Feldheim.

Berkowitz, A. L., and Moskovitz P., eds. (1996). *Embracing the Covenant: Converts to Judaism Talk About Why and How.* Woodstock, VT: Jewish Lights.

Berrin, S., ed. (1997). *A Heart of Wisdom: Making the Jewish Journey from Mid-Life Through the Elder Years.* Woodstock, VT: Jewish Lights.

Bershtel, S., and Graubard A. (1992). *Saving Remnants: Feeling Jewish in America.* New York: The Free Press.

Boorstein, S. (1997). *That's Funny, You Don't Look Buddhist.* New York: HarperCollins.

Brody, L. (1997). *Daughters of Kings: Growing Up as a Jewish Woman in America.* Boston: Faber & Faber.

Camlot, H. (1996). Why synagogue attendance soars on three days each year. Jewish Telegraphic Agency Magazine, August 9, p. 8A Online. http://library.northernlight.com.

Chen, D. (1997). Fitting the Lord into work's tight schedules. *The New York Times*, November 29, pp. 1, B4.

Curtius, M. (1997). California and the west: San Francisco Museum seeks to define Jewish identity for the 21st century. *Los Angeles Times*, November 27, p. 3.

Dames, J. F. (1994). Boomerang God is dead: generation now going back to churches and temples. *St Louis Dispatch*, October 12, p. 1.

Dart, J. and Hong, R. (1998). New beginnings for the high holy days. *Los Angeles Times*, September 19, Metro Edition, p. 4.

Davis, A., ed. (1997). *Meditations From the Heart of Judaism: Today's Teachers Share Their Practices, Techniques, and Faith.* Woodstock, VT: Jewish Lights.

Dershowitz, A. (1997). *The Vanishing American Jew.* Boston: Little Brown.

Diamant, A. (1997). *Choosing a Jewish Life.* New York: Schocken.

Falk, G. (1995). *American Judaism in Transition: The Secularization of a Religious Community.* Lanham, MD: University Press of America.

Firestone, T. (1998). *With Roots in Heaven: One Woman's Passionate Journey Into the Heart of Her Faith.* New York: E.P. Dutton.

Gallup, G. Jr., and Castelli J. (1989). *The People's Religion: American Faith in the 90's.* New York: Macmillan.

Gillman, N. (1996). *Conservative Judaism: The New Century.* West Orange, NJ: Behrman House.

Glazer, N. (1988). *American Judaism.* Chicago: University of Chicago Press.

Goldberg, J. J. (1997). Interfaith marriage: the real story. *The New York Times*, August 3, section 4, p. 13.

Goldstein, S. (1992). Profile of American Jewry. *American Jewish Yearbook*. Philadelphia: Jewish Publication Society.

Goodstein, L. (1998). To bind the faith, free trips to Israel for Diaspora youth. *The New York Times*, November 16, p. 8.

Gordis, D. (1995). *God Was Not in the Fire: The Search for a Spiritual Judaism*. New York: Touchstone.

Gottlieb, L. (1995). *She Who Dwells Within: A Feminist Vision of Judaism*. San Francisco: HarperCollins.

Greenberg, R. (1997). *Pathways: Jews Who Return*. Northvale, NJ: Jason Aronson.

Grossman, C. L. (1997). Setting standards for faith. *USA Today*, April 14, p. 1D.

Grossman, G. C., and Grossman, G. C. (1995). *Jewish Art*. Southport, CT: Hugh Lauter Levin.

Hertzberg, A. (1998). *The Jews in America: Four Centuries of an Uneasy Encounter*. New York: Columbia University Press.

Horowitz, C. (1997). Are American Jews assimilating themselves out of existence? *New York Magazine*, July 14, p. 30+.

Kamentz, R. (1994). *The Jew in the Lotus*. New York: HarperCollins.

Kamentz R. (1997). Unorthodox Jews Rummage through the Orthodox Tradition. *The New York Times*, December 7, p. 84.

Kantrowitz, B., and King, P. (1994). In search of the sacred. *Newsweek*, November 28, p. 53.

Karp, A. J. (1997). *A History of the Jews in America*. Northvale, NJ: Jason Aronson.

Kaufman, D. R. (1991). *Rachel's Daughters: Newly Orthodox Jewish Women*. Piscataway, NJ: Rutgers University Press.

Kosmin, B. A., et al. (1991). *Highlights of the National Population Survey*. New York: Council of Jewish Federations.

Lamm, M. (1991). *Becoming a Jew*. New York: Jonathan David.

Lerner, M. (1995). *Jewish Renewal*. New York: HarperPerennial.

Liebman, C. S. (1973). *The Ambivalent Jew*. Philadelphia: Jewish Publication Society of America.

Linzer, J. (1996). *Torah and Dharma: Jewish Seekers in Eastern Religions.* Northvale, NJ: Jason Aronson.

Linzer, N., Schnell D. and Chenes J., eds. (1998). *A Portrait of the American Jewish Community.* Westport, CT: Praeger.

Levin, M. (1996). *The Guide to the Jewish Internet.* San Francisco: No Starch Press.

Marin, P. (1996). An American yearning. *Harper's Magazine,* December 1, p. 35.

Morgan, T. B. (1964). The vanishing American Jew. *Look,* May 5, p. 42+.

Moyers, B. (1996). The resurgence of faith: America's religious mosaic. *USA Weekend,* October 13, p. 4.

Raphael, M. L. (1988). *Profiles in American Judaism: The Reform, Conservative, Orthodox and Reconstructionist Traditions in Historical Perspectives.* New York: Harper and Row.

Sachar, H. M. (1992). *A History of Jews in America.* New York: Alfred Knopf.

Schrader, E. (1998). Reform Jews seek revival of traditions. *Los Angeles Times,* June 20, p. 1.

Seltzer. R. M., and Cohen N. J. (1995). *The Americanization of the Jews: Reprisals in Jewish Social and Intellectual History.* New York: NYU Press.

Silberman, C. (1985). *A Certain World: American Jews and Their Lives Today.* New York: Summit Books.

Sinert, M. L. (1995). More young Jews keeping kosher, attending synagogue. *The Jewish Advocate,* February 9, p. 6.

Sklare, M. (1993). *Observing America's Jews.* Hanover, NH: Brandeis University Press.

Steinsaltz, A. (1997). *Teshuvah: A Guide for the Newly Observant Jew.* Northvale, NJ: Jason Aronson.

Sussman, L. J. (1995). *Isaac Leeser and the Making of American Judaism.* Detroit: Wayne State University Press.

Waskow, A. (1997). *Down to Earth Judaism: Food, Money, Sex and the Rest of Life.* New York: William Morrow.

Weiner, S., ed. (1996). *The Fifty Eight Century: A Jewish Renewal Sourcebook.* Northvale, NJ: Jason Aronson.

Wertheimer, J. (1993). *A People Divided: Judaism in Contemporary America.* New York: Basic Books.

Wertheimer, J., Liebman C. S., and Cohen S. M. (1996). How to save American Jews. *Commentary,* January, pp. 47–53.

Woodard, J. (1997). Characters of creativity: five artists incorporate Hebrew lettering into their diverse works. *Los Angeles Times,* October 23, Valley Edition, p. 4.

Zucker, D. J. (1998). *American Rabbis: Facts and Fiction.* Northvale, NJ: Jason Aronson.

Index

About the Author

Dr. Debra Gonsher Vinik is a professor in and chairperson of the Communication Arts and Sciences Department at Bronx Community College of the City University of New York. She is the writer and producer of numerous broadcast and cable documentaries on communication issues as well as those of Judaic interest including: ABC's "Embracing Judaism: Reaching In, Reaching Out, Reaching Up" and "Grateful, Am I to You," which explores the morning service. She is currently at work on the documentary "And the Walls Keep Crumbling Down," a look at early twentieth century synagogues of Manhattan, along with a college textbook on public speaking. She lives in New Jersey with her husband and five cats.